The Passions
Of Howard Hughes

By Terry Moore
& Jerry Rivers

GENERAL PUBLISHING GROUP

Los Angeles

Credits for photo insert:
AP/Wide World Photos: pages 3 (all), 5 (top), 6 (top)
The Bettmann Archive: pages 6 (bottom), 7 (bottom), 8 (top and bottom)

For information:
General Publishing Group, Inc.
2701 Ocean Park Boulevard
Santa Monica, CA 90405

Library of Congress Cataloging-in-Publication Data

Moore, Terry.
    The passions of Howard Hughes / by Terry Moore.
        p.   cm.
    ISBN 1-881649-88-1
    1. Hughes, Howard, 1905-1976. 2. Moore, Terry.
3. Celebrities--United States--Biography. 4. Businessmen--United States--
Biography. 5. Millionaires--United States--Biography.
I. Title.
CT275.H6678M66   1996
338.7'67'092--dc20
[B]   96-4599
                                                                              CIP

Printed in the USA
10 9 8 7 6 5 4 3 2 1

General Publishing Group
Los Angeles

Table of Contents

.

Acknowledgments

.

The authors wish to express their gratitude to the following people for their faith and support: Patti Mayes, Milton Shoong, J. Louella Dunn, Lillian Greiff, Link White, John Fiorio and Tom Mobley.

We want to express a very special thank you to Barbara Young, who provided a wonderful place to write, and for all her help and encouragement. Another word of appreciation to the Reed Sprinkles for the Catalina trip on their yacht and for the runway research that Reed helped with. But most of all, our thanks to Howard's aides, you know who you are, for all your help and honesty. The promise of confidence is forever.

And we cannot forget Lester Persky, who believed in and supported the book from the beginning. And Murray Fisher, a truly talented editor, and of course our wonderful agent, Mike Hamilburg.

This book is dedicated to

Howard Hughes

and

the truth.

Prologue

.

Back in the Sixties, Noah Dietrich was having dinner in our home one evening when he asked me if I would consider writing his book about Howard Hughes with him. I was very flattered and told him so, but I asked him, "Why would you need me? You were Howard's right hand man for 32 years." Then he admitted, "Because Howard is still an enigma to me. I've run the Hughes Tool Company and later he moved me to California to help with RKO and his other operations, but I've really only known him where it pertains to business. You are the first person I've ever seen him allow himself to get close to. I couldn't believe it when he used to drag me all the way to your home in Glendale so we could hold a meeting on the way to pick you up. At least I had his attention, so I went along for the ride."

"But Noah," I questioned, "You must have met many of his women over the years."

"Only briefly," he said, "and Howard would never discuss business in their company. I saw a different Howard when he was with you. He became boyish and playful, and that's what I want to capture."

"I don't want Terry participating on any book about Hughes—no offense to you, Noah. I want him out of her life!" That was my then-husband, Stuart Cramer, who spoke up, and I understood his feelings. He had previously been married to Jean Peters, who had left Stuart and gone back to Howard. We liked Noah and his lovely artistic wife, Mary, and they often spent time in our home. Stuart and Noah even shared offices and a secretary. Of course, Noah went on to write his book, and it did very well without my input.

One by one ever since then, I've shed tears over Howard's old guard: Noah, Lloyd Wright, Howard's very private trustworthy attorney, Dr. Vern Mason, who was Howard's favorite physician through most of his life. After Dr. Mason died, I remained friends with his son and daughter-in-law, Patty Mason, who was invaluable in helping me by sharing information about Howard that she had never revealed to anyone. When I asked her why, she told me, "Father said you were the one who made Howard happy."

"Mayday, Mayday," Howard was making the emergency landing call over the air waves in the Constellation he was flying with my mother and me as his only passengers. I was sitting in the co-pilot seat and Mama Blue was strapped in the engineer's seat directly behind us. As I turned around to look, I saw the panic in her eyes. Howard was calm, just going about the business of getting us landed. I felt warmly secure. After all, what could possibly happen? We were with Howard Hughes. He could take care of anything. I truly felt that way about him from the moment we met.

In 1948, Howard had seen me in a movie, *The Return of October*, co-starring me and Glenn Ford, in which I am orphaned and believe my uncle has come back as a horse to win the Kentucky Derby—the thing he wanted most while he was alive. Howard had always considered himself an orphan after losing his parents so young, so he fell in love with my character and me. I was so eager, fresh and vibrant during the production that the makeup man had to hang a sign around my neck, "Please do not kiss." He didn't want the makeup spoiled because everyone just wanted to hug, kiss or bite me. My mother had told me my whole life that I wasn't pretty but I had a nice personality, and if I let it shine through, everyone would think I was pretty. So I shined and bubbled like uncorked champagne all through those teenage years when Howard claimed me as his forever.

I was born to act and my greatest dream was to fly. Howard played my acting scenes with me and I sailed through the skies with him. Howard Hughes, the greatest pilot of the 20th century, taught me to fly and I became the third woman in the world to check out in jet airplanes. He was my teacher and I was his willing, eager student. I was his perfect canvas because he found no previous experiences to undo, only a spirit as strong and as stubborn as his own. I was a teenage girl raised strictly by my Mormon family who had instilled a great love and verve for life into their only daughter.

When Howard was younger, he had almost an aesthetic face and hands that were long and slender. His eyes flashed with youthful determination, an almost flirtatious quality. When I met him, they were deep and penetrating; I felt undressed to my soul. Other times they were compassionate, sad eyes. I always referred to them as "Last Supper Eyes."

Our love grew into a loving-tempestuous relationship and marriage. I wasn't as tall, as willowy, as sexy, as intelligent, as worldly as his other women, but I made him happy. I made him smile and laugh a lot, and all his friends said they'd never seen him behave this way before. We were bonded together in every way. By golly, we even had the same birth signs—sun, moon, and rising—which doesn't happen in a million years. He often insisted we were alike. He'd take my face in his hands, smile and repeat, "Helen (my birth name), you don't know what we have." In many ways, Howard was a hopeless romantic. Wherever we dined, he had them play our song, "Again." "Again—this couldn't happen again—this moment forever, but never, never again... This is that once in a lifetime, but never again."

We were always testing each other's will, and mine was every bit as strong and determined as his. Howard called me his Philadelphia lawyer because I usually caught him whenever he went astray or visited the women he had stashed away before he met me. I always knew what he was up to from the Mormon drivers and secretaries. It was because of me that Howard had hired many Mormons. He liked the fact we were honest, had integrity and didn't drink or smoke, and wouldn't be drunk on some Saturday night and talk about him.

While I was in his life and when it was possible, Howard wouldn't go to or have a meeting unless I was there; in fact, he would insist on it. He said my voice was in the right pitch and because of his deafness, it was in the range he could hear. And if someone made a point that he couldn't hear, I picked it up and repeated it loud and clear. I was with him when he dealt with Robert Gross, the head of Lockheed, Ralph Damon, who headed TWA, General George and General Shoup, all his meetings with Convair and when he test flew and purchased the Martin 202s. I was at his side with Floyd Odlum, who had sold him RKO and I waited for him so long while he worked on the HK 1 (now known as the Spruce Goose) that sometimes I'd fall asleep in the car.

Howard told me his story from his beginnings until the day I left. My genuine interest and intense curiosity drew it out of him over the years. He seemed happy to finally be able to share with someone he knew was trustworthy. Howard liked to pour out his life to me because I loved to listen and relive experiences with him, especially all his love affairs with the beautiful stars I had worshipped and grown up with. It was so exciting, listening to him relate all his intimacies with them. My curiosity wouldn't be satisfied until I had pulled every detail out of him about these amazing love affairs, and about the rest of his life. His best friend and confidante, I was filled with an exuberant, dynamic energy, and

I delighted Howard with my unbridled imagination, always ready for more.

After I finished my first book following his death, I thought I could put Howard to rest, but I still could not. I realized that I had told only a portion of the story: my life with Howard. I still had Howard's whole story from beginning to end locked up inside of me, fighting to come out. I'm tired of all the Howard Hughes books each quoting the other books written either by people who had never laid eyes on him or by employees he always kept at a distance. I see lies, half-truths and rumors reprinted from one book to another until they become accepted as a record of the truth. I feel the time has come to set the record straight.

I have met many multi-millionaires and a few billionaires. They seem to gravitate to me because of my Hughes connection. I've never met one who didn't hold Howard as their idol. The ones I've known are strictly goal-oriented, and their sole interest is for more power. Howard, on the other hand, just grew richer in spite of himself. He was a visionary, an innovator, an inventor. His purpose in life was never to become rich or powerful. He wanted to make a better world to live in. He felt his destiny was to leave his fortune to mankind for medical research.

When it came to Howard, everyone was always looking for a puzzle. The man whom the world came to regard as an enigma, really wasn't. One morning when we woke up, in the early Fifties, Howard asked me, "How many senators does New York have?"

I didn't know if he thought I was that stupid or he was losing his mind. Still I answered, "Two."

"How many does California have?"

"Two." If this was his game, I'd go along with it.

"How many senators does Nevada have?"

I was bored now. "Two," I blurted.

"Exactly. I'm going to buy me a state. I'm going to control two senators and a governor who I will run for President, and no one will ever have that kind of power over me again."

It was as simple as that. Howard was usually misunderstood because he was so direct. The decision to try to control two senators and a governor was made after the Senate investigation that was started when Juan Tripp, the head of Pan American, joined up with U.S. Senator Ralph Brewster and tried to bury Howard. Even though Howard won and made fools of them, the wounds never healed and he was going to make certain it never happened again.

Knowing him then, the tall, handsome, debonair Howard Hughes, on top of life, neither I nor anyone else who knew him could ever imagine that this life of lives would end so tragically. As the world now knows, Howard descended into a drugged, psychotic hell, manipulated by a command center who had not his interests at heart but their own. The friends he could trust could no longer reach him.

His aides gave me so many stories of how well he was doing, but I knew when our correspondence fell off at the end that things were not as they seemed. I didn't walk, I flew to his rescue, all the way to London, where he was in residence at the Inn on the Park. General Lasky's son Jesse and I tried to force ourselves up to his floor. We did make it, but guards with guns forceably turned us away. London's famous entrepreneur, John Mills, our friend who owned Les Ambassadeur directly across the street from Inn on the Park, believed Howard might be a prisoner of sorts because the first thing Howard always did when he was in London was to call him. John and I set up a telescope across the street from Howard's windows. But the only thing we could see was hospital equipment in part of the suite. At least we knew he was alive.

My second effort to rescue Howard came when I made a similar attempt to try to free him from his room at the Xanadu Princess Hotel on Paradise Island in the Bahamas. On this occasion the FBI prompted me to make contact with Howard. But this time we were too late as he had already been moved to Acapulco, apparently on the tip of an informant. Who knows what would have happened had I succeeded?

When I meet people, they always ask me the same questions.

"You were really married to Howard Hughes?"

"Yes."

"He was crazy, huh."

"No."

"Well, why was he so strange in the end?"

"Why was Elvis?"

"I'm not sure."

"Prescriptions. Prescription drugs."

"Oh...that's right."

Why did Howard Hughes take them? No one forced him to.

His fifth airplane crash caused tremendous physical damage, and his trusted physician, Vern Mason, told me that Howard required medication for the rest of his life. But as long as they were regulated and he wasn't permitted to become allergic to the drugs, he was in no danger of becoming addicted. As I later learned in confidence from several of his personal aides, whose names have been changed, three people around him became aware of the situation and deviously got rid of those Howard could trust, brought in their own doctors and allowed him to become an addict.

What do the drugs do? How did they affect him?

They make you psychotic and paranoid. Eventually, you insulate yourself from the world and no longer want people to see you. You can't even bear to wear any clothing because you have tremendous sweats and the odor is horrific. You lose all interest in food and your body dehydrates. Howard became a prisoner of the drugs, and of himself.

That's what happened to Howard Hughes. But Howard was more than a myth, more than this mysterious, tragic character who played out his life before a fascinated world. He was a man. A flesh and blood man with wants and desires much like every other man. He was one of the 20th century's great romantics, a swashbuckler of the highest order. Howard shared these stories of his exploits with me, and I know he would have wanted to have been remembered as something other than the portrait that history has painted of him.

For the first time, in these pages, Howard speaks.

Listen.

CHAPTER ONE

It was good being in the air again. This was where he belonged. This was where he felt comfortable. He'd been uneasy this last day, waiting in Fort Lauderdale. Someone might see him, might get through to him, might serve him with a subpoena.

That wasn't what he wanted, not just now. He wasn't ready yet. But being in the air again, that was good. He loved the feel of the engines, the sound of the engines. Even though he wasn't piloting the plane, he felt in control again, if only for a moment.

Then he looked down at his hands. They looked almost tarnished, like silver when it's not polished for years. And spots—he saw spots on the back of them. They were never there before, were they? His hands had always been large and strong. The most glamorous women in the world—Ava Gardner, Lana Turner, Ginger Rogers, Katharine Hepburn, Mary Pickford, Gloria Swanson, Constance Bennett, Terry Moore, Billie Dove—had all told him they were one of his best features. But now the hands were skinny, the fingers bony. These couldn't be his hands.

He looked up and caught his reflection in the window. Could that be me? My God, what's happened to me? I'm looking at an emaciated ghost of myself. When did my hair go gray? It's almost white. And this beard. How much do I weigh? It can't be more than 125 lbs. Even 120. These lines in my face, when did they appear? I know all the scars from my plane crashes, but these lines make me look so old. And my eyes—so dark and sunken. I must look 90. But what the hell, today's Christmas Eve, December 24, my birthday, so I'm only 67, aren't I?

Looking out the window, he spotted a sight he hadn't seen since he set the round-the-world speed record in 1938, setting down in London after a 25,000-mile flight in his Lockheed 14. There was Buckingham Palace, a stalwart relic of what used to be the British Empire, and there the Tower of London, covered in a light snow. Now he felt the plane bank left. He thought, this is just when I would have started the turn. He felt more power being applied, and he approved. It's just what he would have done.

He liked this plane, a Lockheed Jetstar. He hadn't piloted one yet, but he had it on his list: This is one he was going to fly. He spotted the Thames, remembering that on his 1938 trip he had lined up on this fabled river. Now the Jetstar went to full flaps. He would have waited a few more seconds before undertaking this maneuver. Just then, one of his aides came over and, gently pressing his shoulder, pulled him from his reverie, saying, "Boss, I got to make sure that you're buckled up."

Howard wondered, what kind of jerks do I have working for me? Doesn't he realize how many flights I've made, how many takeoffs and landings I've done? How many crashes I've survived? And he's pestering me about buckling up. Without bothering to acknowledge McDermott, Howard turned back to his window to watch their final approach. He felt the touchdown, first the left wheels—then, just a second later, the right side. With the engines in full reverse, the noise was almost deafening, even for him, inside this luxurious cabin. Then the nose wheels smoothly touched down and the aircraft taxied to the terminal.

He wanted to go up to the cockpit and talk with the pilots, but no sooner had the plane rolled to a stop than a commotion burst out all around him. Three different aides rushed up, grabbing him, pushing him and pulling him into the aisle. "C'mon, Boss, we've got to hurry," McDermott said into his ear. "The limo's waiting right outside the plane. You know you don't want anyone to see you. We're moving now!" Chris and Harley took him by the arms.

Feebly pushing the guards away, Howard snapped at McDermott, "What the hell is the damn hurry? I was just going to get acquainted with the cockpit on this plane."

"Boss," said McDermott soothingly, "we have to get to the suite quickly, the boys have been setting it up for you, and everything is just the way you want."

"Well, I may have changed my mind. I don't know if that's what I want now."

"Gentlemen," said McDermott, ignoring him, "Mr. Hughes is going to the hotel suite now." Before he could begin to protest, Howard was literally swept off his feet and carried into the waiting limousine.

The limo driver had been instructed to drive directly to the service entrance of the Inn on the Park without looking at his passenger. He was to avoid eye contact no matter what. Howard wanted to see the sights on the way to the hotel, but the limo was equipped with blinds, on orders from Romaine Street, so that no one could see in. The problem was none of the passengers could see out, including the man in the back seat who was paying for it.

After what seemed an eternity, the group arrived at the service entrance to the Inn on the Park. Helped out of the limousine by a phalanx of aides who blocked even a glimpse of the mysterious new tenant in the penthouse suite, Howard was whisked into a service elevator held open by a security guard who had received the same orders—not to look at their new guest. Howard tried to make eye contact with the man, if only to see a face other than the ones that surrounded him all the time, but to no avail. Even though he was taller than his aides, they had him in a firm grip, he couldn't see over them, and the security guard refused to look his way. The elevator door closed, the car made its way swiftly to the penthouse, the doors opened and he saw two more guards staring blindly straight ahead.

Ushered through the double doors of the suite—virtually indistinguishable from the others he had lived in in the recent past—he saw a large living room furnished with several couches and tables, easy chairs, telephones and two desks, and, through a door, a fully-equipped kitchen he knew had been stocked for his special dietary needs.

Howard started walking toward a living room window saying to no one in particular, "I'd like to sit here a while and look out at the city." He didn't know that his penthouse suite overlooked one of the best views in all of London. All he had to do was remove the tape from the blackout curtains to see the wonders of Hyde Park and Buckingham Palace. But this was not to be. Before he could get halfway to the window, he was rushed through another door into a rather small bedroom. Its windows were also taped shut and covered by blackout curtains.

McDermott came into the bedroom to inquire if Mr. Hughes was comfortable, and also to tell him that they had five different movies for him to choose from. The boys would have the projector set up in just a matter of moments.

Not bothering to respond, Howard asked, "Tell me, if I'm not mistaken, we're at the Inn on the Park, aren't we?"

"Yes, Boss, that's correct."

"You know, McDermott, my good friend John Mills owns Les Ambassadeur, the club I used to frequent in the 40s and 50s, every time I'd stop in London. It's just across the street from this hotel. I've decided to go down and see if he's there."

McDermott couldn't believe what he was hearing. "But... but what about your movie?" he sputtered.

"I'm not in the mood for a movie just now."

"Just a moment, Boss," said McDermott. "Take it easy. I'll be right back."

He left the bedroom to confer with the other aides. Howard could sense that there was something wrong. He was doing something they weren't used to. He was questioning what was happening to him. He was even walking around. Opening his bedroom door, Howard strode into the living room and announced, "What clothes do I have here? I'm stepping out!"

Before he could utter another word, he was practically run over by three aides who took him back into the bedroom and closed the door behind them. In a very soothing tone, McDermott said, "Look, Boss, you don't want to go outside. We understand there's two fellas waiting downstairs with subpoenas for you. We don't know how the hell they found out you were here so quickly, but they're waiting for you."

"What kind of crap are you giving me?" asked Howard. "That can't be—I want to see my pal John Mills."

Without another word, the boys pushed him onto the bed. Harley said, "Mr. Hughes, don't you think you better take a rest after such a long flight? I have just what you need."

Howard replied, "I don't need any more of that damn

medication, and I don't *want* any more of it."

Harley insisted. "Mr. Hughes, this is what you want. In fact, it's what you need. We know what's best for you. We have instructions from Romaine Street to take care of you, and we're going to do our job."

"Who the hell do you work for?" Howard asked them all. "You're working for *me*, and I'm telling you I want to go downstairs."

He was trying to get up from the bed, but the boys were removing his shirt. McDermott ordered, "Hold him!"

Howard tried fighting them, but it was futile, because he was so frail. He was being manhandled by three aides, all much younger and stronger than him, and they had him down on the bed, expertly tying off the blood flow in his left arm so the vein was popping out. No easy task since his arms were so skinny.

Harley filled the hypodermic with codeine and slid the needle into the vein. As he was being injected, McDermott told Howard, "You know this is doctor's orders, and you know we're only doing what's best for you. And, oh yes, happy birthday, Mr. Hughes."

Howard was still struggling, but he was no match for the aides, and the codeine was beginning to weave its magic. He felt it flowing through his bloodstream, running along his spine, up through the base of his neck and then finally the warmth as it reached his brain. He didn't want it, but he couldn't fight it.

As the aides watched the drug taking hold, they released their grip on him, placed a pillow under his head, and he started to drift off to a place in his past, a place where he was in charge, a time when he was still Howard Hughes. He wondered if he would ever be able to go there again without the help of the warmth and magic of the drugs.

CHAPTER TWO

JULY 14, 1938

Floyd Bennett Field
Brooklyn, New York

It was about 2:30 in the afternoon. The sky was remarkably clear. The sun was glistening off the body of the Lockheed 14 on the final leg of its record-setting around-the-world journey of three days, nineteen hours and seventeen minutes. The "New York World's Fair 1939," which is the name Howard Hughes gave his aircraft at the request of his good friend Grover Whalen, president of the Fair, was on its final descent into New York's Floyd Bennett Field. The entire world was standing by their radios waiting for Hughes to land.

As they circled into their landing pattern, Howard's thoughts wandered back to the time when he had first known he was destined to become a record-setting aviator. It was the spring of 1921 and young Howard had never wanted anything so much in his life. His father, Howard Hughes, Sr., had come to visit him at the Fessenden School in West Newton, Massachusetts, where he had been enrolled since the fall of the preceding year. This wasn't young Howard's idea, but his father wanted him to attend Harvard as he had, and prestigious Fessenden would be a good preparatory school. The Hughes drill bit was on the way to making his family rich, and Howard found himself in the company of other boys, sons of wealthy families who also had ambitions for their young heirs to attend Ivy League schools. Howard hadn't done well in school before, but at Fessenden his grades were satisfactory, and he even excelled in algebra. It was at Fessenden that young Howard had also developed his love for golf. The school had a nine-hole course, and Howard spent nearly all his free time perfecting his game.

It was on the golf course that he had first become interested in airplanes. From the fairway, Howard would see the single-engine planes from a nearby airfield doing their loops, turns and banks, and he wondered what it would be like to fly one of them. He never liked being cramped up in school, being told what to do, being just like the other boys. He didn't want to be part of the crowd. He knew he was meant for other things, better things, special things. Out here on the golf course, that's the way he liked it. And as he watched one of those single-engine beauties go through its paces, he wanted to be up there flying it. He knew he would be in control up there. He knew he would be in charge up there, he knew he would be free up there.

"Okay, Sonny, I'll tell you what," said Howard Sr. to his handsome young son, who was already the tallest boy in his class of 30, "If Harvard crosses the finish line first, you can have anything you want." Howard Sr. had picked his son up at Fessenden and taken him to New London, Connecticut for the traditional boat races between Harvard and arch-rival Yale. Young Howard knew what he wanted, and he joined his father along with all the other Harvard stalwarts in shouting encouragement to the crew of the Harvard Crimson scull.

"C'mon, c'mon!" he heard himself shouting in unison with his father as they stood by the finish line. Howard had never rooted so hard before, and he believed it was his encouragement, his cheering, his applause that got the Crimson to the finish line first. And now, with the victory in hand, it was time to collect on his father's promise.

"Well, Sonny, I'm a man of my word. What do you want the most in the world?"

Without hesitation, Sonny spoke up, "To fly."

"What, what are you talking about, Sonny?" sputtered his amazed father. "What do you mean, fly?"

Sonny tried to describe his fascination with airplanes. How he yearned to be airborne in one of them, how he knew he could learn to pilot one himself. In fact, he told his father, he knew he was destined to become a great aviator. "Father, you promised anything I wanted, and I want to fly."

"Sonny, I thought you might want a new set of golf clubs or a camera or even a new short-wave radio set, but flying—that's too dangerous." Howard Sr. saw the look of disappointment, even despair, appear on Sonny's face, and he continued, "And besides, I wouldn't know where to go, or even how to go about getting you a chance to fly."

Young Howard saw his opportunity: "Father, on the way to the races we passed a place that gives rides in airplanes." He went on excitedly, running his words into one another, "It was a seaplane, and it was tied up along the Thames River, and they're only charging five dollars a person for a ride."

Howard Sr. didn't answer, he just stared at Sonny, and then he turned his gaze toward the sky.

In his most convincing yet endearing manner, his son said, "Father, to quote you, you are a man of your word, and a promise is a promise."

Howard Sr. turned to him with a great smile on his face,

pulled his son to him, gave him a hug and said, "Son, you're right to hold me to my word. Now where is this airplane of yours?"

The rest happened so fast that it was a blur in Howard's memory. He remembered arriving at the bulkhead in the Thames River where the seaplane was tied up. He remembered his father paying the pilot ten dollars, and his surprise that Howard Sr. was going to fly too. Then there was the roar of the engine and the spray of the water in his face as the Curtiss seaplane tore across the river, building enough speed for takeoff. Young Howard's heart was in his mouth as the plane's nose lifted up and he felt the power and exhilaration of being thrust up into the air, high above the Thames and the city of New London.

More than just the experience of first flight for Howard Hughes, this was release. It was release from being one of many. It was release even from being one of the privileged few. Howard knew from the very instant that the pilot pulled back on the stick and the seaplane left the river that this was his fate, his revealed destiny, to spend much of his life here, up in the air, where he would be in charge, where he would be free, where he could escape.

From the cockpit of the Lockheed 14, flanked by its two supercharged Wright G-102 Cyclone engines, Howard spotted the runway at New York's Floyd Bennett Field and put the plane into a slow left bank.

"Holy cow!" exclaimed Harry Conner, the 37-year-old co-pilot. "Do you see what's happening on the field?"

"There must be a million people out there!" said Lieutenant Thomas Thurlow, the 33-year-old navigator.

How can I get away from them? Howard asked himself, shifting uncomfortably in his seat as he expertly guided the big silver Lockheed out of the bank and into the landing that would secure his name forever as part of aviation history.

As the plane roared down the runway, the crowd was already surging toward it to greet their new hero. When Harry Conner and Hughes cut the engines and began going through their after-flight checklist, they realized they wouldn't be able to complete that last duty as the first of more than 25,000 cheering, near-hysterical spectators and fans, led by Mayor Fiorello La Guardia and Grover Whalen, streamed forward to surround the plane. Even though Police Commissioner Louis Valentine had over 1000 police on duty for crowd control that afternoon, no one could have anticipated this kind of public outpouring.

When the pandemonium finally started to die down, the crew began to disembark from the cabin. The crewmen Stoddart, Connor and Thurlow were the first to be greeted by the mayor and Whalen. Then, in need of a shave and wearing his trademark Stetson hat and a white shirt, open at the neck, a six-foot, three and a half inch, 165 pound, movie-star handsome man who was shrouded in legend and myth, a man who had always shunned celebrity, avoided the press, controlled his own publicity, and above all demanded and paid for secrecy, stepped out into the glare of the flashbulbs.

The crowd went wild. Police Commissioner Valentine had ordered a cordon of officers around the aircraft, and they held their ground, eventually moving Howard and his crew in a flying wedge to a reviewing stand where Mayor La Guardia offered congratulations and welcomed them all home in the name of seven million New Yorkers.

The crowd, along with the mayor, was demanding that Howard speak. He had nothing prepared and didn't want to, but he knew the crowd would have to be appeased. So in his Houston drawl, he acknowledged the honor, thanked everyone very much—and that was that. He indicated to

Whalen that he was tired and wanted to leave. Whalen had made arrangements for a press conference at his home under much more controlled conditions.

Ushered into a waiting limousine, they were off to Whalen's townhouse in Greenwich Village. Only there, in the more relaxed atmosphere, did Howard Hughes unwind enough to offer the assembled newsmen a reasonably detailed account of the flight. He also made sure to acknowledge the accomplishments of Wiley Post and the feats of Amelia Earhart, two pioneering pilots whose tragic ends hadn't deterred him from this challenge.

When Howard felt he had given them enough of his time, he made the excuse that he had to go get some rest. The crew would stay behind to fill in more of the details. Actually, Howard wasn't the least bit tired. In fact, his adrenaline was on overdrive, because all he had on his mind was Kate Hepburn.

Whalen showed Howard to an upstairs bedroom and told him to grab a little rest, then come back down in half an hour or so. After 45 minutes the guest of honor still hadn't returned to the salon, and when Whalen sent his valet Juan to wake Mr. Hughes and escort him back downstairs, Juan returned a few minutes later and whispered to his employer that the tall airman was nowhere to be found.

The press at the reception at Grover Whalen's house in Greenwich Village didn't realize that the story they were covering about Howard Hughes' flight around the world was old news as far as Howard was concerned. He was off on a new adventure.

Whalen had hardly shown Hughes to his bedroom when Howard doubled back down the stairs, trying three doors until he found one that opened into a central courtyard that led to Eighth Street. There he flagged down a taxi and told the driver to take him to 244 East 49th, Kate Hepburn's New York City address. When they got to within a half-block of Kate's house, it was obvious that he wouldn't be able to get through to her that way: A large group of reporters was gathered outside the entrance to her building. His romance with Miss Hepburn was no secret, and the press was laying for him.

But to Howard, they were just a momentary inconvenience. He ordered the taxi to the Drake Hotel nearby on Park Avenue. Howard was still wearing the same pants that he had flown in, and luckily for the cab driver, he had some money in them that he had carried along for emergencies. One of the myths about Hughes was that he never carried money; only it wasn't a myth. Howard reached in his pocket and came out with a handful of 50s and 100s. The driver didn't have change for a fifty, and so, for the rest of his life he was able to boast of the time Howard Hughes told him, "Keep the change."

Howard rushed to the front desk in the Drake and ordered a suite using the alias Howard Alexander. After taking the elevator to his rooms, he picked up the phone and dialed Kate's number. He told her he had been outside her place not more than 20 minutes ago, but it was impossible for him to get in without the whole world knowing about it. She asked him for his suite number and told him to sit tight. She'd take care of everything. That was one of the things he loved about her. Sure, they had lots of things in common, like golf, airplanes, movies; in fact, even their bodies were similar, both long and lean. But he was wild about her independence, her ability to take charge, to be in control just like him. It's strange that he would like this side of her, because he could never tolerate it from any other woman.

It was about an hour after his phone call that the doorbell

to his suite began ringing, and ringing and ringing. Before he'd had time to get to the door someone began banging on it as well. "What's going on out there?" Howard shouted through the door. But there was no reply. He shouted again, "Who's there? What is it?"

Finally, he heard a voice say, "Champagne and sandwiches."

What the hell is that, Howard thought to himself. I didn't order anything from room service. Opening the door, he saw a serving cart filled with a tray of assorted sandwiches cut in quarters and two bottles of champagne chilling in ice—Cristal Rodier 1931, the best.

Behind the cart, he saw a bellhop in a forest green uniform with gold epaulets on the shoulders, big brass buttons on the front of the jacket and gold braid running down the sides of the trousers. But this was no ordinary bellhop. Beneath the braided cap—a cap just like the kind worn by an organ-grinder's monkey—was an adorable, familiar face. "Champagne and sandwiches for the world-famous flyer," she cried out in her loudest voice. "Champagne and sandwiches for my flyboy."

Howard broke out in a big grin and shouted, "Katie, it's you!" He ran around the cart and took her in his arms. Kate Hepburn was laughing uproariously as she pulled the little cap off her head, and her chestnut hair came gloriously cascading down over her face and shoulders.

Looking down the hall, Katie said, "Let's get this inside before someone spots us." They pushed the cart into the suite and Howard kicked the door closed behind them. Once inside, he took a long look at her and burst out laughing. She'd done it again—come up with some outrageous prank and managed to pull it off. What a fabulous gal. "How the hell did you manage to get that uniform, the cart and everything else—and get up here undetected?" he asked gleefully.

"Howard, as you've told me many times yourself, it's amazing what you can accomplish with enough cash and determination."

Howard laughed. "Tell me about it. I took a cab over here and luckily it's one of the few times in my life I've ever had some money with me. But of course the goddamn cabby didn't have change for a fifty, so I had to tell him to keep it."

Howard's story broke Kate up all over again. "Let's celebrate with a drink, Howard. Open the champagne."

Never much of a drinker, Howard had difficulty opening the bottle, so she took it from him, popped the cork and poured the bubbly into two flutes. Howard held his glass high and said, "What shall we drink to?"

Katie thought a moment and replied, "To the aviator and the bellboy."

They touched glasses, took a sip, and then Howard kissed her gently on the ear. Putting his glass down, he brushed her hair away from her face, kissed her lightly on the mouth and whispered, "Katie, do it, do it to me."

She whispered back, "Do what?"

"You know what. It's all I've been thinking about. All the way around the world, it's all I could think about."

Katie was holding Howard very close, sliding her hand slowly up his leg to his buttocks. "No, I'm not going to do it."

That's what he loved about her—the teasing, the games, the one-upsmanship. He felt the heat building in his blood, and the pulse quickening in her neck. He knew she loved the games, too.

"C'mon, Katie, do it."

"No, you haven't been a good boy," she said, squeezing his thigh.

"I've been a very good boy, in fact, I've been the best." Howard's breath was starting to come in short gasps as he worked his hand inside her bellboy's slacks.

"You have been nothing of the kind. You didn't call me from all the stops you made along the way."

"I called you from every place except Siberia, and that's because there weren't any phones."

Katie now had Howard's belt buckle undone. She was starting to feel for him. His breathing was becoming spasmodic.

"Are you telling me the truth?" she demanded, starting to stroke him.

"Yes, oh God, I swear, yes."

CHAPTER THREE

DECEMBER 25, 1972

·

*17000 Ventura Boulevard
Encino, California*

It was exactly 9:00 a.m. when the intercom rang in Bill Gay's private office at the Hughes Tool Company on Romaine Street in Los Angeles. His secretary told him that John McDermott was on the line from Inn on the Park, London, to give him a report on the first day in England, and that it was most unusual. Gay ordered his secretary to have McDermott hold the line while she asked Nadine Henley to join him so they could both hear the report together.

Gay took the moment to savor how much his life, and his relationship with Nadine Henley, had changed since the day he first met her in the summer of 1947. A tall, lean 27-year-old, he had been raised a devout Mormon. Through a relative of his in-laws, he had learned about a job opening in the Hughes empire that would earn him enough money to complete his studies in political science, business and philosophy at the church's Brigham Young University in Salt Lake City. He had applied to Nadine Henley and was hired on the spot. Nadine saw in the young Gay a tool of which she could make use, and took it upon herself to make him her protégé. His attributes were diligence, efficiency and above all, politeness. Plus, he knew never to let anyone know what he was thinking. No matter what he was feeling, he was always smiling. Like all the others who came in contact with Gay, she would be oblivious to what really lay beneath the smile.

Back in 1947, opportunity had come knocking for Gay when Hughes himself sent down word that he was in need of an executive personal assistant. He wanted someone who would be his own private liaison, 24 hours a day, someone who would never fail him, someone who could coordinate things for him, someone who would carry out his orders quickly and efficiently and without question, no matter how bizarre. In August and November of 1947, Hughes had testified before the Senate War Committee, in what was known as the Brewster Hearings, during which he had sworn that if his experimental wooden airplane, the Flying Boat—known as the Spruce Goose—didn't fly, he would leave the country. Well, Hughes did eventually fly the Flying Boat, so his testimony was a great success. But while he was in Washington, D.C., his communications with his headquarters at Romaine Street had broken down, and he swore it would never happen again. So he had ordered Nadine Henley to find the right man for the job, and she did. Her only condition in offering the job to Gay was that he was to keep her informed of absolutely everything he did for Mr. Hughes.

That was the first time he had ever met Hughes. He went to Howard's office at Goldwyn Studios two blocks from Romaine Street. Welcoming him warmly, Hughes told him how highly Miss Henley had recommended him. Gay couldn't believe he was in the presence of the man himself. He had grown up with the legend of Howard Hughes, and he had heard stories of his exploits while working at Romaine Street. Becoming Miss Henley's assistant was exciting enough, but being with Howard Hughes himself was the first step into a new world of power.

Of course he would accept the position being offered. Maybe it was meant to be. After all, he was almost as tall as Hughes, and just as lanky, and even though he didn't inherit a tool company, he was just as smart. At that moment, Bill Gay had made up his mind that he was going to rise to the top of the Hughes organization, no matter what he had to do to get there. Even he didn't realize the course it would take, but Nadine Henley knew. She had picked the right man.

There was a knock on his office door. He quickly rose to his feet, straightened his tie and jacket and said, "Come in." As usual, Nadine was dressed in a proper business suit, correct blouse and matching shoes, every hair in place. Her look was officious, yet when she smiled, the picture softened. She couldn't be called pretty, yet she wasn't unattractive. In her younger days, some would have considered her desirable. But her best feature was her soothing voice. No matter what the provocation, she remained unruffled, never revealing the slightest anger, fear, amusement or excitement. Like Gay, she was totally in control—at least of herself.

"Good morning, Bill," she said, entering the office and taking the seat in front of his huge mahogany desk.

"Good morning, Miss Henley. I have John McDermott on the line reporting from Inn on the Park in London. I felt you should hear the report with me. I'm going to put him on the speaker phone."

Gay pressed a button and spoke into the air. "John, how are you this morning?"

"Well, to begin with, it's 5 o'clock in the afternoon here in England."

"Yes, of course. John, I want you to know Miss Henley is here with me."

"That's fine. You both should know that we landed yesterday and the Boss wasn't himself. Ever since the meeting with Ambassador Shelton and President Somoza in Nicaragua, he hasn't been the same. We haven't been able to keep him quiet the way we normally can. He's more independent, he's up and about, he's asking questions and he's fighting the drugs. I'm concerned that we may be losing control of him."

The word "control" triggered a memory for Nadine. She had never imagined that the plot she had set into motion back in the 1940s—and acknowledged only in the most secret parts of her mind—could ever reach this stage. She had never been interested in the money, or the power, or the control, like the rest of them. She was only interested in Howard Hughes, and that's why it hurt so much. That's why she'd had to do what she did. That's why she was going to continue to do what she did.

Her eyes closed as she listened to Gay and McDermott droning on. Her mind drifted back to the summer of 1944, to the happiest and the saddest moments in her life. She was once again the private secretary of Howard Hughes, who had fallen into the habit of continually calling her to his Bel Air home on Sorbonne Road to work on his will. She was the only person he would entrust with that most secret document. It was the sixth time she had been called to the house. From the beginning, he had been constantly making changes and doing rewrites. How could he spend so much time over the most minor details, time over the punctuation, over seemingly meaningless points of grammar? Her insight and intuition were telling her that something was wrong. She dared think Howard Hughes might even be losing it. Let me help you, she wanted to tell him.

Nadine Henley was enthralled just to be near Howard Hughes, the world-famous aviator, the lover of movie stars, the most sought-after playboy in the western world. Here he was, as handsome as any leading man on the silver screen, and she had him all to herself, even if it was only as his secretary. No matter what he asked her to do, no matter how tiresome, she would do it gladly. She knew how much he must think of her to entrust her with the writing of his will.

She would sit with her notepad in the living room as he paced in front of her dictating his endless additions and deletions. And while he paced, in his white shirt, the first few buttons open to his chest, sleeves rolled up past his elbows, she would gaze up at him. His dark, almost black hair was longish for the style of the day, and it was combed straight back. It made him look younger and more handsome than he already was. That day, he wore beige tropical wool pants that seemed to hang on his body with the pleats billowing outward. His shoes were black cordovan wingtips, worn without socks. Appraising his long athletic body, she knew he could have been a champion golfer if he had chosen to pursue it. He certainly had the look of an athlete, but he had turned his interests elsewhere. She remembered all the women he was reputed to have romanced.

Nadine wasn't a particularly sexual person, but every time she was near him, she would feel herself tingling with excitement. The feeling would start in her throat, then flow down past her stomach to that place she wouldn't dare even to think about. She lay in bed alone at night and wondered what it would be like to have Howard Hughes make love to her. She thought about different ways to entice him, but their relationship was always strictly business. She addressed him as Mr. Hughes and he called her Miss Henley. Perhaps he's just too shy to say something to me, she thought hopefully. Why else would he have me here so often? He could have me do this in the office. He could call me up with it.

She was watching him as he paced back and forth, not talking, only pacing, and Nadine finally spoke, "Mr. Hughes, is there a point I can help you with?" Howard just looked at her, as if seeing her for the first time. She was sitting with her legs crossed, her skirt at the proper length on her knees, her white silk blouse open at the neck accented with a brightly-colored scarf. She had bought the scarf at a garage sale. She was wondering why she was thinking about it when she realized that Mr. Hughes was staring at her in a way he never had before. Could he be thinking of me as a woman and not as a secretary?

He stopped pacing, walked up to her chair and then moved around in back of her. He had never done this before. Not in all the previous times she had come to his home in Bel Air, or anywhere else for that matter. Nadine began to feel a little uncomfortable. She didn't know why, and her throat became very dry.

Howard stood behind her chair staring at her crossed legs with the memo pad resting on them and the pencil in her hands. Nadine started to turn around to face him, but in a voice she had never heard before, he said, "Miss Henley, don't turn around." She was extremely flustered, but she obeyed. She wanted to obey.

There was no sound, no stirring for a moment or so. Nadine just sat there, legs crossed, pad and pencil in hand, staring straight ahead. She could sense his closeness, but she dared not turn or speak. She felt his hand lightly touch her neck. She felt his fingers move down her shoulder and down between her breasts. Startled, she exclaimed, "Mr. Hughes!"

"Miss Henley, don't talk. Don't say a word."

So she sat there, frozen. Could this be happening? She couldn't believe what she was feeling. His hand, inside her blouse, was working its way inside her brassiere and grasping her left breast. Nadine was breathing in deep, quick gasps as he pressed his lips against her ear and darted his tongue in and out and flicking her earlobe, all while he was gently massaging and squeezing her left nipple. She had never experienced anything like this. Then, with his right hand, he began stroking the inside of her thighs.

He pushed her legs apart. She resisted just for a moment, but then the memo pad and pencil fell to the floor as she opened her thighs for him. His hand reached for the top of her stockings, then the crotch of her panties. He started to rhythmically rub the outside of her panties between her legs. Nadine could feel that she was getting moist, and so could he. Her breathing was much harder now, and Howard himself was puffing for breath. He slipped his fingers around her panties and inside her. She was so wet that his long, strong fingers seemed to go all the way up to her mouth from the inside. He took his hand from her breast and walked around in front of her. He pushed her legs apart, and she saw that he was undoing his trousers.

Nadine was moaning with pleasure. She had never felt ecstasy like this before. She didn't believe it was possible.

"Miss Henley, help me take my pants down," Howard commanded.

Like a slave, she unhooked his waistband, pulled down the zipper and the pants crumpled to the floor. She saw that he wasn't wearing any underwear and that he was totally erect.

"Miss Henley, take off your blouse," he said. As if in a trance, she took off her blouse. "Now undo your brassiere." Again, she obeyed.

Nadine took his penis in her hand and found herself rubbing it in circular motions over both her breasts.

"Mr. Hughes!" she screamed.

"Be quiet, Miss Henley. I told you to be quiet. Are you ready?" She stared at him. "I said, are you ready, Miss Henley?" She nodded and Howard slid his penis down between her breasts, down past her belly. Then, pulling her panties to the side and lifting her hips, he entered her.

She lay back, sprawled on the chair, almost hysterical with pleasure as he pumped away madly. She was grabbing him, touching him, feeling for him, moving along with him—and then it happened. He couldn't hold back any longer and exploded deep inside her. She too burst from the inside out and the outside in. Gasping for his breath, Howard fell upon her in the chair, then onto the floor as he almost lost consciousness.

Nadine pondered Howard at her feet with idolizing eyes. This was the Howard Hughes she had always dreamed about. This was the moment she had always dreamed about. This was going to go on forever. This was all she lived and breathed for, and now the moment was here. Now at last he was hers.

It took Howard about 25 to 30 seconds to compose himself. Then he stood up and pulled his pants back on. Looking directly at her, he said coolly, "Miss Henley, this never happened. I am never going to speak about this again, and you will never mention it either to me or anyone else, ever. This is a direct order. Do you understand me?"

She felt the tears beginning to well up in her eyes. Her mouth went dry, her palms wet. This was absurd, unbelievable. She felt herself starting to go faint. She wanted to run away, but she was glued to the chair, unable to move. She was sitting there legs open and psyche exposed in front of Howard Hughes, the man she loved, the man she would do anything for. But he was talking to her like she was just another one of the properties he owned, one of the airplanes he wanted to discard, some employee whose name he didn't even know.

She felt betrayed, and her shock and shame was swept away in a flood of rage. I'm going to get even with him. I don't know how, and I don't know when, but if it's the last thing I ever do, I'm going to get even with this son of a bitch. Those were the thoughts in her mind as she sat in Bill Gay's office that December 25, 1972.

Bill Gay was saying to her, "What do you think, Miss Henley? What are your suggestions?" His query brought her back, back from that hateful, shameful memory of 28 years before, back from that searing, burning hurt of long ago. Her solace was that she had gotten even, and she was going to keep getting even with Howard, even if it killed him.

CHAPTER FOUR

JANUARY 10, 1973

·

*Inn on the Park
London, England*

The huge salon of the penthouse suite at the Inn on the
Park was filled with sunlight this afternoon. Everything
had been relatively quiet since arriving here from Managua
a little more than two weeks before. The palace guard, as his
aides were sometimes called, had Mr. Hughes tranquil and,
of course, secluded in accordance with standing orders from
Bill Gay.

There were six of them who formed the inner circle. It was
their job, indeed, their only purpose for being, to cater to
every whim, wish, desire or need of Howard Hughes, no matter how eccentric, as long as it had the approval of the man
who had given them their employment; the man to whom
they gave their gratitude and unwavering loyalty: Bill Gay.

In addition to taking care of Mr. Hughes, the aides handled all communication to and from Howard Hughes. That
procedure, ordained by Gay, had been going on for quite a
few years now. Nothing could get past them; only the messages that Bill Gay wanted Howard Hughes to know about,
only the news that Bill Gay needed Howard to acknowledge and only the information that would benefit Bill Gay

and his two cohorts Nadine Henley and Chester Davis.

Even though years before Howard thought he had banished Gay to some obscure position, even though Howard was still in control, even though Howard was still the boss, Gay had outmaneuvered him. Howard had made the mistake of letting Gay too close to him, of giving him too much control over his personal contacts. As paranoid and secretive as he later became, Howard was too open, too honest, too naive a visionary. He didn't take the time to wonder what made this man so efficient, what made him so diligent, why he was always so damn polite. And above all, Howard Hughes didn't take the time to look beneath the smile of Bill Gay.

Glenn Kaiser, one of the guards, was sitting on a couch in front of the TV set in the living room. He was watching the news on the BBC. Kaiser had started in the Hughes organization in 1953 after a stint as a construction worker and a failure as the manager of a sawmill in Montana. His brother-in-law was a friend of Bill Gay in the Mormon Church and got him the interview for the job. He was hired as a driver, and his loyalty to Gay won him his present position.

Also on duty at this time was Chris Mays, who was in the kitchen having a glass of milk. He was a milling machine operator before starting at the Hughes organization and before being hired by Gay.

The newsman on the BBC was announcing that about one half hour before, the Supreme Court of the United States had handed down its decision that reversed all prior lower court rulings in the TWA lawsuit against Howard Hughes.

"Chris, get in here right away! You aren't going to believe this!" Kaiser shouted out.

"What's wrong?" Mays cried out on the run.

"The boss has won the TWA suit," said Kaiser.

"The 170 million-dollar judgment," the BBC announcer

went on, "which was $143 million plus penalties and interest, is now null and void. After litigation that began June 30, 1961 and has ended today, Howard Hughes is vindicated, as well as being $170 million dollars richer."

Kaiser said, "I've got to tell Mr. Hughes the news right now. He'll flip when he finds out." Kaiser got up and started toward Hughes' bedroom.

Mays caught him by the arm. "Hold it, Glenn. We'd better check with Romaine Street. There's no telling what they want him to know. We've had no instructions on this matter."

"But this is too exciting," Kaiser exclaimed. "I'm sure they'll want him to know."

"You've been with us long enough to know that we don't make any moves without instructions."

Five minutes later, John McDermott came to the suite, and before Kaiser or Mays could open their mouths to speak, McDermott said, "I know, I know. I heard the news in my room and I called Romaine Street. Bill thought it was great news and a great triumph. I've already issued a statement for the press that Mr. Hughes is very happy with the outcome, and that he always had great faith in the United States judicial system. We should tell Mr. Hughes immediately. So boys, let's go tell the boss."

McDermott knocked softly on the door to Howard's bedroom, then again harder. When there was still no reply, he slowly opened the door. The room was pitch black except for the flickering light of the motion picture projector and its bright reflection on the now empty screen. Howard had had another bad evening with acute constipation, a problem that had been going on for many years. The vast quantities of drugs that had been given to him, especially codeine, had only worsened this condition. His room had a dank and musty odor. With the windows sealed closed and the curtains and drapes taped shut, there was hardly any movement of the air in the room. It looked and felt and smelled just like all the other rooms in all the other hotels that Howard had occupied before.

McDermott saw that the boss was napping and motioned for the other aides to back out of the room. They always liked to keep him sleeping. Their job was easier that way.

Kaiser was still so excited that he said, "Maybe we should wake him. He'll give us hell when he finds out we held back the news."

"Quiet, we'll tell him later," said McDermott.

"Who's there? What's going on?" Howard asked, half awake. He could just make out the three figures standing in his doorway. "Well, what is it? Damn it, I was just falling asleep. Get me a glass of Poland water, ice cold, and I want to see you pour it!"

"Mr. Hughes, we have some great news for you," said McDermott. "You've won the lawsuit."

"Which lawsuit?" asked Howard, still trying to focus.

"Why, the TWA lawsuit," Kaiser interjected. "You've won it after all these years. Congratulations, boss."

"Congratulations," chimed in Mays and McDermott.

"Now just a minute," said Howard, trying to get the cob-webs out of his head. "You mean we won in the Supreme Court?"

"Yes," McDermott replied. "They overturned the lower court decisions by a vote of six to two. We only got the news a few moments ago. It means you don't have to pay the $170 million. This is a great victory, Mr. Hughes."

Though he was still uncomfortable from his constipation, Howard was listening very closely now. He was also tired, not just from being unable to sleep properly, but also from the drugs. They were crippling him both physically and mentally for years, too many years. He was trying to concentrate on what he was being told. "You mean I've won that goddamn case that shouldn't have gone to the courts in the first place?" At last, his mind was working, he was becoming the Howard Hughes of old, before that last plane crash, before the drugs, before he began to let other people take control of his life.

He knew he was legally immune from any anti-trust litigation brought by the stockholders of TWA because his management of the airline had the approval of the Federal Civil Aeronautics Board at the time, only none of the lower court judges had looked at that basic premise. He knew it would take the power and authority of the Supreme Court judges to recognize his autonomy, and he repeatedly sent messages to his lead attorney, Chester Davis, to Nadine Henley, to Raymond Holliday, who was running Hughes Tool in Houston, and, of course, to Bill Gay. The messages all had the same theme: "Wait for the Supreme Court ruling!"

All Howard got in return were prophecies of doom. In letters, in phone messages, the reply was always the same, "We can't take the chance that the Supreme Court will rule in our favor. We have to be prepared to pay the judgment of $170 million. You have to sell the oil drill bit division of Hughes Tool." All Howard could think about was the fact that he had allowed himself to be manipulated into selling the division. That business was the legacy left to him by his father, the business that funded all the other business and private ventures all his life. That was his golden goose. He made $150 million in the sale, but the business made more than five times that much while he still owned it. What the hell was he thinking? How the hell did he let it go this far? Why did he let them talk him into it?

McDermott could sense something was wrong. He had seen the boss in this mood before, and he didn't like it. He knew Hughes was about to explode. "McDermott," Howard shouted, "why did you force me to sign? Why did everyone push for the sale? Don't you morons realize that I didn't make $170 million—I probably *lost* close to a *billion* over the next few years. I never should have gotten rid of the tool-bit division. Get me Chester Davis on the phone!"

"But Mr. Hughes," McDermott pleaded. "You won the case, and all you've really done is gone public with the tool-bit division."

"Don't you understand, you bunch of idiots," Hughes screamed, "I don't own it any longer. I don't have control over it anymore, and to make matters worse, I didn't have to sell it. We won the goddamn lawsuit! My father's legacy to me is gone! Now get the hell out of here—and get me Davis on the phone! *Now!*"

All three aides backed out of the room quickly, and Chris Mays said he'd get Chester Davis on the line.

"What's wrong with you?" McDermott shot at him. "We follow procedure. I'll put through a call to Bill Gay. Let *him* decide how to calm the boss." McDermott made the call to Romaine Street and talked to Kay Glenn, who in turn connected him to Gay in his Encino office.

Gay immediately asked, "How did Mr. Hughes like the news?"

"At first he didn't understand, but then he got angry, very angry. He said we made him sell his father's legacy."

"That's an ungrateful reaction from a man who just saved 170 million."

"Mr. Hughes doesn't see it that way. He says he didn't make 170 million, he lost close to a billion from what the tool company could have made for him."

"He's not out of it yet, I see," said Gay, letting his guard down a bit. "If we hadn't convinced him to sell the tool-bit division and to go public with it, we never could have set up Summa." Realizing that he might be saying too much, Gay stopped short and asked, "What else?"

"He's ordered us to get Chester Davis on the line for him, and he's really working himself up. I'm afraid we're in for a really terrible time. You know how he gets. Making all of us crazy with orders about the smallest details."

Gay cut him off: "Stop complaining. You boys are being well taken care of, and now you're going to be in even better shape with Summa. Number one, there's going to be no call from you to Davis. Tell Mr. Hughes he's too busy with the paperwork from the court's decision. I don't care what you tell him, but no call to Davis. And number two, whatever it takes, calm Mr. Hughes down. We need him for the meeting with Governor O'Callaghan and Chairman Hannafin. I don't care how you do it, give him all the drugs you want, just keep him calm. Convince him that the deal is to his benefit. I'm counting on you and the boys, as always." And with that, Gay hung up.

Gay's next call was to Nadine Henley and Chester Davis, Hughes' general counsel and vice-president of Hughes Tool. Davis was instrumental in getting the Supreme Court's decision to overturn the lower courts. Born Caesar Simon in 1910 of an Italian mother and French Algerian father, his name was changed to Chester Davis when his mother remarried and moved to the United States. He resigned from a large Wall Street law firm in 1961 and started his own firm, representing Hughes in his defense of the TWA suit. Through the years he had worked his way to status and power equal to Nadine Henley's and Bill Gay's. It was an uneasy, unofficial partnership, since each of them had their own reasons for participating in the conspiracy. Dressed in his usual dark suit and dark tie, always quick with a smile and even quicker with his temper, the balding Davis pushed the button on his desk telephone that connected him with his co-conspirators.

"Chester, how are you? Congratulations on a great victory. It was long overdue," said Gay in what he hoped would be an admiring tone.

"I agree. Bravo," Nadine chimed in.

This was a peculiar group, each always jockeying for position over the others, each contemptuous of the other, at times even detesting one another. Yet they all begrudgingly accepted one another because each had their own hidden agenda.

"How did the old man take the news of my winning the TWA suit for him?" Davis boasted.

"I 'm not sure I like the term 'old man,'" chastised Nadine. "Mr. Hughes is only one year older than me, and I don't think of myself as an old woman. Do I make myself clear, Mr. Davis?" A very long silence ensued, with Davis trying to think of a reply that would slap Nadine Henley down in the obnoxious manner for which he was so well known, but he thought better of it and remained silent.

"I said, do I make myself clear, Mr. Davis?"

"Perfectly clear, Miss Henley, and let me apologize. I had no intention of insulting either you or Mr. Hughes," he replied finally in a tone so contemptuous that it was obvious he was craving a confrontation. But she didn't take the challenge.

"Okay, now that that's cleared up," Gay interjected, "to answer your question, Chester, Mr. Hughes doesn't think you're the genius you apparently think you are."

"Now hold it just a goddamn minute!" shouted Davis.

"No, you hold it!" Gay interrupted without raising his voice. "Mr. Hughes is not the least bit impressed with the 170 million he doesn't have to pay. He says that the sale of Hughes Tool—which all of us forced him into, in case you've forgotten—has probably cost him about one billion dollars over the next five years."

There was silence on the line and Davis finally said, "Well, I've got to give Mr. Hughes credit. He finally figured it out, but what the hell, it's too late. Everything is signed, sealed and delivered. And if we hadn't held the fear of the $170 million judgment over his head, he never would have given in. Because we won the lawsuit, the $170 million will stay in Summa, along with all the other Hughes holdings. And we three are the executive committee of Summa."

Gay said solemnly, "We may be in control, but that's not good enough. We have to own it."

Again, silence. Then Nadine Henley cooed soothingly, "Bill's right, you know, we won't really control it until we own everything. We have much work ahead of us. This is only the first victory. Chester, I want you to start getting the proper names on the gaming licenses in Nevada. Bill, I want Mr. Hughes to be made tranquil, but I want him available to sign whatever we need or to meet whomever we designate. I know that's dangerous, but it will be necessary. Do we all agree?"

Davis and Gay, as if on cue, replied, "Yes, Miss Henley." Davis said his good-byes with his characteristic pomposity, and Gay told Nadine he would instruct the aides as to their "care" of Mr. Hughes.

In the back of his mind, Gay smiled to himself for letting each of the others think they were calling the shots, when all along he knew perfectly well that no one would get anything signed, nothing could be approved, nothing would be accomplished, unless he wanted it so, because he held the keys to the kingdom.

John McDermott had received his orders to keep Mr. Hughes "calm" and make sure he was "available." McDermott knew this meant they would have to increase the drugs. He called a meeting of the aides, and they decided Chris Mays and Harley Smith would start administering higher dosages of codeine and Valium if Mr. Hughes refused to cooperate. The palace guard had learned long ago how to control Mr. Hughes. When there was relatively little going on that required his attention, they would decrease his use of drugs ever so slowly. When he was needed to agree to something, or to sign documents or even on rare occasions to make an appearance for a meeting, they would increase the drugs to the point where he would need them so badly, so intensely, that just the threat of withholding them would make him submit to anything. They became masters at decreasing or increasing the drugs, addicting him ever so slowly, ever so patiently, ever so persistently, almost to the point of no return.

And ironically, who did Howard Hughes have to blame but himself? Didn't he hire Bill Gay, didn't he order him to hire the men to do his bidding, to carry out his commands without question, no matter how bizarre? In fact, he had wanted them to insulate him from the demands put on him by the outside world. To guard him. That's right, to guard him. And now the inconceivable had happened: Howard Hughes had become a prisoner, a prisoner of his own guards.

Mays and Smith knocked on Hughes' bedroom door, then again, louder, because the boss' deafness was growing worse. "Come in, come in!" Howard shouted finally. "Where the hell is Chester Davis? I want a full explanation of this name Summa. I didn't pick it, and what's more, I don't like it. I've never owned anything that didn't have my name on it. Who the hell picked this goddamn name anyway? Listen, I've made notes concerning a reversal of the Hughes Oil-Tool division sale. I want to dictate a letter on this matter." Hughes was really into it now. He was rattling off command after command, and what frightened the aides was that he was hitting the proverbial nail right on the head. They hadn't seen him this lucid since they arrived on that first day in London.

"Something must have been wrong with me," Howard was saying. "I would never have sold the Tool Company. I don't know how I could have agreed to the sale. It was my father's legacy." Howard was running his words together, and he was weeping. He kept repeating, "I let him down. I sold his legacy. What's happened? How could I have done it?"

Chris Mays was almost starting to have feelings of remorse, seeing the boss in such a pitiful state. He was about to say something when Smith motioned for him to hold Hughes' arm as he tied it off with rubber tubing. Instead of Howard fighting them as they feared, he just kept on murmuring and weeping about the Tool Company as Smith slid the hypodermic syringe into the vein that would carry the codeine on its way to weave its spell of magic and relief.

Howard Hughes slid down on his pillow and started to drift off. The two aides watched in relief as a smile began to appear on his face. Howard had drifted back to a time when the Hughes Tool Company was still his—and so was his life.

CHAPTER FIVE

JANUARY 3, 1931

·

La Casa Grande
San Simeon, California

He could feel the electricity in the air at the party that was going on all around him. This has to be the most exquisite ceiling I've ever seen, thought 25-year-old Howard Hughes, gazing at the ceiling that had been brought piece by piece from the Palazzo Martinengo in Brescia, Italy and reassembled with painstaking care here in the Assembly Hall of the castle that the fabulously wealthy and legendary William Randolph Hearst had built at San Simeon.

The Assembly Hall was so large, so majestic, that it was easy not to notice even the enormous Sixteenth Century fireplaces at both ends of the room. Fine Flemish tapestries hung from the walls, large solid silver candlesticks adorned the mantelpieces, and the huge couches and chairs were on the same baronial scale as the mahogany desks and tables scattered throughout the room. The mixture of architectural styles from centuries gone by, as well as the interior design, created an aura of extravagant but informal elegance, not only in the Assembly Hall but in every room, every building, every outdoor wonder, that helped to weave the myth, the legend of San Simeon.

"I hope there isn't a hole in the ceiling," said the beautiful Marion Davies, laughing as she pulled Howard's arm. "Wouldn't it be terrible if it rained and we had a roof leak right here in the middle of my birthday party?"

"Mr. Hearst wouldn't allow it to rain!" Howard responded in equal good humor. "He wouldn't let anything spoil your birthday!"

"Then why are you standing here all alone in the middle of this room and not talking to my other guests? I simply won't allow it," Marion went on in her whimsical way. "I've got someone for you to meet. There are many who want to make the acquaintance of the handsome, dashing, young movie producer, Howard Hughes."

"You have to excuse me, I couldn't get over the majesty of this ceiling. I really admire Mr. Hearst for putting this castle together. And spending so much money on it."

"Don't let W.R. hear you call it 'the castle.' He refers to it as 'the ranch,'" Marion scolded as she put her arm in his and started walking him around the Hall greeting her guests and introducing young Howard at the same time. Most of the people he had only read or heard gossip about, but some he had met on the train from Glendale to San Simeon, at the Beach House in Santa Monica, or at Wyntoon, an entire miniature village in northern California, or at the Ritz Tower in New York, or the fantastic 135-room St. Donat's castle in Wales.

Howard, as well as other guests, were asked to be at the Glendale station no later than 7:35 p.m. for the ride that took them to San Simeon. It was a private train with sleeping cars and a dining car paid for by W.R. and driven on tracks laid by W.R. just for the purpose of transporting himself and his guests to San Simeon. The festivities had begun the moment Howard boarded the train, and shy as he was, he found himself getting into the party mood. Even though Howard never drank much alcohol, the booze flowed all around him and the waiters were tripping over each other trying to fulfill the gastronomic requests of W.R.'s privileged guests.

The train arrived early in the morning at San Luis Obispo, where it was met by a waiting fleet of limousines that would take them on the hour and a half drive to San Simeon. Howard couldn't believe his eyes the first time he saw the structure with its vast grounds and multiple guest houses, all furnished with the opulent eccentricity of a fairy tale castle. Howard marveled at the money Hearst must have spent on this wonderland, and wondered if he would ever be in a position to do something on a scale like that. He was thrilled that Hughes Tool Company had already provided him with the capital to become completely independent and to make his first movies.

At his first sight of San Simeon, Howard realized that there was more to life than mere independence. What he saw there was immense power—and immense control. Just having the wealth that Mr. Hearst enjoyed gave him the power to draw legendary people of means, people of stature, people of accomplishment to him here at San Simeon or anywhere in the world. A suggestion, an indication, a slight intimation by Mr. Hearst was enough for even the great men and women of his time to fall over backward in their zeal to please him. That was control. That was the lesson young Howard learned the day he arrived at San Simeon, and it was one he would never forget.

"Isn't that Douglas Fairbanks and Mary Pickford over there?" Howard asked Marion Davies.

"Why, of course," replied Marion. "Haven't you met them?"

"No, I'd be too embarrassed."

"Never mind, you'll meet everyone as the evening goes on," she assured him. Marion then introduced Howard to Jack

Warner, head of Warner Brothers Studios, all duded out in a cowboy outfit—as were all the other guests. That was the custom for W.R. and Marion Davies. They had a tradition of great costume parties. Any excuse at all would make for a party, and Marion's birthday—or W.R.'s—was the best of all. She chose "Cowboys and Indians" as the theme this year. Everyone, of course, got into the act and the outfits were fabulous. For those who didn't have the time to pick up a costume, W.R. had a trainload of outfits delivered to San Simeon on loan to him from the movie studios. The studios always obliged, since their owners were often invited guests and everyone wanted to be part of the fun. The costumes would arrive in the afternoon, and there was great amusement for those who picked out their costumes from among those that W.R. had provided, as well as for the other guests who would offer commentary on the impromptu fashion show.

Lunch was served around 2:30 and afterwards the guests would enjoy themselves on the fabulous grounds, playing tennis or swimming in either the indoor Roman Pool, decorated with eighteen-carat gold-filled tiles made in Venice, or the outdoor Neptune Pool, which held 345,000 gallons of mountain spring water heated to seventy degrees and surrounded by Carrara marble sculpture in the Greco-Roman style. They would also make the rounds of Hearst's pride and joy, an incredible private zoo containing lions, tigers and even an elephant. On the day of a party, extra chefs, waiters, bartenders and other servants joined the three chefs and score of servants already employed there full-time by Hearst. Two orchestras also arrived, continuously spelling each other for the pleasure of those fortunate enough to receive an invitation to this magical private realm, high up on a mountain, the place called La Casa Grande, the Great House, at San Simeon.

"Jack, I want you to meet Howard Hughes," Marion said to Jack Warner.

"We've met," said Warner. "It was at the premiere of your movie *Hell's Angels* at Sid Grauman's Chinese Theater. I loved it, and I hear it's been doing great business. Congratulations, Mr. Hughes."

"Please, call me Howard, Mr. Warner, and I certainly remember saying hello to you."

"Well, Howard," Jack Warner went on, "you remind me of Coop in your cowboy outfit. Except you're a little taller than him." Howard felt greatly complimented to be compared to Gary Cooper, and with a sense of humor that he had always possessed but lost in later years, replied, "Aw, shucks..." which brought a big laugh from both Marion and Warner.

Jean Harlow came over, wearing an all-white cowgirl outfit complete with white boots, ten-gallon hat and a see-through, white chiffon, fringed blouse. She had William Powell on her arm, and of course, everyone knew it was Howard Hughes who had discovered Harlow as the replacement for Greta Nissen, who couldn't handle the dialogue when Howard changed *Hell's Angels* from a silent to a talkie. That was Harlow's big break, and it catapulted her to stardom. She gave Howard a big kiss, meant for his mouth, but he discreetly turned his head to the side and wound up with a big lipstick smooch on his cheek. "Mr. Hughes, what a surprise. We heard you were coming, but nobody believed it," exclaimed Harlow. "Happy birthday, Marion darling, and you all know Bill Powell."

Powell tipped his glass to them suavely, but before anyone could say another word, Harlow had Bill by the arm and they were off visiting other notables. "Howard, you know the word is that you and Jean were a hot romance," Marion Davies whispered to him.

"I know that's what everyone thought, and I did nothing to keep that rumor from the press because it was great publicity for the movie, but I can assure you, Marion, there was nothing to it. In fact, I never saw her sex appeal and I made the mistake of selling her contract to Irving Thalberg at MGM for only $60,000. If I had known she was going to be such a hit in *Hell's Angels*, I never would have let her go."

"Well, Howard, you better keep that secret, because everyone thinks you're such a genius for gambling your money on turning *Hell's Angels* into a talkie after spending so much on it as a silent. And then you went on to top yourself with *Two Arabian Knights* when your director Louis Milestone won an Academy Award last year. Howard, you're fast becoming a legend, so we'll let everyone keep guessing about you and Jean, okay?"

"All right, but you're embarrassing me by saying all these swell things. I'm going to get a big head." Marion realized Howard was totally sincere in what he had just said, and she adored him for it. Here was this tall, gorgeous, rich young man who was also genuinely modest, and she felt like protecting him, mothering him. All the women in Howard's life would have this feeling of mother love toward him. It was one of his great charms.

This was still the cocktail hour, but it would go on for more than two hours before everyone was called to dinner. Howard's height gave him an advantage as he surveyed the party going on around him. He recognized Norma Shearer, Gloria Swanson, John Barrymore, Charlie Chaplin and Merle Oberon. And then he spotted an exceptionally attractive girl wearing an Indian head-band complete with white feather and a wonderful beaded Indian costume including the moccasins.

"Who's that?" he asked Marion.

"Oh, let me introduce you. She's Liz Whitney."

"You mean of *the* Whitneys?" Howard was always impressed by the old rich families, the society families.

"Yes, dear boy," answered Marion. "W.R. loves to mix his society friends with showbiz and theater people. And don't be so astonished. Liz Whitney and her crowd are just as interested in socializing with the movie stars as you are in meeting them. They're just people like you and me," said Marion with a laugh, introducing Howard to Liz Whitney as well as to John Farrow and his wife, actress Maureen O'Sullivan, and then, in rapid succession, to Hedy Lamarr, Charles Boyer, Basil Rathbone and Randolph Scott. All were in the requisite western gear and all looked great, especially Randy Scott, who was long and lean like Hughes.

Over the orchestra's playing and the din of the party crowd, the announcement was made that dinner was finally being served. Weaving his way through the crowd, Hearst himself came over to escort Marion into the dining room.

"W.R., I don't think you've made the acquaintance of Howard Hughes. Mr. Hughes, let me introduce you to Mr. William Randolph Hearst," said Marion.

"Please, not so formal," said Hearst with a laugh. "My friends call me W.R., and I know we're going to become friends, Mr. Hughes."

"Please call me Howard, Mr. Hearst, er, W.R., and let me thank you for the invitation."

"You have to thank Miss Davies, since she's up to date on who's on the guest list. But I must tell you that you've made quite an impression on her with your accomplishments, and I must admit, on me as well. I really enjoyed *Hell's Angels*. That was quite a discovery in Jean Harlow."

"Howard gave me the scoop on Jean, and I'll fill you in later, W.R." said Marion as she took them both by the arm and led them into the dining room, known as the Refectory.

On the way in, Dolores del Rio wished Marion happy birthday and was introduced to Howard, and the couple told him about their custom concerning house guests. "You see, when some people get an invitation to be our guests," explained W.R., "they take it for granted that they can stay as long as they wish. Now I would simply tell them enough is enough. But my dear Marion thought of a way that's much more subtle."

Marion delightedly continued, "You'll see in just a moment how long our dining room table is. Well, W.R. and I sit directly across from one another in the center of the table, and I seat our newest guests close to W.R. on one side and myself on the other side. As the days go on, I move those guests who have been overstaying their welcome until they're finally seated at the end of the table."

"Only a fool wouldn't get the damn hint by then," said W.R. Howard and Marion joined him in a laugh as Mervyn LeRoy and Constance Bennett walked by and asked what was so funny. W.R. answered, "You'll only know if you're staying a while." And that started Marion, Howard and W.R. laughing again.

As they entered the Refectory, Howard once again couldn't believe what he was seeing. The room was enormous, the ceiling was made of ornate inlaid panels. Imported from a French castle, he guessed. From the massive arches above all the doorways he got the impression that he was in a mighty medieval fortress. Hanging from the ceiling were banners from Sienna, and a gigantic French tapestry was draped on one of the massive walls. The dining table, with huge solid silver candelabras set upon them, ran almost the entire length of the room and had to seat at least 50 people. And there were other tables set up about the Refectory to accommodate the rest of the party guests. But he couldn't stop gazing at the incredible length of the dining table and thinking about the anecdote he had just been told by Marion and W.R. My goodness, he thought to himself, you'd really have to be staying here a long, long time to be pushed to the outer limits of this table.

He saw place cards on the tables, and he was about to start searching for his when Marion said, "I told you, Howard, I have someone I think you'd like to meet. Come, let me seat you at the main table."

She led him to a seat that was only two to her own right, and he looked up to see W.R. taking his chair almost exactly across from him. What an honor, thought the young and very impressed Howard Hughes. But I'm glad I'm only staying the night, because I'd be embarrassed to start seeing my seat being moved to Outer Mongolia.

Howard felt a nudge on his right shoulder, and he turned to see a rather plump lady standing behind the adjoining chair in a large sombrero. She gave him a wide smile, and like the gentleman he was, he got up to help her to her seat. She looked straight up at him and said, "Why, thank you, tall, dark and handsome."

This had Howard smiling to himself, since he loved a compliment as well as the next man, but he was interested in only the most beautiful of women. Even though, he answered, "Thank you, lovely señorita, and let me introduce myself."

"Oh, that's not necessary. I know all about you, Mr. Hughes. I specifically asked Marion to seat me next to you. You see, I want to write a feature story all about the exciting new film producer who gambles his own money. I'm Louella Parsons."

"Let me tell you what a pleasure it is for me to meet you, Miss Parsons," said Howard in his most endearing tone, since he knew how powerful Louella was, being syndicated in all the Hearst publications around the world, "but I don't think your readers would be interested in me."

"On the contrary, Mr. Hughes, my readers will be fascinated to learn more about the man who discovered Jean Harlow, and they'll also want to know what drives you, Mr. Hughes. You're the kind of person that legends are made of, and my readers won't be denied."

Hughes realized he was up against a very sharp cookie, and he also knew she had the full backing of W.R, so he made an immediate decision that he never regretted for the rest of his life. He would give her certain items that he normally would not grant to other members of the press.

As if on cue, Louella said, "And let me remind you, Mr. Hughes, that W.R. will also be grateful for your cooperation with me."

"You need not remind me, Miss Parsons, since I already feel in his and Miss Davies' debt for inviting me to this wonderful affair. So I've already decided to say yes. Just call my office and we'll set an appointment."

"Excellent, Mr. Hughes, you've made me very happy." Howard felt he had handled this situation very well. He had kept his relationship with her formal, as he would always do with the press, but he also made an ally. He would give her just a little more than was already public. Howard would let her print how he changed the charter of his company to the Caddo Rock Drill Bit Company of Louisiana, a subsidiary of Hughes Tool. He would explain that since he was the only stockholder of Hughes Tool and therefore Caddo, he amended the charter to allow for the financing of motion pictures. Being the owner and sole stockholder of Hughes Tool would be one possession he would never part with. He already knew that properly nurtured, Hughes Tool would allow him to amass treasures, power and control that would far outshine even the Hearst empire.

"Oh, I see you've already met Howard Hughes," said Marion, leaning toward them.

"Yes, we're going to become great friends," said Louella.

"That's wonderful for Howard," said Marion. "Now he can count you and W.R. as new friends as well as myself. That's what I try to do, put people together."

"Marion has a wonderful reputation for matchmaking. Did you know that, Mr. Hughes?" said Louella.

"As a matter of fact, I was made aware of that attribute by Cary Grant on the train ride up to San Simeon," replied Howard.

"I don't want to tarnish my reputation, Howard," said Marion, "but I've told you I had someone special for you to meet."

What was about to happen would alter Howard's life forever.

"Mr. Hughes, it is my pleasure to present Miss Billie Dove," Howard heard Marion say. He just sat there looking at the place card to his left, wondering why he hadn't noticed it before: Billie Dove. He looked to his left, and there she was, gazing back at him. In that instant he was smitten, more than smitten, more than infatuated, he was afraid he was falling in love...love at first sight. He had heard of it, but never believed it was possible. Billie Dove, one of the greatest actresses of her time, and he was her biggest fan. He knew she had started as a Follies girl, and that just added to his passion. He had loved her from afar ever since he saw her in *The Black Pirate* starring opposite Douglas Fairbanks. She was a great star, and here she was. He couldn't take his eyes off her, and his imagination ran wild as his gaze ran up and down her lithe body.

"Well, Howard, what have you got to say?" asked Marion with a laugh. Louella was waiting, Marion Davies was waiting, and Billie Dove, trying to avoid Howard's stare, was waiting. But all Howard could do at that moment was to just sit there while he felt himself growing hard beneath his napkin. Thank God I'm sitting down, he told himself. And thank God I've got Hughes Tool all to myself, because whatever it takes, whatever it costs, I've got to have Billie.

CHAPTER SIX

FEBRUARY 10, 1931

.

Aboard the Hilda
Off the Coast of Santa Barbara, California

The shore looked closer than it actually was. His captain had assured him that they were approximately a mile and a half off the coastline, and the boat was holding steady at five knots in a lazy, circular course nearly two miles in diameter. The captain's orders were to maintain this slow pattern until further notice sometime the next morning.

Howard had been anticipating this moment ever since he was introduced to Billie Dove by Marion Davies on that extraordinary evening at San Simeon more than five weeks ago. He had nothing else on his mind but her. Nothing.

Howard had never been smitten like this before. In his relatively young life, he had been married and divorced and known his share of women. And as a motion picture producer, he had come to realize what many in his producer's position before him understood; that women, young women, beautiful women, all the women who wanted an opportunity in the movies would make themselves available to him. But this was different. Billie was different. She already was a star, a big star, and she didn't need producer Howard Hughes.

For three weeks since their meeting, Billie had been ignoring all his pleas and overtures. But that didn't deter him, and neither did the fact that she was married. Like everyone else in Hollywood, he knew her marriage was rocky and it was just a matter of time. In fact, Howard had made up his mind to speed up the process that would lead to Billie's divorce.

His pursuit of her had the whole town talking. He would find out where she was having lunch or dinner, and he would take a table directly across from her, and just stare at her throughout the meal. He would follow her when she went shopping, when she went walking, when she would take a drive. Wherever she went, day or night, there was her shadow, Howard Hughes. And when he couldn't be there, he would have her paged on the phone, he would call, and call, and call. It wasn't a mere infatuation, it was a compulsion, an obsession. Howard Hughes was obsessed with the beautiful, erotic and married Billie Dove.

At the beginning of the fourth week of his relentless chase, she finally said, "Yes. Yes, I'll see you, yes, I'll go out with you, yes, I'll have dinner, lunch or breakfast, only give me a chance to breathe, Howard. You have to stop always being there."

The only word that Howard heard her say was "yes," and he took it as his cue to complete the conquest. He began flying her in his own airplane to the vineyards in Sonoma County for brunch and then on to the Coronado Hotel in San Diego for a late dinner. Just the smell of her was driving him wild, but Billie kept saying "no." Howard would take her to dinner at the Ambassador Hotel in Los Angeles and then on to late dancing at the Biltmore, and Billie still said "no." Howard would fly her to the Grand Canyon and back to L.A. in time for dinner, and it was still "no." Howard gave

Billie a fabulous diamond necklace, and still the answer was "no." He was at his wit's end and fast running out of things to do when Billie expressed an interest in yachting.

Howard took this suggestion quite literally and turned his attention to finding the largest yacht available in the shortest amount of time. Thank God for Hughes Tool, he said to himself, or I'd never be able to afford somebody like her. He decided to call upon Noah Dietrich, the man he had hired in 1925 and since then entrusted with the running of the day-to-day affairs of the growing Hughes empire. It was quite a paradox, this association of Hughes and Dietrich. Noah Dietrich was seventeen years older than Howard, and physically it was like Mutt and Jeff, with Howard at 6'3½" and Dietrich nearly 5'8." Noah was a preacher's son, and Howard was the son of a wildcatter who had left to Howard, in addition to the drill bit company, his gambler's instinct and his powers as a visionary. Howard had called upon his father's gifts to him many times in his life, and the hiring of Noah Dietrich was certainly one of those occasions.

Howard had placed an ad in the *Los Angeles Times* in November 1925 looking for an executive assistant. He had been in California for almost a year since buying out his relatives and taking total control of Hughes Tool Company. His interest was in making movies and not in the management of business affairs. Dietrich answered the ad and met Howard in his suite at the Ambassador Hotel. After Howard questioned him about his background and was satisfied that Noah had a solid knowledge of business as well as being a CPA, he hired him a few weeks later.

Howard made it clear to Noah that part of his job was not only to handle the business but also to perform certain personal missions that would be entrusted to him. Howard didn't want "no" for an answer to any of his requests; he only wanted them carried out, and he wanted Noah to make sure the finances for all his adventures would always be available. Since then, Noah had run all the enterprises admirably and had carried out all his personal assignments with discretion and dispatch. This made for a very agreeable relationship with his employer.

Now came another challenge. It was three o'clock in the morning when the phone rang at Noah Dietrich's bedside. He knew it had to be Howard. Who else would be calling at this hour? There would be no "hello" and no apology for calling this late and waking Noah and his wife. Dietrich picked up the phone reluctantly, because he knew it was going to be another impossible task that Hughes would want accomplished no later than yesterday.

"Noah, I'm glad I caught you in."

"Where else did you think I'd be at three o'clock in the morning, Howard?"

"Well, here's what I need you to get for me."

"Whatever it is, couldn't it wait till tomorrow?"

"No, it goddamn can't! Billie Dove has let me know that she likes boating. She actually said 'yachting.' So I've decided to get the best and biggest yacht you can find, and once she sees that I'll go to the ends of the earth for her, she'll be mine."

"Howard, listen—you've gone too far this time. A large yacht can cost a fortune, and I'm sure she'd be just as happy with a speedboat ride."

"Noah, are you crazy? This is Billie Dove we're talking about. She's the biggest star in Hollywood, and I'm going to get her the biggest boat. It's taken me four weeks to get this far with her, and I'm not going to blow it over the size of a boat. She's driving me crazy, Noah, and I've got to have her. I don't care what it takes. Just get me that goddamn boat!" Click.

Early the next morning, Noah started making inquiries on

Mr. Hughes' behalf. The only yacht that could be located on such short notice was located in Santa Barbara, and it was a beauty. She was 170 feet in length and it took a crew of 18 to man her properly. She was called "The Hilda," named for Hilda Boldt, the widow of a steel magnate, who now was the owner. Dietrich phoned Howard with the news that he had located a yacht that he thought would meet his requirements. On the phone, Hughes told Dietrich that it sounded great and he should buy it for him. Dietrich said, "Howard, I think you should try it out first—you know, test-drive it. See how it feels, and besides, they want $450,000 for it, so you don't want to make a rash decision."

"Maybe you're right, Noah. Set up a test run for tomorrow. We'll see how it feels." The next day, Howard flew Noah up to Santa Barbara in his airplane where he met the captain and crew and they took a short cruise for about two hours. He liked the smell of the sea air. He liked the overall size of the ship. He liked the teak decks. He loved the master stateroom with its king-size bed. He was impressed with the way everyone in the crew called him "sir." He liked everything about it.

When they got back to the dock, Howard said to Noah, "I have to call Billie right away. I'm telling her we're going for a weekend cruise, just the two of us along with my crew. This is it, Noah. I've got her now."

"Hold on, Howard," replied Noah, astonished. "We haven't even made a deal for the boat yet, not to mention the crew. Mrs. Boldt is asking $450,000 and in today's market, I think I can get it for a quarter of a million. Give me a week, a few days at least, and I'll save you $200,000."

"I'm going cruising this weekend, and that's just a day away, Noah. See what you can do by then."

Noah called Mrs. Boldt and explained that Mr. Hughes

wanted to test-cruise "The Hilda" once more this weekend before making up his mind. Pretty shrewd herself, Mrs. Boldt sensed that Dietrich was stalling and, knowing the reputation of the young Howard Hughes, told Noah that the next time Mr. Hughes would be cruising on "The Hilda," he would being doing so as the new owner or not at all. Dietrich, knowing that Howard would blow his stack if he didn't have the boat, told Mrs. Boldt that in that case he was prepared to offer her $250,000 for "The Hilda." Mrs. Boldt countered with $400,000. Dietrich said there was no way he could come up with that figure without consulting with Mr. Hughes. Mrs. Boldt then offered what she termed a solution. She would accept $350,000, but only if it was in the form of a cashier's check and only if it was delivered the next day. She further stated that this was $100,000 less than her asking price and, if those terms were not suitable, the ship would be taken off the market as far as Howard Hughes was concerned. Dietrich knew she was gambling, but he also knew she had a winning hand. He called Howard to tell him of his conversation, but the only reply he got was "Buy it!"

Now, as dusk was approaching, Howard was lounging back in a deck chair on the aft deck of his new yacht. He was sipping a freshly squeezed orange juice that had just been handed to him by one of the crew, and he was gazing alternately out at the sea, then at the Santa Barbara coastline as "The Hilda" slowly cruised in a giant, gentle circle. Turning to the table just a few feet from him, he saw that the steward had followed his orders to lay it out wonderfully in a gleaming white and blue tablecloth with the initial "H" emblazoned on it as well as on the white and blue napkins. The silverware also had the initial "H" stamped onto every piece. Champagne was chilling on the ice, and the table looked beautiful as it sat there in the sunset, set for two.

Howard's patient quest would soon be at an end. This was going to be his time with the woman who had been in every conscious thought he had since the moment he met her at San Simeon. So what if it cost him $350,000 for this ship. He would have paid ten times that amount. As long as he had Hughes Tool, he could have whatever he wanted, and right now he wanted Billie Dove.

When the sun had gone down, the chief steward informed him that dinner was ready to be served. Howard gave instructions to ask Miss Dove to come to the aft deck for supper. He had run this scenario in his mind over and over again. He knew every move he was going to make, every word he was going to say. He had even dreamed about every reaction Billie was going to have. He knew he was going to take command. Then, backlit by moonlight, materializing as if by magic, Billie appeared on the deck, and every plan, every dream, every thought he had of being in control went straight overboard. He knew right then and there that he was about to be completely at her mercy.

She looked even better than he had envisioned, and Howard was breathless at the sight of her. One of the stewards asked if she would care for a cocktail before dinner, and she replied, "Just a glass of champagne—and one for Mr. Hughes."

Still sitting in his lounge chair, Howard said nothing. He just watched Billie. The steward handed her a chilled flute of champagne and then brought one to him. He watched as Billie brought the glass slowly to her lips, watched as she darted her tongue around the rim and then inside to taste the cold bubbly. He saw the way she lifted the glass and arched her back and neck to take a swallow of the golden liquid. Every move she made, every gesture, every glance was erotic to him. My God, she was even barefoot.

Billie motioned for him to take a drink, and he obeyed.

She was still standing about eight feet from him, bathed in moonlight, slowly, rhythmically moving to a musical beat that could be heard only inside her head. It was driving Howard mad, and he started to get up—but she gestured for him to stay where he was. Billie continued to sway to her own beat, and Howard's gaze returned to her feet. He wanted to feel them, to touch them, to kiss them. He let his eyes roam up her legs, past her calves to her thighs, and then he noticed for the first time that she was wearing shorts, rather baggy white sailor-style shorts with gold stars on them that buttoned just below her belly button. Her midriff was bare below a halter top, also in dazzling white with gold stars, cut low above her breasts.

She was still swaying in the moonlight, and Howard was beside himself. Without realizing it, he had his hand on his crotch and was actually beginning to rub himself. Billie saw what he was doing and motioned for him to come to her. At her side in an instant, he went to reach for her—but Billie stopped him, asking for another glass of champagne. He complied with even more alacrity than his head steward. This made Billie laugh. Howard noticed how big her eyes were and how they sparkled when she laughed.

"Billie, I have to hold you, I have..."

"I know Howard, I know," she said soothingly, caressing Howard's cheek. "Patience, darling, patience. We have all night, all year, we have forever. Now drink your drink and tell the crew we'll serve ourselves."

"But, Billie," Howard protested, "I had them prepare something very special and they want to impress us."

"Just do as I say," answered Billie, "I have something very special for you too."

He told the steward to put the whole meal on the table, including dessert, and that they would not be required until later. Howard sat Billie down at the table and took the chair next to her, neither one saying a word. Howard poured himself his second glass of champagne, which was most unusual for him, and then a third for Billie. She began to pick at her crab cocktail, which was sitting on a huge bed of ice. As she took another long draft of champagne, she studied Howard through half-closed lids. He was handsome, very tall and lean, and still very much a boy. As shy as he was, it was hard to believe he had so much wealth. She had to admit she loved the attention and the gifts he had lavished on her, and she knew she was ready to give in. But she was a few years older than Howard, and if he was going to have her, it was going to be her way. She would tease him and torment him and whip his desire to the point of frenzy.

"Howard, come over to the lounge with me and bring our wine," she told him. "I want you to rub my feet." He couldn't believe what he was hearing. She laid back on the lounge chair and crossed her legs. He walked over to the side of the lounge, gave her a glass of champagne, sat on the end of the chair, trembling, and put her feet in his lap. It was just as well they weren't talking anymore, because he lost the use of speech when she began moving her feet over his crotch, feeling for him with her toes.

"Now be a good boy, Howard, and give me a good foot massage. If you do it well, I'll have to reward you."

Howard took Billie's feet in his big hands, and his long, strong fingers began working, shooting fire through the soles of her feet up her lovely legs to her spine, around to her breasts and back down to her crotch. With the same rhythm as Howard was rubbing her feet now, she was rubbing her toes on the fly of his pants, and the pace grew faster, faster, faster and more frenzied. She knew what he was doing, and she enjoyed the game. Howard was massaging her calves, then her thighs. Billie slowly moved her legs apart, and as Howard pushed her baggy shorts to the side, he saw that she had no panties on, and he began to moan. As he moved his hand higher, she began to dig her toes deep into his groin, and sweat broke out on Howard's brow as he felt her groping for him with her feet.

Slowly, hesitatingly, he opened his belt buckle, unzipped his zipper and, seeing Billie's eyes telling him to go on, he pulled off his trousers. Howard had no underwear on and his turgid penis sprang free. Billie at once had it between her feet and was stroking it with her toes as Howard continued working his way to her crotch. She took his hand and began rubbing his fingers through her pubic hair, then slid them inside her. She began moaning now, moving her lower body in a slow, circular motion, all the while rubbing Howard's penis with her feet. Howard could feel how wet she was and he knew that she was as ready as he was. Unbuttoning her shorts, he slowly rolled them down over her belly and her mound of jet-black hair as she arched upward to let him pull off her pants.

He began to move on top of her, but Billie stopped him. "No, Howard," she cooed, "not yet. I want you to kiss me first. I want you to kiss me like you've never kissed anyone before."

"Anything, Billie, anything."

"Get the champagne and pour it over my feet and up my legs and onto my pussy," she ordered him. Howard did as he was told.

"Now, be a good boy, Howard," commanded Billie, "and lick it all up."

He started kissing her toes, then he licked off her calves, and as he reached her thighs, she reached down and began stroking his erection. Howard was shaking so hard, he didn't know if his heart could take it. He had licked his way all the

way up her taut thighs to the warm place between her legs—
and he couldn't go any further. He had never kissed a woman
there before. He thought it was wrong, or just not manly. But
Billie kept stroking him slowly, seductively. "C'mon Howard,
you have to lick up every last drop of the champagne."

"But, Billie…"

"No 'buts,' Howard, lick up the rest of that champagne or
there's no reward," she said, rubbing him faster and harder.
Tears came to Howard's eyes as the excitement built toward
bursting. Here was this incredibly gorgeous, sexy woman
open before him, and he didn't know what to do. But his
mind was made up for him when she moved her hand from
between his legs and pushed his head down between her
own. "That's right, that's right, just like that, yes!" she
squealed in ecstasy.

Howard had never done anything like this before. It was-
n't all that bad. In fact, it was incredibly exciting. If this is
what he had to learn to become more worldly, that was fine
with him. While he was licking, kissing and probing Billie,
she began to push herself into his mouth, at first gently,
then harder and harder. She was moaning, wailing, almost
sobbing as she writhed against him, pulling and pushing on
his head, and then she let loose with a scream from deep
within her as her entire body convulsed around him. Spent,
they lay there soaked in one another. Then he raised his
head and watched her stomach heave in and out with the
gasping breaths she was taking. As he looked up at her
beautiful face, transfigured with joy, she opened her eyes
and gave him a warm, wonderful smile.

"And now for your reward," she said, grasping his man-
hood and drawing it slowly into her mouth as she continued
smiling at him. Thank God for Hughes Tool, thought
Howard gratefully.

CHAPTER SEVEN

MARCH 17, 1973

·

*Inn on the Park
London, England*

It was 10:30 p.m. in Howard Hughes' penthouse suite at the Inn on the Park. The big meeting was scheduled for later that night.

"Hey, Stan," shouted Chris Mays from an easy chair in the salon of the vast suite, "You better go look in on the boss. It's about time to get him cleaned up!"

"In a minute, just a minute," answered Stan, "just a few more bites of my sandwich and I'll have him looking like Cary Grant." He'd been through this ritual many times before. He was now a full-fledged member of the palace guard, but he hadn't been hired by Bill Gay, and he wasn't loyal to Bill Gay either. He was there because the boss himself wanted him there. It was a unique relationship that started in the Beverly Hills Hotel in 1961, and had continued these last twelve years. Stan was a barber by trade, and it started innocently enough when he was asked to give some very special barbering to a very important person, and sworn to keep the whole affair secret. When the mysterious VIP turned out to be none other than the reclusive billionaire Howard Hughes, Stan felt very special to be included as one of the few to have contact with "the Man." He was also paid one thousand dollars for the first haircut.

When he was told about a month later that Mr. Hughes appreciated his skill and wanted to keep him on retainer, he was won over. Stan liked and respected Mr. Hughes from their first meeting, and he was intrigued by all the secrecy surrounding the entire Hughes myth.

From his very first exposure, Stan knew something was wrong, very wrong, but who was he to question? Maybe this is the way all eccentric billionaires behave, with phobias about germs, giving elaborate instructions on how to complete even the simplest tasks, letting their hair grow below their shoulders, never going out in public. Hell, how should I know, he thought, how many billionaires do I know? Only Howard Hughes. But he knew something was wrong, very wrong.

Stan had been drawn in, however, and he was aboard. Aboard for the whole ride ever since 1961. Even so, he still wasn't considered an insider, but that was okay with him, because Stan didn't like the way the aides treated Mr. Hughes. Even though they said it was on orders from Romaine Street, meaning Bill Gay, Stan still didn't like the way Mr. Hughes was kept isolated, insulated from affairs that Stan thought Hughes should have been consulted on. It was as if he had been quarantined from the outside world. But Stan was determined to help him return from exile. That is, if he wanted to return.

That was the question that had been gnawing at him since he first came to work for Mr. Hughes. He didn't really want to turn a blind eye, but the money was more than he had ever made. Then there were the perks—yes, the perks—expense accounts, gourmet cuisine, trips to Europe for his family. How could he turn that down? But if Mr. Hughes ever made it known to him, made it known clearly,

Stan would help, he was sure of it.

"Hey, Stan, it's a quarter to eleven," said Chris, as he tapped him on the shoulder, "C'mon, you know they want him looking good. Bill Gay, Davis and Miss Henley have been waiting a long time for this meeting. The Governor and the Chairman of the Gaming Commission are already in London. You've got to do a good job. I hope the boss doesn't give you a hard time."

"I'm going in to him now," said Stan, stopping off in his room to get his barber's bay, filled with all the equipment he'd need to groom the boss. He had heard the aides discussing the upcoming meeting, and he knew it had something to do with the Las Vegas properties.

Stan knocked on Hughes' bedroom door, but there was no reply. He knocked again. No reply. He knew his employer was half deaf but refused to wear a hearing aid, so Stan slowly opened the door to the darkened room—and that same dank smell every time he entered the bedroom.

"Mr. Hughes, Mr. Hughes," Stan said quite loudly, standing next to his bed. Hearing only grumbling, he listened closer, but he couldn't see any signs of life. The bedroom door was ajar and he was looking at Mr. Hughes by the light from the salon. "Mr. Hughes," he said once more, "it's time for your haircut and trim. C'mon, let's get up." Stan hated waking him, because he knew how difficult it was for him to have even a fitful sleep. "It's me, Stan. Everyone is waiting on you, and I'm going to get you looking good!"

In a groggy, pleading voice, Howard said finally, "Is that you, Stan? Give me another half hour or so, I'm having a really nice dream. Be a good fellow, just a little more time." And he turned his head, sinking back to sleep, back in time.

In the dream, he was talking to Dan Beard, known as the Chief, who was dressed in his buckskin clothes complete with fringe and Teddy Roosevelt-style Rough Rider hat. The Chief ran and operated Camp Teedyusking in the Pocono Mountains of northeastern Pennsylvania. It was the beginning of the summer of 1916, and Howard was ten years old, and it was the first time he had been away from home. At first young Howard, known as Sonny, was disturbed about leaving home. But after arriving in camp and having a talk with the Chief, who also happened to be one of the founders of the Boy Scouts of America, Sonny was looking forward to the adventure of being away from his parents.

Howard's mother, Allene Hughes, had been in contact with Dan Beard before Howard enrolled in the camp this summer. By letter she had explained that Sonny was a very shy boy and was prone to illness and headaches. She was in great fear of an outbreak of either typhoid or infantile paralysis or some other disease that might be carried by unseen germs. She and her husband, Howard, Sr., felt that a place in the clear, clean outdoors such as Camp Teedyusking would be just the ticket for Sonny. Especially with the hot summer coming that would undoubtedly bring the spread of germs to Houston. She would require reports as often as possible on Sonny's health. Reports that would cover his weight, height, heart, feet, color, teeth, digestion, bowels, sleep, and the exact nature of his contact with any other boys who may have something contagious. "Please work with Sonny," she concluded her letter, "as he is a nervous child and has a very difficult time making friends with other children."

Having dealt with many parents, Chief Dan was sympathetic to a family's customary concerns, especially the first time a child was away from home. But in young Howard's case it was most unusual for a mother to express the deep fears that were so clearly evident in Allene Hughes. He saw a fine boy in young Howard, and Beard knew that if Mrs.

Hughes would simply let nature take its course and let Sonny spend the summer in camp with the other boys, he would return to her a stronger and more fit young man.

"Tell me, Howard," said the Chief, "what do you want to do here in camp this summer?"

"Well, Chief, first of all, please call me Sonny. That's what my family calls me," the ten year old replied. "I 'd like to learn about camping and fishing and hiking and sleeping outdoors. But Mother says I have to be alert not to get hurt, and I have to be careful about germs. You know, you can't see them."

"I know, Sonny," said the Chief as delicately as possible. "What else did your mother warn you about?"

"She said I have to be cautious about who I become friends with."

"Why's that, Sonny?"

"Because you never know if they've been sick or might be getting sick."

"Do you have many friends at home in Houston, Sonny?"

"Not really, Chief, only Dudley Sharp. He's real neat and Mother says he's okay because he's my father's partner's son. We hang around together and take saxophone lessons, and we're interested in a lot of the same things."

"Tell me, Sonny, does Dudley's mother worry about the germs the same as your mother?" asked Chief Dan.

"No sir, Chief," said Howard. "Mother says Mrs. Sharp doesn't see the germs as clearly as she does. That's why she tells me to be so careful. Most people don't see them and don't know what kind of trouble they can cause, like polio and stuff worse than that. Sometimes Mother puts gauze around my nose and mouth when she thinks the germs are coming."

"Well, Sonny, you may feel that's carrying things too far, but I'm sure you know she does it because she loves you so much."

"I know, Chief," said Howard. "Mother tells me she loves me all the time, and that she's not going to have any more children, and she's afraid of losing me."

Chief Dan smiled, trying to make young Howard feel welcome, and said, "Well, nobody's going to lose you here. You're going to have a great summer at Camp Teedyusking, and you're going to become a real Buckskin Man."

Howard remembered that summer and the one after that when his friend Dudley went to the Chief's camp along with him, and the great times they had as Buckskin Men. He let his mind drift and wander. He was gliding, flying in the air all by himself, without an airplane, and then he was floating. Floating in a pool, and the pool became a lake, and the lake became the ocean, and he was back with Billie Dove aboard his ship, "The Hilda."

He remembered that first night with Billie and how exciting it was. He remembered how soon afterward he signed her to a five-picture contract at $85,000 a picture. He remembered going to Europe with her and telling her how much he loved her. He remembered wanting to marry her, but that she still needed to get her divorce. He recalled her estranged husband Irvin Willat putting the screws to him and demanding $325,000 in thousand-dollar bills to let her go and ordering Noah Dietrich to get the money and get it in cash from Hughes Tool. He remembered his lawyer Neil McCarthy had turned the money over to Willat and then flying Billie to a town in Nevada and waiting the six weeks for her divorce to become final. He remembered how excited he was that he was going to be married to her at last. He played golf three or four times a week at the Wilshire Country Club with his pro in between trips to see her in Nevada. On the day the six weeks were up and Billie's divorce was final, he flew her back in his plane and celebrated with Cary

Grant in Los Angeles. He remembered setting a date for his wedding and, in the meantime, Billie taking golf lessons from his pro so they could have another interest in common.

And then he remembered hearing that Billie was having an affair with his golf pro. And he recalled that the pro had told him during one of their many rounds of golf that he had "the clap"—gonorrhea. And Howard remembered his mother, his wonderful darling mother, telling him, warning him, begging him to be careful of germs, to watch out for them, for you never knew when, you never knew how, you never knew who could give them to you.

He remembered never seeing Billie ever again. He remembered burning all the clothes he had, burning all the sheets and pillowcases and bedspreads that he and Billie had slept on. He remembered his mother's warning about those unseen germs and decided then and there never, ever to take a chance like that again. He would be in total control of all women in his life from then on, even if it meant putting them in houses and guarding them 24 hours a day. Sonny would never let anyone get that close again.

Howard was still floating and dreaming when he heard a voice urging him, "Mr. Hughes, c'mon, boss, you have to let me clean you up. Please, Mr. Hughes, it's been over an hour since you asked me to give you a little more time."

"What the hell is it?" demanded Howard. "What's going on?"

"I've got to get you cleaned up for the meeting, boss," said Stan.

"Meeting?"

"The big meeting, Mr. Hughes," said Harley Smith, who had padded quietly back into the room. "Bill Gay and Chester Davis are here, and the Governor of Nevada and the Chairman of the Gaming Commission."

"Give me a few minutes. I've got to concentrate on just what the hell I've got everyone here for. I'm still drowsy."

"I'm sorry, Mr. Hughes," said Smith, "but Stan has to start shaving you now. It's your own orders to have this meeting. It's what they say you've wanted ever since you fired Bob Maheu."

"It is?" asked Howard, bewildered, addressing no one in particular.

CHAPTER EIGHT

MARCH 18, 1973

·

Inn on the Park
London, England

The scent from the plush, deep-red leather of the VIP booth of the Grill Room at the Inn on the Park was the aroma of luxury, the fragrance of wealth, the rich smell of control. Bill Gay sat deep within the comfort of the banquette and let his hands feel the warmth of the leather. The Inn was abreast of the English garden, overflowing its myriad banks of flowers. His view from the other side, seemingly part of the hotel grounds, was the sylvan acres of Hyde Park. What a shame that the resident who was making all this possible couldn't enjoy the majesty of this setting, because it was almost too late for Howard Hughes.

Chester Davis sat across from Bill Gay and wondered what was going through his mind. He found himself studying Gay. Tall and lean, with no extra skin on him, he wore his hair short, nearly military style, and the small dark eyes, blinking nervously, had the cold stare of a cobra. He always seemed to be plotting something. Gay rarely laughed, never raised his voice, never took a drink. Davis didn't trust anyone who didn't have a drink, at least once in a while. But the thing that bothered him most about Gay was that he always wore a dark gray, navy blue or black suit with a white shirt and tie. Until this moment, he hadn't been able to figure out why that was so disturbing to him. What frightened Davis was that the dark, ominous Gay looked like a funeral director. Everything neat, everything in place, solemn, impersonal, courteous, strictly business.

Well, it's too late now, he reflected—in for a penny, in for a pound, and besides they were about to complete another major step in the takeover plot.

"Jesus, Bill, I can't stand this waiting. What if the old man decides not to go through with the meeting?"

"I've asked you before, Chester, and I don't intend to ask you again, do not, I repeat, do not use the Lord's name in that manner. But in answer to your question, as we speak, Stan Dean is cleaning the boss up for the meeting."

"Are you sure he can be trusted with the governor? It would be disastrous if he said the wrong thing."

"Remember, Chester," explained Gay, "we've been getting him ready for this meeting for almost three years."

"What the hell are you talking about?" Davis said impatiently.

"Use your head and think back," said Gay. "It was early in 1970 when Mr. Hughes decided to turn the handling of the TWA case from you to Bob Maheu."

"So?"

"So that's when Maheu made the blunder of deciding to set his strategy for the TWA defense without consulting you. Mr. Hughes was horrified when the Attorney General recommended damages in excess of 131 million dollars."

"We were pissed," said Davis. "I had assurance that Brownell wouldn't ask for more than five million."

"Those assurances were worthless. A year later Judge Metzner awarded the plaintiff the maximum, 145 million to be exact."

"I couldn't fuckin' believe it."

"You couldn't believe it. Imagine how Mr. Hughes felt when the news came a day before his birthday. No wonder he turned it over to Maheu," Gay added.

"That son of a bitch Maheu shouldn't have tried to take me off the case. He was trying to cut my balls off!" shouted Davis.

"Control yourself, Chester, and I've asked you before, no profanity."

"Who the fuck are you trying to kid with this holy Joe act?" exclaimed Davis, his face reddening. "You and Nadine Henley are in this thing just as deep as I am. Stop worrying about my goddamn language and start worrying about Hughes not fucking us up with the governor."

"Okay, okay, Chester, just calm down."

A slight smile flickered on Davis' face. He noticed that as Gay got more upset, his eyes began to blink almost uncontrollably.

"As I was saying," Gay continued, "Maheu's big mistake was trying to take you off the TWA litigation, but it was the year before when he actually made the fatal error that led to his fall from grace."

"Committing Hughes Tool funds to buy a helicopter commuter service that was already deep in shit was a stupid decision," said Davis as he pulled on his left ear, a habit he was totally unaware of, but one that almost anyone he came in contact with found extremely annoying.

Gay smiled. "Mr. Hughes certainly didn't need to take on more debt, especially another airline, when TWA was already in trouble, and a large judgment was hanging over Hughes Tool. I had the boys tell Mr. Hughes as subtly as possible what his great white knight Bob Maheu had committed him to, without his permission. Well, even in his mental state, Mr. Hughes blew his stack."

"I knew Maheu was in serious trouble when he called all the Hughes executives to that meeting in L.A. He was almost groveling when he said he would never again commit funds without consulting us. It must have galled him to ask for our help when his reputation was on the line as the man who deals for Howard Hughes." Davis laughed. "And the son of a bitch couldn't understand why Hughes wouldn't take his calls anymore."

"Right," said Gay. "I made sure of that by having the aides give him hints that Maheu was running everything into the ground, driving his Vegas properties into bankruptcy. We just planted the seed in Mr. Hughes' head and let his imagination and the medication do the rest."

Gay let these last words sink in. "Chester, when Maheu made the decision to remove you from the TWA litigation, he didn't want to ruffle your feathers, so he said he was keeping you on for other Hughes matters and for his overall new strategy concerning TWA and the purchase of Los Angeles Airways."

"So?" said Davis.

"So he put it all in a memo and sent it over to Mr. Hughes at the Desert Inn. Of course, one of the aides got it first and read it to me according to my standing orders."

Chester, holding back a smile. "And you told him not to give it to Hughes?"

"Better than that. I told him to destroy it on the spot and never mention it."

Davis made a mental note never to trust this devious son of a bitch. "Now I understand why Maheu needed our help," he replied evenly. "He was completely cut off from Hughes."

"Not quite completely," said Gay. "We let certain things through, nothing that could help his cause, only enough to let Hughes feel he's on top of everything. You see, Maheu's mistake was thinking he really was in charge. But all he really had was a contract for a big salary, and an overly generous expense account..."

"And a house on the Desert Inn golf course so big that people called it Little Caesar's Palace," added Davis.

"Yes, but that house, like everything else, was owned by Mr. Hughes. You see, Maheu was held on a leash—a very long leash, but still a leash. And when he got out of hand with his flamboyant lifestyle—and an executive jet for himself—we just pulled in the leash. No way were we going to let Maheu really be in control of 150 to 200 million dollars worth of Las Vegas properties. He forgot that in order to carry out his plans, he had to get Hughes' personal permission. In order to get that, he had to go through the aides, and that meant going through me. He didn't realize that I held the key."

"How in the hell do you keep those aides in line, Bill? I've never met them, but I speak to them on the phone. Why would they want a job where they're locked up with Hughes for weeks, even months at a time?"

"Loyalty and perks."

"Loyalty to whom?"

"To me, of course. Most of the aides weren't too successful in their endeavors prior to coming to work for Mr. Hughes. They had done everything from construction work to mechanics to being a wax salesman, and probably many things in between. Everyone started as a driver, just as I did. Except for one of them, they all came to me for a job either through a relative or a friend connected with the Mormon Church. Mr. Hughes liked what I did for him. I handled little problems for him quickly and efficiently, and I never questioned his orders, nor did I ever, I mean ever, talk about any of the duties I performed for him. Well, those attributes, especially my silence, impressed him. It impressed him to the point that he wanted me to hire men just like myself to work in his Romaine Street headquarters.

"The only men I knew that I could trust were Mormons. Mormons are brought up to have integrity, to be trustworthy and loyal. I also knew that, by hiring them, they would be indebted to me. Also remember, none of us smoke or drink."

"Yeah, I noticed that," said Davis sarcastically.

"Well, it was very important to Mr. Hughes, because he was already beginning to show signs of his germ phobia, so he didn't want anyone smoking around him. And he liked the fact that none of us would get drunk and talk too much. It was easy. Nothing like hard labor, just running errands, chauffeuring people to and from hotels, airports and houses. The only things I demanded of them were to keep their mouths shut and never talk about their duties, and, most importantly, that their loyalty was not to Mr. Hughes but to me. They know I am the one who can move them up in the organization—or fire them."

"That I understand," said Chester, "but it still doesn't explain your hold over them. How you get them to guard Hughes but follow the policy we dictate."

"I'm coming to that. Mr. Hughes has always told whoever he wants something from that he's going to leave them a large sum of money in his will. Well, Chester, I've hinted to the boys that we're doing what we're doing so that I can make sure that Mr. Hughes' money goes to the Mormon Church."

"You no-good son of a bitch," screamed Chester. "We're going through all this just so your fucking church can get the money?"

"What's wrong with you, Chester?" asked Gay, blinking out of control. "Of course, I have no intention of turning over such wealth to the church. But if that belief eases the conscience of the boys, so be it!"

Davis just smiled at Gay.

"And don't forget the perks," Gay explained, "we give the boys a more than ample salary—more than they'd ever made before, even though it still isn't that much. And where else are these fellows going to get a job where they get a new car, the lowest interest loan to buy a house and be allowed to fly their wives and their families to vacation with them? They stay in fabulous hotel suites and eat the best food on the menu."

"You're right," agreed Davis. "Where the hell else would guys with blue-collar backgrounds live the life they're enjoying?"

"And all I ask," stated Bill Gay, "is that they shut up and follow orders—my orders."

"That's all well and good, but how are you going to control the outcome of this meeting with the new Governor of Nevada and Chairman of the Gaming Commission? How do you know Hughes will behave himself?"

"I'm about to tell you," answered Gay, with a note of exasperation in his voice, "but only on one condition: You have to stop pulling on your ear."

CHAPTER NINE

MARCH 18, 1973

·

Inn on the Park
London, England

Harley Smith had left the room having seen that Hughes had finally acquiesced to the cleanup and haircut. Stan was alone in the bedroom with just his boss and the dank odor that he swore would always remain in his nostrils.

Howard was sitting on the edge of his bed, staring out as if into space, seemingly lost in thought. One might conclude that Hughes was contemplating his strategy for the meeting that was soon to take place. But Stan knew that was probably not on his employer's mind. He knew from past experience, from other times when he had to get Mr. Hughes ready for whatever important function the aides deemed necessary, that the boss never thought about the immediate situation until it was actually time to perform. It was strange he should think of it as a performance, but how else could he define it? Mr. Hughes was like a great actor who could be feeling lousy, have a million other things to worry about, yet when the curtain goes up, goes out and gives an award-winning performance just as the script has called for. Only in this theater, the script was written by Bill Gay, Nadine Henley and Chester Davis.

Stan Dean was not only Hughes' personal barber, but over the years had also become his male nurse. Howard felt comfortable with Stan, and as he came to require more personal attention, it seemed only natural for him to wear both hats. It was in his capacity as nurse that Stan observed the physical condition of his employer as he was preparing to get him ready for the meeting, and he was shocked by what he saw. Stan wondered why he hadn't noticed the gravity of Mr. Hughes' deepening deterioration before. He felt it must be like living with someone for many years and, as they lose weight, or put it on, you don't seem to notice it.

Mr. Hughes was bone thin. He had an open sore at the shoulder that wasn't healing. His color was awful, in fact, it wasn't so much the color being bad, it was more like an absence of color. And there were needle tracks on both arms. His hair was always fine, but now it was terribly long, almost shoulder length, and the color had long since gone yellowish white. And the beard he had adopted in the mid-60s, worn in a short Van Dyke, had grown like a wild weed almost to mid-chest. Worst of all were his nails, which were anywhere from three-quarters of an inch to a full inch long on both his hands and feet. Stan came close to the point of nausea as he began to comprehend the reality of his condition. What could possibly have made Mr. Hughes allow this to happen to himself, and what kind of people are those who have allowed it, and worse, taken advantage of it. I must find a way to help him, thought Stan, and I only pray to God that he'll give me an opportunity.

"Okay, Mr. Hughes, I'm going to trim your hair now," said Stan. "Let me help you to your chair." He reached under Howard's arm and half pulled, half pushed him into the chair. He then got a sheet and wrapped it around his otherwise naked body. For many years Howard had adopted the habit of staying completely nude in his bedroom. Stan went to get his barber shears and comb, then prepared three bowls of warm water for Mr. Hughes to soak his hands and feet in, so it would be easier to trim his nails.

Stan remembered that on a number of other occasions when he was required to clean him up, the boss hadn't spoken a word. But to Stan's great surprise, Howard came out of his reverie, like a man suddenly waking up, and said, "Stan, I want you to get me looking real sharp. This is an important meeting for me, and I want to make a good impression."

Stan couldn't believe his ears, and he noticed that Mr. Hughes' eyes were remarkably clear. "Yes, sir," he replied. "I'm happy to see you're feeling better. Just a minute ago, I didn't know if you were going to make it to the meeting."

"That's ridiculous," said Howard sharply. "The aides have been preparing me for weeks. I'm finally going to get that son of a bitch Maheu out of the picture once and forever."

Stan couldn't hide his surprise as he began cutting the hair from around the boss' shoulders and neck.

Howard went on: "He thought he was going to run Las Vegas, but I found out in time and stopped him."

Stan felt his way carefully. "How'd you find out, Mr. Hughes?"

"I have my ways. I know what's going on in all my businesses."

Stan didn't comment. He just continued cutting his hair and listening.

"Well, aren't you going to ask me how I know what's going on?" demanded Howard. Without giving Stan time to answer, he looked around and then said in a conspiratorial tone, "I can sense things, Stan, you know, feel them. It's instinctive, almost like a psychic ability."

Stan was flabbergasted, but he said nothing. The best thing he could do for his employer was to try to get him well physically and, as the opportunity arose, to do what he could to help him back to the world of reality before it was too late. He decided to just go along with Mr. Hughes, at least for the present. "So that's how you knew about the Maheu situation, from psychic feelings?"

"Yes, Stan, and of course, the aides filled me in on the situation. I sensed that something was very wrong with Bob Maheu. Then the boys told me that he was trying to buy the Los Angeles Airways deal with my money. Hell, I never gave him permission. I never told him to fire Chester Davis. I only told him to take care of the TWA case." Howard continued talking, almost inaudibly but coherently, "The least Maheu could have done was to keep me informed. I had established a system of memos with him, but they stopped. He even stopped calling me."

Stan had been with the Hughes entourage at the time of the Maheu situation, and he had wondered what caused the rift between them, but he wasn't privy to the particulars. And he wasn't that friendly with the aides. He was considered the low man on the totem pole, so no one filled him in. But since Mr. Hughes was in such a talkative mood, Stan dared be more bold and asked the question that was preying on his mind. "Mr. Hughes, how do you know, why are you so sure that the aides are giving you the right information about Maheu or anything else concerning your organization?"

Stan held his breath and waited for Mr. Hughes to answer.

"Loyalty, Stan, loyalty. The boys are grateful to me for their jobs and, of course, the benefits that I've instructed Nadine Henley to give them. Besides, I've let them know that I'm thinking about leaving a substantial amount to the Church of Latter Day Saints."

"I didn't know you were leaving money to the church. I'm a Mormon, too, Mr. Hughes."

"I'm thinking about it. It's part of a plan I have," said

Howard. "And Stan, I want you to know that I'm very aware of all that you've done for me over the years. I know how inconvenient it's been for you and your family, but I don't know anyone else I can trust as I trust you."

"Thank you, Mr. Hughes. I feel it's a real honor working for you."

"And, Stan, I want you to know that I plan to take very good care of you in my will."

"Mr. Hughes, I don't know what to say."

"Don't say anything. Just keep giving me your loyalty," said Howard in a benevolent tone, thinking to himself how clever it was to use this ploy of promising money in his will. It had always gotten him what he wanted and worked better than actually giving money. Howard had figured out long ago that when you give money, they know what they're getting, but when you promise them money in your will, their own greed lets them imagine the amount to be much greater than anything he would ever consider giving them.

"All right, boss," said Stan. "Your hair is all trimmed now, so I'm going to start on your beard."

Howard thought to himself, maybe I really will do something for this fellow. It'll just have to wait until I complete my plan.

Trimming his beard, Stan said, "I'm going to have you looking real sharp, boss, just like you said. Tell me, why did you say this is such an important meeting for you?"

"When I first sensed that Maheu was screwing up, I started worrying about all of my holdings in Nevada. You see, Stan, I had Maheu in charge of all Nevada, acting on my behalf. He was on the gaming licenses, and that gave him tremendous power. But I still felt he had my best interests at heart. And he was telling me that the casinos were doing well, so I put my feelings aside. The only thing that had me overly concerned was that damned TWA judgment."

"But you won that case," said Stan, and he reflected once again how amazing it was that Mr. Hughes was so alert. He guessed that the medication was being decreased and figured that if he could take charge of it, if only for a little while, he might be able to help his boss get off the drugs entirely.

He was shaken out of those thoughts when the boss exclaimed, "Goddamn it, Stan, at that time the judgment was $160 million or so and it didn't look like we were going to win. And then I got the first of Raymond Holliday's reports."

"He's the head of your Tool Company division, right, Mr. Hughes?"

"That's right, Stan, only it's not my damn company any longer. That division is public now. If I'd been in my right mind, I never would have let it go. As I was saying, Holliday brought me this report showing that Toolco needed X amount of dollars to keep on hand for the TWA judgment, and when you added up the needs of my other companies, including the Nevada operation, we were going to come up short. Then about two weeks later, Holliday brought me another report showing that my Nevada operations would probably lose almost 14 million dollars that year under Maheu."

"How could that be, Mr. Hughes?" asked Dean. "I thought your casinos and hotels were going great."

"That's the same damn question I asked," said Howard, almost speaking to himself. "Who the hell ever heard of casinos losing money? That's when I knew that son of a bitch Maheu was stealing from me. And would you believe, he had a bigger and better private jet than I ever had. Where the hell did he get the money for that? I can tell you not from me. But I sensed what he was pulling and the aides confirmed it. Then he stopped communicating with me. That proved it, as far as I'm concerned."

Stan was finished with the beard and began trimming the boss' nails. Taking his left hand out of the water, he began clipping the taloned fingernails. "Mr. Hughes, I still don't understand what's so important about this meeting with the Governor of Nevada?"

"That's the best part of my plan," said Howard, as if he were repeating this explanation by rote. "I had to protect myself from Maheu. He's a very devious man, you know. So I decided to have his name taken off the Nevada gaming licenses and put the licenses in the names of people I could trust."

As Stan started on the other hand, he prompted, "Is that what you did, boss?"

"Yes, I made up a proxy that allowed Raymond Holliday, Chester Davis and Bill Gay to be on the licenses, and took Bob Maheu off. I made sure in my proxy that they could run the properties and, of course, that made them happy, but they didn't like the fact that I also made sure that they cannot, I repeat cannot, sell, dispose or transfer any of my Nevada holdings." As he looked up at Stan, Howard couldn't keep from smiling at how shrewd he was.

Stan was dumbfounded how sharp and clear Mr. Hughes' mind was operating. He was positive that the drugs or, as the aides and Mr. Hughes himself called them, his medication, had been decreased at least a week or more prior to this meeting. He hoped that the boss would insist on less and less medication and start to come back into the real world and not the world of self-imposed prisoner. Stan began trimming Howard's toenails. "Now that I'm getting you all cleaned up and barbered, will you please try and keep it up?" Stan pleaded. "Please, Mr. Hughes, you'll feel better—like you do now."

"We'll see, Stan. We'll see."

"Okay, boss. One last question, though, if you don't

mind: Why do you want to see the governor?"

"It's not that I want to see him," explained Howard. "He insists on seeing me. You see, since this proxy involved so much property and money, the governor wanted to make sure it's really what I want to do. Ever since that Clifford Irving fiasco, they don't believe it's my real wishes. He insists on a face-to-face meeting. That's why I want you to make sure I look good, Stan, so the governor can see I'm all right. I have to make sure the proxy is accepted so I won't have to worry about Maheu any longer. And I'll meet with the governor or the devil to take care of this."

Stan completed sprucing up Mr. Hughes. This included giving him a complete sponge bath and splashing Old Spice after-shave on him. Stan also put him in a new white terrycloth robe and bedroom slippers, then stood back and admired his work. The man in front of him was neat, clean, trimmed and seemingly in charge of all his faculties. A far cry from the long-haired, long-nailed, foul-odored figure of only an hour ago. Stan Dean really felt that maybe the man he liked and admired so much was on his way to recovery.

"Stan, be a good fellow and bring me that medicine bottle over there," ordered Howard. Without question, Stan handed the bottle to his employer, who popped four of the blue tablets into his mouth and swallowed them with a bottle of Poland water that he had Stan get for him from the supply that was always kept in the refrigerator in the kitchen.

Stan realized only after Mr. Hughes had taken them that they were ten-milligram Valium tablets. "Mr. Hughes, you shouldn't have taken so many pills. You want to be sharp for your meeting."

"It's okay. I'm used to it. I want to be very much at ease, and these will help." There was nothing more Stan could do at this point, so he just stood there and waited for Mr. Hughes to give the next order. Howard had closed his eyes, but he wasn't sleeping. Stan could see the movement behind his eyes, the lines on his brow, as if he was thinking deeply, concentrating.

Finally, Howard broke the silence. "Stan, I'm going to trust you with my biggest secret." Stan didn't know what to think. What could it possibly be? The only thing that came to his mind was that Howard Hughes was going to tell him where his will was kept.

"Well, Stan, what do you say? Can I trust you to help me and to keep silent?"

Stan had promised himself that if the opportunity presented itself, he would do everything he could to help. "Yes, Mr. Hughes, you can count on me," he said proudly. But nothing in the world could have prepared him for what Howard finally said.

"Okay, Stan, this is why I need your help. The boys don't think I know what's going on, and let's keep it that way, because I'm going to escape. I'm going to fly again—and I'm going to escape."

CHAPTER TEN

MARCH 18, 1973

Inn on the Park
London, England

It had been five minutes since Chris Mays had come to the table where Bill Gay and Chester Davis were sitting in the Grill Room. He brought the news that Mr. Hughes was about ten minutes from being ready for the meeting with the officials from Nevada. Gay instructed Mays to return to the penthouse and make sure that Mr. Hughes looked presentable, and even more important, that he complete a last-minute review of the subjects that Gay wanted him sharp on.

As Davis and Gay made their way toward the bank of elevators, Gay reflected on how rich and wonderfully appointed this hotel was. It was the first time he had been to the Inn on the Park, and he made a mental note to compliment McDermott and the other aides for planting the suggestion to stay there in Mr. Hughes' ear. He marveled at all the flowers and greenery that surrounded him, not only here on his walk to the lifts, but all over the Inn. Mixed throughout the hotel, arranged in vases and laid out in all strategic areas were pink, white and yellow tulips. All a feast for the eyes. And as he walked, he knew he was stepping on antique Persian carpeting from Tabriz and Feraghan, the finest he had ever beheld. Gay felt very much at home in these luxurious surroundings, and why not, he thought to himself. In just a very few minutes, he and his partners, in their dark secret, should be a major step closer to the kind of wealth that would make the opulence of this hotel seem like that of a Woolworth's five and dime. The kind of wealth that could buy him his own 707, a fleet of 707s, the kind of wealth that gave him a headache just trying to calculate it. The wealth of Howard Hughes.

"I'm so nervous, I'm afraid I'm going to piss in my pants," said Chester Davis as they walked toward the elevators. "You know, Bill, I've never met Mr. Hughes."

"I know. But you have nothing to worry about, Chester. You're in good favor. You won the TWA litigation."

"Yeah, but he figured out that we pushed him into selling Toolco so we could take it public."

"That's water under the bridge, it's old history. No need to let it concern you."

"How can you be so sure?"

"The aides keep me informed. In fact, they keep me informed on a day-to-day basis, and if it's required, an hour-to-hour basis." The two men were walking at a very leisurely pace, taking their sweet time.

"Now to get back to the question you asked before we were interrupted by Mays," said Gay, "and to alleviate your apprehension, I've already been over this ground with Miss Henley."

"Well, I'm real pleased that you've alleviated Nadine's fear of this meeting," Davis said in his most sarcastic tone, "but I'm the one who's on the firing line, so why don't you just fill me in, too, Bill."

"All right, Chester, but you must stay calm. Mr. Hughes *wants* this meeting to take place, and he wants it to go off like clockwork."

"What the hell are you talking about?"

Both men stopped walking, and Gay turned to face Davis. "That's right, Chester. You see, we convinced Mr. Hughes that Maheu was absolutely, no question, stealing from him."

"But that's nonsense."

"We know that, but Mr. Hughes thinks otherwise. In early October 1990, I had Raymond Holliday prepare a report showing that Toolco needed money to be set aside for the TWA judgment if it ever came to be. I also had him show that Hughes Tool would, for the first time, be in the red by more than 10 million dollars with the way the Nevada Properties were being managed. As you can imagine, this had him very concerned—but not convinced yet."

Davis was smiling in admiration.

"To push him over the edge a couple of weeks later," Gay went on, "I had Holliday give him a second report, one zeroing in on the Nevada operations only, primarily the casinos. It showed that Nevada would lose somewhere between 13 and 14 million dollars under Maheu."

"And whoever heard of casinos losing that kind of money?" Davis chimed in.

"That's exactly what I knew Mr. Hughes would say. We put the bug in his ear that Maheu had to be stealing, that no one could be that incompetent. We kept reminding him about Maheu's house, his jet, his entire lavish lifestyle. Between the whispers, the medication and the isolation that Mr. Hughes has committed himself to, it was a foregone conclusion that he would condemn Maheu."

"And when you cut him off from speaking or writing to Hughes, he was dead in the water," said Davis with a laugh.

"Absolutely," said Gay, as they continued their stroll toward the elevators. "I had the aides convince Mr. Hughes that Maheu had to be out forever, especially off the gaming licenses. We persuaded him to okay a proxy signing over the casinos to us. Us being you, Chester, Raymond Holliday, and me."

"That's how you got Holliday to give Hughes the reports."

"In any event," said Gay, "we finally got Mr. Hughes to sign the proxy and I had it notarized by one of the aides, but Mr. Hughes was still clever enough not to give us final authority."

"I know," Davis acknowledged, "but it gives us enormous leverage. Even with everything that you do to Hughes, he still has his moments of clear sight."

"That's true for the present, but in time, Chester, we will not only control everything in the Hughes empire, we will own it."

They had arrived at the elevators and had to wait for an aide with the key to admit them to the penthouse level. The buttons in all elevators that stopped at the penthouse had been removed and replaced by locks that were turned by special keys to which only the aides had access. This was just one of the measures taken to make sure no one could ever get near Howard Hughes.

"As I was saying, Chester," said Gay, "since this proxy turns the running of the casinos over to us, the governor intends to make sure it's really what Mr. Hughes desires."

"I understand his apprehension," said Davis, "especially in light of the Clifford Irving hoax, and the publishers' experts swearing it was Howard Hughes' signature. Who can blame him for not trusting the handwriting? But the fingerprints? I don't see how he could refute them."

"We have to understand, Chester," said Gay in a solicitous tone. "This is a new governor, not our old friend, Paul Laxalt. After the news broke that Mr. Hughes had met with President Somoza and Ambassador Shelton in Nicaragua, the governor insisted on meeting with Mr. Hughes personally."

"It would be a slap in the face," said Davis, "if Mr. Hughes met with a foreign dictator but refused to meet with the new governor of the state where he has a fortune in holdings."

"Exactly, and that's why we're here. So remember, Chester, Mr. Hughes wants this meeting. In his mind, he's getting rid of the crook, once and forever. We've convinced him of that. That's why it's all going to go as smooth as silk."

"What about his medication?"

"We've been weaning him off it very slowly these last few weeks, but not enough to lose control. He's been taking 10 milligrams of Valium, and I'm sure he'll be very mellow and cordial. He's still very convincing when he wants to be, and in this meeting, he wants to be."

Harley Smith arrived at the elevators and greeted Gay warmly. Davis looked at him with disdain, the same way he looked at all the aides, as Smith pushed the button for the elevator and the three men stepped in. Smith inserted his key into the keyhole where the button for the penthouse used to be and turned it.

All three men stood in silence as the elevator raced toward the penthouse suites, since the Hughes entourage had taken over the entire top floor of the Inn. While Gay and Smith stared at the shine in their shoes, Davis openly admired himself, feeling triumphant, in the mirrors that surrounded them.

The elevator came to a quiet stop, and the doors opened to reveal an armed guard in uniform behind a large desk. The guard nodded acknowledgment at Smith, who said to him, "Harry, this is the gentleman we've told you about, Mr. Bill Gay."

Harry almost jumped out of his chair and saluted military style. "It's my pleasure to meet you, sir."

Gay allowed a smile to cross his lips, because with this small gesture, he realized that even though he hadn't been with the Hughes entourage during its travels, his influence and power had preceded him. What this small gesture confirmed was that he was indeed the man in charge.

After the guard logged in their names, Smith ushered Gay and Davis into the salon of the Hughes suite, and Mays came over with Glenn Kaiser to pay his respects.

"Where is the governor?" demanded Davis. No one answered, since none of the aides volunteered information without instructions from Bill Gay.

"You fellows heard the question," said Gay.

Taking the cue, Kaiser announced, "The governor and Commissioner Hannifin are in a suite on this floor. They're waiting for word that Mr. Hughes will see them. I might add that they're becoming quite impatient. The governor just reminded us that it's almost 1:30 in the morning."

Just then Stan Dean came out and whispered to Mays that Mr. Hughes didn't want to be kept waiting. Mays whispered the news to Gay, who thought to himself, Isn't this just like the Howard Hughes he remembered? Everyone had been assembled awaiting his pleasure, and between extra sleep, bouts of constipation, and the time it took for his haircut and clean-up, Hughes had kept them all on call for over a day and a half. Now, at last, he was ready for the meeting at 1:30 in the morning, and *he* didn't want to be kept waiting.

Gay wondered to himself what it would be like to see Hughes again. Fifteen years had passed since the last time he had spoken to him in person. And he would never forgive Hughes for all the menial tasks he had ordered a man of his ability to perform. And blaming me for his breakup with Jean Peters, Gay thought, was ridiculous. And whoever said they were married anyway? The boss had been afraid that Noah Dietrich was trying to have him committed to an institution so he could take over his organization. The boss knew if he had a wife, they would need her permission, so the next thing we knew, Hughes said he was married. He hardly ever saw her, so how could he blame *me* for the consequences, Gay said to himself. Anyway, no woman could live with a man with Hughes' habits and phobias, having to use Kleenex to touch everything in his presence. No one realized those phobias were the keys to the kingdom, no one except me. The boss always put more and more demands on me, without giving me the compensation that I deserved. Well, the tables are almost fully turned now, and I'll soon be calling all the shots.

The governor and commissioner arrived in the suite, and a silence fell over the entire room. All eyes were fixed on the bedroom door of Howard Hughes as it opened slowly and a tall, slightly stooped, white-haired, neatly groomed, very frail looking man began making his way into the main salon. He was dressed in a full-length white terrycloth robe and had slippers on his feet. Smith escorted him into an easy chair and everyone continued standing. Hughes made a deliberate show of taking a hearing aid out of the pocket of his robe and inserting it in his ear. Then he looked his visitors in the eye and said in true showmanship style, "The better to hear you with, gentlemen. Please sit down." He never acknowledged Chester Davis, but said to Gay, "Good to see you after all these years, Bill." He wanted to add, but kept it to himself, You've done pretty well for yourself considering you're just a chauffeur.

Howard felt the old juices flowing, the old excitement returning. He felt up to the challenge, and he knew the challenge was just beginning with this meeting. The real challenge was escape.

Howard knew the meeting would go well. He felt by turning over the running of Nevada to Gay and Davis, it was the lesser of two evils. He knew that as long as he retained ownership, he still had ultimate control. He wanted to tell his former errand boy, Bill Gay, "Don't worry, you'll have the proxy because it's what I want, at least for the time being, but what no one knows is that I'm going to take control again." He kept that to himself.

The meeting lasted a little more than one hour, and everyone came away feeling like the victor. The governor and chairman were convinced that Howard Hughes was Howard Hughes, and that the proxy was his wish. Gay and Davis felt they had won, too. And Howard felt he had completed his first step back to taking charge again. He liked that feeling, and he wanted more of it. After all, he thought, isn't it my money, aren't they my businesses, isn't it my life? And these aides, who do they think they work for? Surely not for Bill Gay, not Chester Davis, not Nadine Henley. They work for *me*, and I'm going to take a small step to show them who's in charge right now.

The governor and the chairman had departed, but the others were still in the room, and Howard called over Bill Gay, as he had in years past. "Bill," he said, "I want you to do something for me."

Gay immediately got concerned and realized that Mr. Hughes was more alert and rational than he had planned for him to be. He thought he had been a little too sharp in the meeting. And now, unconsciously, Gay started blinking rapidly. From deep within his subconscious, his deeply conditioned fear of Howard Hughes took hold and even though he wished to suppress it in front of the aides who were still present, he couldn't.

Gay snapped to attention and said, "Yes, sir, Mr. Hughes, what can I do for you?"

Howard had already achieved what he hoped for. By

Gay's obvious subservience, Howard had put doubt in the minds of the aides as to who was really in charge.

Before answering, Howard looked every aide in the face, and after what seemed an eternity, he turned his gaze back to Gay and said, "What you can do for me, Bill, is get me Bob Hunt."

Gay was stunned. He didn't want Bob Hunt in London. Hunt was a longtime friend of Howard Hughes and a former executive at Lockheed. Hunt and Mr. Hughes always talked airplanes in the old days, but Gay wanted things just the way they were. "But Mr. Hughes," he said, "I don't know where Bob Hunt is."

"Then find him," ordered Howard in a strong voice, "and get him here in this suite within the next two days. Do you understand me, Bill?"

Gay nodded. "Yes, Mr. Hughes."

"Good," said Howard as he rose unhurriedly from his chair and gazed at the occupants of the suite with a triumphant glow upon his face, "I'm going to take a nap now. This meeting has tired me."

He turned and strode, walking tall and unattended, back into his bedroom. Howard practically collapsed on his bed, but managed to prop up his back with pillows. He was physically and mentally spent from the ordeal of the show he had just put himself through. Reaching over, he took four more 10-milligram Valium—just to ease the excitement of beginning his return to control, and his planned escape. He closed his eyes and for the first time in a long time, fell asleep with a feeling of confidence, without the help of that goddamned syringe.

A smile came over Howard's face and softened his features as he sank deep inside himself, back in time to when he was in his favorite city, Las Vegas. It was the Vegas of the late Forties and early Fifties. He used to fly himself to McCarran Field and check into the El Rancho Vegas or the Flamingo or the Desert Inn and stay up most of the night seeing the shows and catching the lounge acts. That was the Vegas he loved, when he could go almost unnoticed from show to show and casino to casino. A time when people still dressed to go to dinner, and Howard would be in his beige woolen slacks, white shirt and brown wingtips with a coat over his arm but with his tie in the coat pocket for those rooms that insisted that a gentleman wear one.

Howard was never a gambler in the sense of the typical compulsive horse player or sports bettor or even the poker player or craps shooter who just had to gamble. But he loved to go to downtown Vegas, Glitter Gulch, and get lost in the crowd, to feel the excitement of the people in the casinos. He would go from the Mint, to the Nugget, to the Horseshoe and, on occasion, take out a stake of $10 and sometimes even $20, change it into silver dollars and step up to the crap table.

Howard was intrigued by the game of craps. The odds at roulette, blackjack and especially the slot machines were so in favor of the house that he felt they were sucker bets. He thought he had the best odds at the crap table, so that's where he chose to take a shot on occasion with his ten-spot or his 20. Most of the time he'd lose it all, but once in a while he'd win a few bucks. At those times, Howard was just like any other visitor to Vegas, just having fun and seeing how long his money would last. But most people couldn't make their money last as long as Howard, because they simply didn't have as much as he did, and he gave that fact a lot of thought as his dream took him back to a night in those early days when he went to the Desert Inn at about 2:30 a.m. one night, after watching a show, and stopped to watch a crap game.

He'd been walking from the showroom through the casino, since all entrances and exits from anywhere to anywhere make you walk through the casino in all Vegas hotels, when Howard heard the loud, happy shouting and laughing that comes only from a winning crap table. It drew him over, and he walked up to the long oval table and stood by the only player's space left open. Looking around the table, he saw that the shooter had just made his point, and the whole table was betting with him, betting that he would do it again.

The stickman announced, "All right, place your bets, same lucky shooter," and then he looked at Howard. He'd have to place a bet or step away from the table, because there were many others who wanted to get in on a hot game, so Howard reached into his pocket and pulled out $32, which was all the cash he had on him, because it was his habit never to carry money. But since he was in Vegas, he figured this would be sufficient. So he placed all his money on the table and told the dealer to give him dollar chips. Howard hadn't been recognized at this point, and the dealer pointed to the sign on the inside of the table that stated this was a ten-dollar minimum game. Howard didn't like the idea of having to make such a large bet, but he decided the table looked good, the excitement was infectious, and what the hell, he was Howard Hughes. He could afford it, so he bet $10 on the pass line.

The next thing he saw was the shooter rolling the dice toward his end of the table, and as he watched them bounce off the wall and come to a stop, he saw it was a seven. The stickman said, "Seven, a winner, pay the line." Howard had won, and he was genuinely excited when the dealer placed two five-dollar chips beside his ten singles on the pass line. Howard took back his original bet and let the house's $10 ride. Seven again. Twenty dollars ahead, he bet another $10, and again it was a winner. The guy to Howard's right slapped him on the back and shook his hand every time the shooter threw the dice. Even Howard was getting caught up in the fever that takes possession of the crowd around a winning crap game, and for the first and only time in his life, the gambling instinct took him over.

He could really win a lot of money right here, right now, Howard thought, and he told the dealer he'd like $5000 in $100 chips. The dealer told the box man, who told the pit boss that the tall guy at the end of the table wanted a marker for $5000. The pit boss, who didn't recognize him, walked over and asked very courteously and confidentially if he had previously established credit at the casino. Howard said no, and the man asked what his name was. When the tall stranger told him "Howard Hughes," the pit boss asked him to step off to the side, figuring this guy was wising off. An argument was beginning when Walter Kane, a sort of talent scout for Howard, happened to spot the two of them in a heated discussion and came right over.

"What's the problem, Mr. Hughes?" asked Kane.

The pit boss' mouth dropped open and he said, "Mr. Kane, you know this man?"

"Of course. This is Howard Hughes, the famous film producer and aviator. I work for him."

Well, it took only a few moments for the apologies and for the $5000 marker to be made out. Howard had Kane sign it on his behalf, which was most unusual, but it was allowed since this was Howard Hughes, and everyone knew all the stories and rumors about him. The dealer placed 50 $100 chips in front of Howard, and he bet 10 of them— $1000 on the pass line.

"Seven, pay the line," cried the stickman as the shooter continued on his hot streak. Howard let the $2000 ride as the shooter threw a nine, which meant that he had to throw another nine before he threw a seven. All the eyes of the players at the table were on Howard to see what he was going to do. Was he going to take odds, was he going to make come bets or place bets or hard-way bets? Not at all. Howard just wanted the shooter to make his point. All eyes shifted back to the man with the dice as he threw them once again—and they came up nine! A giant shout went up from all the players, including Howard. He was up $3000, and he felt like he was going to break the bank.

But inevitably, as with all hot streaks, as with all good things, eventually it came to an end. And to Howard's consternation, he had $6000 out on the table when the shooter finally crapped out. Even though that left him $9000 ahead, all he could think of was the six he'd lost. Since he wasn't a professional gambler, or a compulsive gambler, or even a good gambler, he had made the mistake that all gamblers finally make: He didn't quit while he was ahead.

Instead, he decided to win back the $6000 that was on the table when the streak ended—money he considered rightfully his. Well, Howard sat there the rest of the night shooting crap. Taking full odds, making come bets and place bets, and most of all betting the hard way, Howard Hughes soon learned that they were all the hard way. After playing for 10 hours straight, all he accomplished was to lose his $9000 winnings along with four thousand of his $5000 marker.

In Howard's mind, this experience taught him a great lesson: that he was never going to be a sucker on the gambler side of the table again. If and when the occasion arose, he would own the casino—all the casinos—and the hotels too. Since you can't beat the house, he would become the house. It took a long time, but it's a lesson Howard never forgot, and on May 3, 1966, he began to become the house. That was the day he received a check for half a billion dollars— $546 million, to be exact—when he sold his stock in TWA.

Howard didn't think about all that money in terms of how much wealthier he was, his thoughts were of how to avoid the huge capital-gains taxes he'd have to pay by taking it as income. It had been years before when Howard had thought about moving to Las Vegas. And now he had good reason to fulfill that wish. Howard had been made aware of the tax advantages of investing capital gains into real estate, a pastime at which he had proved himself extremely shrewd. But he was also made aware in earlier years by Noah Dietrich and attorneys Lloyd Wright and Greg Bautzer about his Sub-Chapter S Corporation which really wasn't intended for companies as large as his, but nevertheless, Howard used it to his advantage. Howard was able to take the income from casinos to offset the huge interest income on his capital. Therefore, he reasoned quite accurately, the more properties he bought, hotels and land, the more capital gains he would be able to offset. In other words, if he bought enough hotels and casinos, Howard Hughes wouldn't have to pay taxes on either capital gains or the interest on his income. He figured it out, it was the American dream come true, you just had to be rich enough. The rich get richer, and Howard intended to prove it in spades.

By becoming the biggest player in Nevada, Howard would have enormous political clout, the kind of pull that would enable him to call the shots on who would be elected both as governor and as U.S. senators from the state of Nevada. This was a plan he had nurtured for many years, and now that he was there, he would back all the candidates to cover all his bets, investing in everything from ranches to land to airports to gold and silver mines, all to offset income—and to make Howard Hughes the number-one high roller ever to hit town.

It had all come about just as he had mapped it out, but as in that crap game of long ago, all good things had finally come to an end once again for Howard. Between the medication and the whispering campaign against Bob Maheu, and the fear of someone breaking into his suite in the Desert Inn to serve him with papers on the TWA judgment in the anti-trust suit, Howard had gone along with the decision to move him to the Britannia Beach Hotel on Paradise Island in the Bahamas. How ironic it was, he thought, that the biggest player in the history of Vegas would end up sneaking out of town like a thief in the night, but what the hell, he was halfway down the rabbit's hole already.

Those four 10-milligram Valiums were kicking in, and Howard was sinking deeper and deeper into sleep, moving back in time even further, back to a time when life was good, when he was still up in the clouds, still behind the controls. Yes, this was better, much better. This was where he belonged.

CHAPTER ELEVEN

JULY 7, 1946
·

Over Culver City Field
Los Angeles, California

T his is just the way I knew she would feel, thought the
smiling pilot as he pulled back on the controls and
throttled up to feel the full power of the two 3000 horsepower engines of the Hughes Aircraft XF-11. It had taken
almost 3000 feet of the 9000 foot runway to build up to the
takeoff speed of 110 miles per hour. The aviator put the
plane in a big, lazy, slow left bank that would be approximately two miles in diameter as he continued his climb to a
little more than half a mile high. He looked out the left side
of his Plexiglas bubble cockpit and saw the red, blue and
white insignia of the United States Air Force painted on his
wingtip. A deep feeling of pride and achievement flowed
through him as he prepared to put the XF-11 through its
paces on this its maiden test flight.

It was unusual for a civilian to test-fly a new plane ear-
marked for the Air Force. But this was a most unusual test
pilot. This man had a combination of credentials, influence
and affluence that no one else possessed. It was his own aircraft company that designed and built this sleek, twin-tailed,
400 mph aircraft designed for photo reconnaissance. Back in

1935, this same man had set the new land speed record with the then incredible speed of 352 mph in his company's H-1. In 1937, he set the transcontinental speed record from Los Angeles to Newark, New Jersey, in a plane he bought from the world-famous aviatrix, Jackie Cochran, and had refitted with a 925 hp Wright Cyclone engine. And in 1938, he set an astonishing record of three days, 19 hours and 17 minutes for a flight around the world. So it may have been unusual for a civilian to test fly a plane for the Air Force, but the unusual was the natural thing for this test pilot, Howard Hughes.

The military wanted this flight performed at its test-flight base in the middle of the Mojave Desert, but Howard had enormous powers of persuasion, and he charmed them until they were convinced otherwise. Besides, he had been test-flying his own airplanes ever since the days when he made his movie, *Hell's Angels*. Howard had tested many aircraft since then, and he wasn't going to let his XF-11 be the exception.

But right from the start, things didn't go smoothly. Howard retracted the landing gear, but the landing-gear light stayed on. The damn gear felt like it had tucked in, but the light was still on. In the down position, the gear would cause drag, and he wanted to get the best performance possible out of the XF-11, even though this was its maiden flight.

He flew to a higher altitude, and then by starting a descent and pushing forward on the controls sharply while at the same time retracting the landing gear, the light finally went off, indicating that the gear had been raised and tucked away. He tried to contact his chief engineer, Gene Blandford, and his aircraft company's manager, Glenn Odekirk, who were on the ground along with the military personnel watching the progress of the test. But he couldn't make contact and wouldn't discover until later that his radio was tuned to the wrong frequency. Still uncomfortable about the landing-gear light problem, he flew low over the field so his people on the ground could get a look at the underside of his plane. Odekirk and Blandford took off in another Hughes company plane to do an air-to-air visual inspection. Viewing nothing out of the ordinary, they landed and Howard continued on the test flight.

He was a little over an hour into the test when it happened. The XF-11 was at 5000 feet and southeast of Culver City Field by about one and a half miles. The twin-engined craft suddenly and violently pitched right and started to descend. Howard thought the door to the landing gear had somehow broken off and attached itself to the right wing. He could try to come in for an emergency landing or continue to fly on and find the cause of the descent. In true seat-of-your-pants flyboy style of years gone by, Howard chose to ride this one out. He used every trick, every skill he had ever learned about flying to keep the XF-11 airborne and level. Besides, he thought, I have on my lucky snap-brim felt hat, and it's never let me down.

He worked and reworked the rudder, the ailerons, anything to keep altitude. Sweating and wiping his brow with his shirtsleeve, he tried increasing power, decreasing power. Nothing. Then the right engine died, and the plane began losing altitude even faster than before. The engine that was still working was making terrible noises as it took the full strain of the rapidly descending aircraft. Howard knew it was too late to even attempt a landing at Culver City Field. He looked north as the XF-11 descended from 1500 feet toward 1000 feet. He knew if he was going to bail out, it should have been at 2500 feet. No use crying over spilled milk, he thought. He was headed toward Beverly Hills, and he fought to keep the falling plane on course. He caught sight of the lush expanse of the Los Angeles Country Club and felt if he could keep the craft in the air just a little longer, he might be able to land her on one of those magnificent fairways.

Wouldn't that be something, Howard thought to himself. Forget Lucky Lindbergh, there will be headlines about Lucky Hughes, and why not—I always wanted to be a golfer. It surprised him that his thoughts were running to headlines and levity, and not to fear of his impending crash. He was less than 500 feet directly over the manicured lawns, the swimming pools, the tennis courts and the lavish homes of Beverly Hills. He realized now that only a miracle would allow him to reach those long green fairways at the country club. The XF-11 was under 100 feet and falling. Howard had no control at all now. He knew the name of the game had become survival, and he didn't want to hurt anyone on the ground. Putting both feet up on the console of the cockpit, he braced himself for the inevitable. If only the plane could clear this last house on North Linden Drive. He pulled back on the controls, trying to give the plane a little more lift. The damn country club was only one block away now. Howard closed his eyes and gritted his teeth—hoping, hoping—and then he heard the sickening crunch of metal as the right side of the XF-11 slammed into a house at 803 North Linden Drive, and everything went black for Howard Hughes.

Torn loose from the rest of the fuselage, the left side of the craft hurtled onward into the house next door on Whittier Drive, finally skidding to a stop in an alley. All was quiet for a moment, and then a monstrous explosion echoed for miles around as what was left of the XF-11 blew up along with the house on Whittier. As if in a movie serial in which the hero miraculously escapes, Howard crawled out of the wreckage and collapsed a few yards from the burning plane with his clothes on fire.

Fortunately for him, Marine Sergeant Floyd Durkin was in

the vicinity and when he heard the sound of the crash and explosion, ran to the site and was amazed to see the pilot tumble from the crushed cockpit on fire. The sergeant ran to Howard's aid, smothered out the flames, pulled him to safety, and only then checked to see if he was still breathing.

With what seemed to be Howard's last breath, he asked Sergeant Durkin, "Did anyone else get hurt?"

The sergeant said he didn't think so, and then Howard mercifully passed out. Sergeant Durkin didn't need to be a doctor to know that the man he just helped was mortally wounded. He was sure the ambulance he heard was coming for a dead man.

CHAPTER TWELVE

JULY 7, 1946

·

$Good$ $Samaritan$ $Hospital$
Los $Angeles,$ $California$

Howard lay unconscious at Good Samaritan Hospital, where he had been taken on orders from his personal physician, Dr. Verne Mason. A very grave medical bulletin was issued that gave him a small chance of survival. It listed his injuries. His chest was crushed. There were fractures of the posterior portion of seven ribs on the left side and fractures of two ribs on the right side. A fracture of the left clavicle. Possible fracture of the nose. A large laceration on the left side of the scalp. Extensive second- and third-degree burns of the left hand. A large second-degree burn on the lower part of the left chest extending from the nipple line to the medial scapular. Another large second-degree burn on the left buttock. Numerous cuts, bruises and abrasions of both arms and both legs. Numerous small cuts on the face. His left lung had collapsed. And, not surprisingly, he was in shock.

The radio air waves and the newspaper headlines were filled with the news of the famed aviator/movie producer Howard Hughes' crash and escape from certain death. They went on to describe in detail his rescue by the Marine sergeant, and to say that his life hung by a thread. Reporters, top executives of the Hughes organization, Air Force officers and some celebrities began gathering at Good Samaritan awaiting word of his condition. That was day one.

Day two began on an ominous note with the news that the patient had hemorrhaged into his left lung during the night. The lung was tapped three times, and the blood was removed. His doctors, Mason and Dr. Lawrence Chaffin, were of the opinion that only intervention by a higher authority could save Mr. Hughes. Dr. Mason started him on injections of morphine to ease the excruciating pain. As Howard lay in bed, he fought to regain consciousness. He would not allow himself to die, he would not allow himself to give up. He would fight back and he would remember this moment to give him strength for the rest of his life. As he was coming to, he was running the flight over and over again in his mind, just like a motion picture. Later that morning the inconceivable happened, according to his doctors. Howard Hughes regained consciousness—and he was not only awake but demanding a detailed report on the crash.

On day three—still on the critical list—Howard announced that the cause of the crash was a problem with the right propeller and ordered his executives to help the Air Force in their investigation into the accident. His doctors expressed amazement at his fortitude, to say nothing about the fact that he was still alive. Hundreds of cards, letters of good wishes and baskets of fruit and flowers overflowed into the hallway outside his hospital room. Many of Howard's Hollywood friends were clamoring to see him, but he wasn't up to it, and he didn't want them to see him in his present condition. He didn't want to see anyone except for his Hughes Aircraft people, and he ordered an armed guard put at his door to keep all uninvited guests away.

On day four, the President of the United States, Harry

Truman, sent a telegram expressing his concern and his prayers for a speedy recovery. He also forwarded to Howard the medal that Congress had voted him for achieving the around-the-world speed record in 1938. Howard had never bothered to pick it up, and the President thought it would bring him good cheer. But the only thing Howard really wanted was his lucky snap-brim felt hat. Where was it, he wanted to know. He was sure it had survived the fire because he was still alive. The word went out, and a policeman found it in the wreckage and turned it over to the Hughes people in the hospital. It was filthy, water stained and crushed. But, like Howard, it had survived. His second in command, Noah Dietrich, sent it out to be cleaned and re-blocked, then had Dr. Mason return it to Howard who was as delighted as a little boy getting a train set for Christmas. He ordered Dietrich to give $500 to the policeman for finding it.

Still listed in critical condition on day five, with Dr. Mason still giving him large and steady doses of morphine since the pain was so intolerable, Howard lay in bed going over, with his company personnel, the sequence of events that led to the crash. His executive secretary Nadine Henley took it upon herself to become his personal guardian and set up a temporary office in the next room to his. If it was possible to get past the armed guards, it wasn't possible to get to Howard Hughes without going through Nadine Henley.

On day six, with his doctors expressing their cautious prognosis that Howard had a good chance of recovery, Howard's aunts, Annette Lummis and Martha Huston, came to see him, but he wouldn't let them in. And when Dr. Fred Lummis, husband of Annette and a noted surgeon, asked permission to examine him, Howard not only refused but insisted angrily that Dr. Lummis would try to kill him. Howard wouldn't explain the reason for this outburst, but

he swore never to see his relatives again, and he never did.
Their attempt to visit him, however, seemed to exhaust
Howard, and he slept through the day and night with the
aid of drugs to help reduce the pain.

Days seven, eight and nine were marked by steady recovery for Howard, with the running of the Hughes empire left
in the capable hands of Noah Dietrich. Controlling the flow
of correspondence and well wishers to his bedside, Nadine
Henley was sincerely dedicated to his welfare and recovery,
but also thrilled and gratified that, in her own secret way,
she had him all to herself. She had exclusive rights on him,
and she intended to guard that prerogative. She remembered that night at Mr. Hughes' house in Bel Air two years
before. She was sure that he had changed his mind about
her since then, that when he recovered and realized what a
fine job she had performed for him here in the hospital, he
would see her in a different light—not only as a fine secretary and personal administrator, but as a wonderful companion, and more importantly, a woman.

On day ten, Howard took the news of his upgraded condition—from critical to guarded—as an excuse to allow his
Hollywood friends in to see him. He was feeling much better and whenever the pain became too much, he would
order a magic shot from Dr. Mason. The doctor had warned
him sternly about the morphine, but Howard knew he had
the willpower to stop it at any time. Hadn't he just willed
himself back from death's door? His doctors were at a loss
to explain his amazing survival, but here he was, well on the
road toward a full recovery.

"Miss Henley," ordered Howard, "tell me who's been
coming to see me, and I'll tell you who to let in."

"Are you sure you're up to it, Mr. Hughes?" asked Nadine.
"Shouldn't the doctors approve your plans first?" She didn't

want him to see his Hollywood pals. She especially didn't want him to be near some of the glamorous women who were sure to upstage her.

"I don't give a damn what the doctors think. Just read me the list, please, Miss Henley," he said with a hint of exasperation.

Without further argument, Nadine read off the names of the biggest stars in Hollywood who had come to visit. Howard listened and as the list got longer, his smile grew larger: "Cary Grant, Ava Gardner, Katharine Hepburn, Linda Darnell, Jean Peters, Errol Flynn, Jane Russell..."

"That's enough," said Howard, laughing. "Call Cary and Ava and see if they could come over sometime today. Tell them I'm sorry I couldn't see them before, but I'd really appreciate a visit now."

"Yes, Mr. Hughes." Nadine went to her office in the next room and placed the calls.

It was an hour and fifteen minutes later when Cary Grant arrived, escorted past the armed guard by Nadine Henley. She had never met him before and like a few million other women, was an adoring fan of his. But she never let on as Cary walked in and told Howard he was looking better than he had any right to. Howard proceeded to tell him all about the crash. He kept talking until he became aware that Nadine was still there and asked her to leave. She apologized and warned that the doctor didn't want Mr. Hughes to have visitors for more than fifteen minutes, which was a lie. But both men ignored her as she walked out of the room, leaving the door ajar.

Nadine paced in the hall outside Howard's room for the entire half hour that Grant spent visiting with him. Every time she would hear laughing followed by coughing from Mr. Hughes, she would become concerned. But there were no calls for assistance forthcoming, so she concentrated on helping the guard turn away hospital staff who wanted to get a look at Cary Grant. At last she heard Cary and Mr. Hughes exchange good-byes, and Howard informed her that he was going to take a nap and was not to be disturbed.

It was about 45 minutes after Grant left that the most beautiful woman in Hollywood made her entrance. The guard standing watch at Howard's door couldn't believe that he was actually standing face to face with Ava Gardner. She was asking which room was Howard Hughes', but he was too dumbstruck to reply. Accustomed to this reaction, she asked again, but this time she was answered abruptly by Nadine Henley. No less astounded by Ava's breathtaking beauty, she knew absolutely that she did not want Howard to be alone with this woman.

"I'm sorry, Miss Gardner, but Mr. Hughes can't see you," said Nadine in her most officious voice.

"I don't understand," said Ava. "You called a little while ago and said Howard asked to see me today."

"I'm truly sorry, Miss Gardner, but Mr. Hughes' doctors have forbidden any more visitors," said Nadine as she moved directly in front of the closed door to Howard's room, blocking it. "You see, Mr. Hughes has had a relapse."

Ava Gardner turned red with anger and, pushing Nadine Henley aside, announced bluntly, "Listen, honey, unless he just died, he'll want to see me!" Winking at her, the guard held the door open as Ava marched past Nadine into Howard's room. "Howard," she announced, "what the hell is going on here? C'mon, get up!"

He came awake slowly, still groggy from his nap. It took him a moment to focus and realize it was Ava. Then a smile broke across his face from ear to ear. For the moment all his pain was gone. "Ava, I'm so happy you came," said Howard with a boyish grin.

"I'm glad you are, but that Nazi bitch sure as hell isn't.

Who the hell does she think she's talking to?" said Ava, standing defiantly with one hand on her hips and the other pointing at Nadine Henley, standing in the doorway. One of Ava's many charms was her tempestuous personality—and a mouth like a truck driver. This outburst only endeared her more to Howard.

"Don't pay any attention to her. That's Miss Henley, my secretary. She's just overly protective," he explained.

"I'm sorry, Mr. Hughes, but you must get your rest. No more visitors, doctor's orders," Nadine lied in a breaking voice.

"What the hell are you talking about?" shouted Howard. "Get out, and keep the doctors out too."

"Yes, Mr. Hughes," answered Nadine in a defeated voice. "But Miss Gardner won't be allowed to stay more than ten minutes."

"I said get out and stay out—and Miss Henley, close the Goddamned door this time," he ordered.

This was the best that Howard had felt since he had been admitted on the day of the crash. And why not, he thought, Ava Gardner could bring a dead man back to life. She came over to his bedside and started gently touching the wounds on his face. Howard noticed that she was dressed in a sheer, very white, billowy silk crepe blouse. It had a plunging neckline, and he could see she was wearing a black bra underneath.

She also had on a mid-calf black crepe sheath skirt with a slit halfway up her thigh. He could see she hadn't any nylons on, and her skin had an astonishing luminescence. She stroked his cheek and told him how worried she was when she first heard about the crash. Howard touched her lips with his unburned hand. And then it happened: He couldn't believe it, with everything he had been through, and the massive medication that the doctors had him on, but he was actually getting a hard-on.

He started to smile and then laugh. "What is it, Howard?" she asked. "What's so funny?"

"You wouldn't believe it."

"C'mon, tell me."

"Well, I didn't think it was possible, not in my condition, but the answer has to be you. Only you could do this to me," said Howard in his most boyish manner as he moved his good hand to Ava's breasts.

She pushed his hand away and said soothingly, "No, no, Howard, we can't have you getting excited here in the hospital."

"It's too late," he said as he took his good hand and slowly pulled off the bedsheet. "See what you do to me?"

She looked down at his chest and stomach and saw bandages over his healing wounds, but she also saw what stood proudly erect between his legs.

"My, my, we are having a speedy recovery, aren't we? Are you sure this is okay?" she cooed as she took him in her hand and began to gently stroke him.

"I'm sure I'll die if you don't," he said smiling.

About 20 minutes had gone by since Ava Gardner had arrived, and Nadine was still fuming, incensed that that brazen hussy had barged past her into Mr. Hughes' room, and even angrier that Mr. Hughes had practically thrown her out. Doesn't he know I want to protect him, doesn't he know I'd never let anything bad happen to him, doesn't he know I love him? Nadine was marching back and forth in front of his door while listening for any sounds from within. Suddenly she heard Howard moaning, and it was getting louder.

She shouted at the guard, "Get the doctor, quick, Mr. Hughes is having a relapse!" At the same time, she pushed open the door and rushed into the room in time to hear

Howard moaning, "Oh, God, yes, yes!" and to behold a scene that would be burned into her memory forever—a memory she would never, ever forget or forgive: the sight of Ava Gardner on the bed, her blouse and bra off and those magnificent breasts free, and Howard, her Howard, getting the best blow job of his entire life.

Nadine stormed screaming from the room, and she continued to scream for a full 15 seconds. And when she stopped, she silently renewed her pledge to get even with Mr. Hughes. She didn't care if he had a hundred more plane crashes. She would never stop getting even—never, never, never. Not until he was dead.

CHAPTER THIRTEEN

APRIL 22, 1973

.

*Inn on the Park
London, England*

It had been five weeks since Howard Hughes had asserted himself and demanded that Bob Hunt be brought to him here in his suite on the top floor of the Inn on the Park. It had been five weeks since he had decided to take control again, five weeks since he had made his plans to escape. Five long weeks, and he was pissed. Pissed that it had taken five weeks for Bob Hunt to show up. Pissed that he couldn't stay away from that damned syringe filled with the warm, magic liquid that they called his "medication."

Howard felt he was making progress, but it wasn't fast enough, and he knew he needed help. He hoped it would come from his friend, Bob. The aides gave him every type of excuse ever invented to keep Hunt away, but Howard persisted and insisted. Now, finally, Bob had arrived and would be coming into the suite in just a few minutes. Thanks for coming, Bob. You've got to help me, but not as you've done in years past; not for a business acquisition, not help for a political favor, not help toward the purchase of jet planes. No, my friend, this time I'm talking about help of a different kind. This time I'm fighting for my very life.

Bob Hunt had come to Howard's aid many times and for many reasons. Once as the go-between for Hughes and Hunt's then boss, Robert Gross, the chairman of Lockheed. That was the time when Hughes was looking for financing for the large number of Lockheed L1011s he had ordered for TWA. Even though that plan hadn't come to fruition, Bob had done all in his power and authority as a Lockheed vice-president to make it happen for his friend Howard Hughes. Another time Bob tried to help Howard in a bidding war with Bell Helicopter, and even though Hunt came up with what could have been the correct bid, Howard had rejected his advice—but that hadn't deterred their friendship. Bob Hunt always seemed to be there for Howard.

When Hughes was thinking about the purchase of Western airlines, it was Bob who had acted as his sounding board as well as unofficial emissary. It was Bob the aides had turned to in November of 1970 to arrange secret transportation for Hughes and his entourage when they moved unannounced and surprisingly from the Desert Inn in Las Vegas to the Britannia Beach Hotel on Paradise Island in the Bahamas. Bob came through like the steadfast confidant that he was when he arranged for a Lockheed Jet Star to be waiting on the tarmac of Nellis Air Force Base just outside of Las Vegas. When Howard and his aides arrived, off they went to their new destination, courtesy of Bob Hunt and the cloak of secrecy in which he had covered the entire mission.

But what really formed a kinship with Howard happened in September 1958 when Hughes was in the midst of the worst personal depression he had ever suffered. The aides around him feared that Howard was going through a complete mental breakdown. Holed away in Bungalow Four at the Beverly Hills Hotel, he was in complete physical and mental disarray. Howard, of course, didn't want, and wouldn't allow, hospital care. In desperation, one of the aides called Bob Hunt and asked if he could talk to Howard and try to get him back to the world of reality. Bob gladly obliged, and slowly progress was made.

Howard's only outside contact at this time was with Bob Hunt. They discussed everything from wing spans to vertical lift to horsepower, from designated routes around the world to the price of airline tickets; anything and everything to do with airplanes. Aviation was Howard's first love, and over the course of a few months, talking every day with Bob, he had begun to return to what was for him normal. And as far as Howard was concerned, Bob Hunt was the main reason for his recovery. Bob was a man he could count on. And above all, Bob was a man who could keep a secret.

Harley Smith was on duty along with John McDermott when Bob arrived at the penthouse. They were immediately aware of his physical stature. He was 6'4" tall and his posture was as correct as one of the Queen's guards. He was dressed impeccably in a Brooks Brothers' double-breasted, tropical wool suit in dark brown, starched white shirt with striped tie and cordovan shoes. He had a full, thick head of hair with gray at the temples. His voice was deep and commanding, the kind of voice that takes charge. From the aides very first sight of him, they knew they weren't going to like having this guy around. They knew things weren't going to be the same. They knew they were going to have to find a way to get rid of this intruder in their own private little world. They knew, and Bill Gay knew, that Bob Hunt had to go.

Bob could feel the animosity, but he expected it. He had been around Howard and had done enough favors through the years to become familiar with the self-importance that the aides attached to themselves. He knew he would be considered a thorn in their side. Tough shit. He was there to help his friend Howard, and he wasn't about to let a petty pecking order of overpaid gofers stand in his way.

"Tell Howard I'm here," he commanded, staring at Harley Smith.

Smith stood there not knowing what to do, looking at McDermott for guidance. McDermott, not wanting a confrontation on the first day with Hunt, and having received no specific instructions from Bill Gay on how to handle him, nodded to Smith to carry out Hunt's wishes. Bob watched as Smith knocked on Howard's door, waited a moment and then entered.

A few moments later Smith came out. "Mr. Hunt, the boss wants to see you now. He's very anxious, and you know you have to speak up real loud, because he refuses to wear his hearing aid."

Bob entered Howard's bedroom and at once noticed the white light flickering in the darkened room on the now-empty movie screen from the projector next to Hughes' bed. And then it hit him—the odor, that dank odor that went up your nose and into your mouth at the same time. It took all the control he could muster not to throw up right then and there. While he composed himself, his eyes adjusting to the light coming from the movie projector, he realized that Howard was sitting on the side of his bed only two feet away from him, and he was stark naked.

"Howard, what the hell is wrong with you?" asked Hunt incredulously.

"Is that you, Bob? Where the hell have you been?" asked Howard, barely hearing him.

"Sure, it's me, who the hell did you expect?" answered Hunt.

"What?" said Howard. "What did you say?"

"Damn it, Howard, put on your hearing aid."

"What? Speak up!" said Howard in exasperation.

Bob took one step next to him, bent over to his ear and shouted, "Howard, put on your damn hearing aid or I'm turning around and leaving."

Bob Hunt was then the only person on earth who could speak to Howard Hughes that way. Bob also knew from past experience that unless he acted firmly with Howard, he wouldn't be able to help him. Howard looked irritated but pointed finally at a drawer. Opening it, Bob retrieved a hearing aid for each ear and handed them to Howard. Hughes looked at the devices in his hand and, like everyone who needs hearing aids and refuses to wear them, reluctantly and deliberately put them in his ears, adjusting them until the high-pitched squeak stopped and he was able to hear Bob saying, "Can you hear me now, Howard?"

Hughes nodded.

"Good," said Bob. "I'm shocked to see you like this, because I thought everything was fine when I heard you had the meeting with the governor. God, Howard, you look like shit."

Howard didn't say anything for about half a minute, and then he shouted, "Where the hell were you? I've been waiting five weeks. I thought I could count on you!"

"What are you talking about, Howard?" answered Bob. "I only got your call three days ago. I dropped everything and got here as fast as I could."

"Those sons of bitches," said Howard, "they've been telling me they've scanned the globe looking for you!"

"I don't know what the fuck's been going on. Just tell me what you want. I'm going to help you, just like I helped you back in '58 at the Beverly Hills Hotel. You know you can count on me, Howard."

Hughes stared at Bob, looked deeply at him. He knew he would have to trust him completely and, more urgently, would need his help to carry out his plans. Howard knew that even though Bob Hunt had always been there in the past for him, this time would be the ultimate test of his loyalty and friendship.

"Bob, of all the things you've done for me, none has ever been as serious as what I'm about to ask of you now. And, of course, everything has to be shrouded in the strictest secrecy."

Bob was well aware of Howard's penchant for secrecy. Sitting beside him on the edge of his bed, he said nothing as Howard went on, "Bob, I've made up my mind that I'm going to fly again."

Startled, Bob stood up and said, "Howard, what are you talking about? Look at the condition you're in. You haven't flown in years. You don't have a current pilot's license. I could go on and on."

Hughes raised a skinny arm in his direction to quiet him and said in a surprisingly firm voice, "You could name another hundred reasons, and you'd probably be right, but it won't change the fact that I'm going to fly again. And the reason that I'm flying again—and this is the part that has to be the most secret covert operation that you've ever done for me—is because I'm going to escape. That's right, escape."

Bob sat down again, and it took him a full minute before he could say anything. He was thinking that his friend might be in worse mental shape than anyone realized. Worse than in 1958 when it looked like he suffered a nervous breakdown. But he knew that Howard always had a way of bouncing back from what looked like the edge of the precipice. Bob had learned over the years not to count Howard out, no matter how dark the situation seemed.

Collecting his emotions, he said, "Howard, what do you mean escape? Escape from what?"

"From this prison that I've made for myself." In a conspiratorial voice, he went on, "In my desire for secrecy, both personal and professional, I've built these walls around me. I've built them to the point where I'm not in total control anymore. I've built them to the point where I'm just about a prisoner. Can you imagine, Bob, a prisoner of my own guards." Bob didn't say anything. He sat across from his friend and listened, nodding from time to time.

"But when the time came for the meeting with the governor, I realized that I had an opportunity to change all that. I saw that I still could muster my authority by asserting myself. I decided to regain control, and I made up my mind to fly again. It's in the air that I've always felt in command and, most of all, free. I was starting to feel like my old self, so I ordered the boys to get you here. I told them I wanted you here in a couple of days and you see, it's taken five goddamned weeks."

Bob spoke softly, "But I'm here now, Howard, and if you want to fly again, I'm going to help you."

"I knew I could count on you, Bob, but it's bigger than just flying. I've got to escape."

Bob listened attentively and tried to comprehend what his friend was saying. "I'm asking you again, escape from what?"

"Bob, ever since my last plane crash way back in '46, I've taken drugs for pain. It started with morphine, but I quickly got off that. It was replaced by measured doses of codeine. Well, over the years, I always knew I could control it. I don't mean to oversimplify, but I could always control it. The boys would always make sure that I could get whatever I needed. Doctor's orders. They call it my medication."

Bob interrupted, "Okay, Howard, that's the first step, realizing you have a problem."

"But I didn't really realize I had a problem until I ordered them to get you here. I knew I had to stop taking the codeine, so that's when I stopped letting them administer the shots to me. But for the last five weeks I've been giving *myself* the codeine. I've been giving *myself* the shots. Bob, I'm a goddamned addict! I have to escape."

Bob realized this was a dramatic confession his friend had just made, and he understood the courage it took to admit his problem. He knew he had to tread very carefully to get his friend back where he belonged. "Howard, you don't have to escape to get off the medication. Give me the authority and we'll change everything about your operation."

"No," said Howard. "Don't you think I've thought of that? No, Bob, I have to do it my way. I have to get my life back. First, I'm going to wean myself off the drugs, and then we're going to fly the hell out of here."

Bob knew Howard really didn't have a plan for escape, but the fact that he realized he was addicted and wanted to get off the stuff was enough to make him want to help. He knew if Howard could get off the drugs and start flying again, then there was a pretty good chance his friend would become the Howard Hughes of time gone by and assume control of his empire again—and, more important, his life.

"By God, Howard, I'm going to get you back in the pilot's seat," announced Bob. "First, I want this room of yours cleaned up. It stinks. Next, I want your barber to clean you up. You need a shave, a haircut and your nails trimmed. If I'm taking you flying, I can't have you looking like some sort of screwball. And you need clothes. You can't fly naked."

Howard started laughing.

"What's so funny?" asked Bob.

"I'm one of the richest men in the world, and you know, Bob, I don't even have any clothes."

Hunt looked at Howard and then the two friends started laughing so loudly that Harley Smith came bursting into the room.

Howard shouted in a voice that the aides had never heard

before. "Get the hell out and don't ever come in again without knocking!" Smith stumbled back out through the door in hasty retreat, and that got Howard and Bob laughing even harder.

"Okay, Howard, back to business, I'm about the same height as you, so I'll go out and get you the clothes you need."

"Don't forget I'll need a snap-brim Stetson. I can't fly without that hat."

"Where the hell am I supposed to find a Stetson in London?"

Howard gave Bob a sorrowful look. Bob knew he always flew with that Stetson. He knew it would bring Howard's confidence level up and help him feel at home in the cockpit.

"All right, Howard, I'll find you the damn hat," Bob said with a warm smile.

"I knew I could count on you. And trust me, I'm going to get off that damn medication, and I'm doing it my way. Remember, Bob, above all, secrecy. That's the ticket, secrecy. No one can know about the escape."

Bob shook Howard's hand and went into the salon, where he ordered McDermott to send Stan Dean in to Mr. Hughes. He then went about the business of stowing his gear in one of the other bedrooms of the vast suite. Tomorrow he would go about outfitting Howard—and finding that damn snap-brim Stetson in London.

A few minutes later, Stan Dean knocked on Howard's door.

"Who is it?"

"It's me, Mr. Hughes. Stan."

"Come in." This surprised Stan, because he usually had to knock several times and shout to be heard. He entered and saw Howard sitting there smiling at him.

"Stan, get me cleaned up real good, like you did for the governor. I'm going to fly again."

"You bet, Mr. Hughes. It's about time." Stan was delighted with the news. Moving him to the old naugahyde recliner, he covered Howard with a bath towel and began covering his face with hot towels.

Howard sat back deep in the chair and let the warmth of the towels begin to relax him. He closed his eyes and relished the thought of sitting in the pilot's seat again. Lulled by the heat of the towels and Stan's skillful neck massage, he began to drift back now, remembering the old days—before he had ever heard of that magical medication codeine—when he flew just for the hell of it. When he flew just for the thrill of it. When flying itself was all the escape he thought he'd ever need.

CHAPTER FOURTEEN

LATE SPRING 1935

.

In the Air Approaching
Santa Catalina Island, California

It was about five miles dead ahead, and it appeared larger than it really was. He knew it was only 22 miles long and eight miles wide at its widest, but it looked like a lush tropical jungle with vegetation growing wild on its mountain peaks as it rose from the warm waters of the Pacific Ocean 24 miles south-southwest of the city of Los Angeles.

Twenty-nine year old Howard Hughes had flown to this destination before and, as always, was impressed with the majesty of Catalina Island. He knew the history of Juan Rodriguez Cabrillo discovering it in 1542 and naming it Santa Catalina in honor of Saint Catherine. He knew the legends of English, Dutch and even Chinese pirates who preyed on ships in the waters surrounding Catalina. He knew there were stories of pirate treasure that was still buried on Catalina's shore, and of sunken treasure ships off its coast. He knew, too, of the modern-day pirates with their gambling ships anchored just beyond the three-mile limit. He knew how adventurous and romantic Santa Catalina could be, and that's what brought him speeding to the rendezvous he had been longing for in the two weeks since he had spotted her.

For no reason in particular, Howard had flown down to Palm Springs that weekend. He had started out simply to get in some air time free from the pressures of business—practicing his loops, banks and rolls to the north over the San Gabriel mountains, then south along the coastline over the beaches of Malibu, Santa Monica, Newport and Laguna, then inland over the high deserts toward Palm Springs. He had decided to drop in at the Racquet Club, which had been opened only a few months earlier, in December 1934, and was already becoming a popular celebrity watering hole among the Hollywood in-crowd.

He was sitting at the Bamboo Bar with Charlie Farrell, a handsome *bon vivant* who was partnered with Ralph Bellamy as one of the investors behind the club. Howard was telling Charlie about the Boeing pursuit biplane that he had flown down in. That's when she walked into the dining room. She was accompanied by two other young women. All were dressed in white tennis skirts with white sweaters wrapped loosely around their shoulders over their white tennis blouses. She was laughing and talking animatedly, apparently unaware of the sensuous vibrations that her athletic young body was sending in the direction of young Mr. Hughes.

Howard stopped in mid-conversation with Charlie and stared at her. Even from where he was sitting, he could—with his keen aviator vision—make out the color of her eyes beneath the blonde hair. They were a very deep blue. No, more than blue, they were almost violet. With that lithe figure, he imagined she might be a dancer. He had to meet her.

"Charlie, do you know that girl sitting over there with the other girls in white?" asked Howard. There was no need to point them out.

"I guess you mean the blonde, right?"

"Well, yes, I find her extremely attractive."

"So does every other man in the room." Charlie had the rundown on them as he had on anyone who was anyone—or who was *going* to be anyone—and especially on anyone who frequented his new Racquet Club. "They've been playing tennis and stopping for a bite of lunch for the past two days. They're contract players for Paramount. And the one you have your eye on is an English girl named Ida Lupino. From what I hear, she's star material."

"I knew it," said Howard with a big smile. He wanted to meet her now more than ever, but he had always found it almost impossible to make the first contact. He always needed someone else to introduce him. He didn't know if it was because of his upbringing or his innate shyness or because of his hearing problem, which was growing worse year by year. But, whatever the reason, he always needed an intermediary.

"Charlie," said Howard, "Do you think you could..."

"...Introduce you to Ida Lupino? Come with me." Exchanging a conspiratorial leer, they stepped down off the bar stools and crossed the room to the trio's table.

"Ladies," said Charlie at their table, "let me have the pleasure of introducing to the three prettiest ladies who have ever graced my new Racquet Club, my good pal, the famous aviator and movie producer, Howard Hughes."

While the others laughed and chattered pleasantries, Howard just stood there, staring at Ida. Speaking only to answer yes or no, he finally stammered out an invitation to dine with him. She said she had come to Palm Springs with her friends and her mother. Always the gentleman, he offered to take everyone out to dinner. He ended up taking Ida and her mother not only to dinner but to lunch the next day and then dinner again. He couldn't help himself, he was infatuated with the lovely young girl from England. It quickly became more than a desire for her—it became a need. But all Howard's generosity and boyish charm went for naught when they had to leave for Los Angeles to continue shooting a picture Ida was working on at Paramount.

As soon as he returned home, Howard ordered Noah Dietrich to find out everything he could about Ida Lupino, and that evening Noah called back with his report. He said she had been born to a stage family in London on February 4th, 1918. Her father Stanley Lupino was one of England's most popular comedians, and her mother Connie, from another famous English stage family, had been acting her whole life. Her father's brother Barry managed the famous Drury Lane Theatre, and Ida had studied at the Royal Academy of Dramatic Arts.

Howard never interrupted Noah, listening intently as Dietrich went on, "It seems Ida got lucky when she met an American producer named Allan Dwan who was in England making a film called *Her First Affair*. For whatever reason, Dwan gave her the lead in the picture. She bleached her hair blonde, changed her eyebrows, and the British press hailed her as 'The English Jean Harlow.' She got some other roles, all of the sultry siren variety."

"If you met her you'd know why," added Howard.

Noah Dietrich, having been through this before, said with a note of disdain in his voice, "Do you want me to continue, Howard?"

"Yes, yes, of course, Noah."

"In 1933 Paramount was looking for someone to play the lead in their production of *Alice in Wonderland*, and one of their scouts, seeing her overseas, took notice of that dewy-eyed look. He reported back to the home office and on his say-so, Paramount offered her a sweet deal as a contract player, and they screen-tested her for the part of Alice. She came to Hollywood with her mother two years ago." Noah stopped to have a drink of water.

Impatiently Howard urged, "Go on!"

"There's not that much more," Noah continued. "She didn't get the part of Alice, but Paramount thinks she's a potential Clara Bow. They gave her a role in *Search for Beauty* and last year she played a stage-struck girl in *Ready for Love*. This year she finished *Panic in the Spring*, and she got the third lead in *Peter Ibbetson* starring Gary Cooper, which she's working on now."

"Now I know she was telling me the truth when she said she had to return to L.A. Tell me, Noah, did you find out anything about her personal life? You know what I mean."

"Well, this part you're going to find quite interesting. It seems our Miss Lupino loves having a good time. She rented a very nice house, complete with swimming pool, and gives expensive parties for the movie crowd. She's also been seen on the arm of numerous leading men in nightclubs around town. All in all, I'd say you've picked a gal who's headed for the top."

"That's what Charlie Farrell said," said Howard.

"Just remember one thing," said Noah in an admonishing tone.

"What's that?"

"She's seventeen years old, Howard. Jailbait. Don't forget it."

"She hardly gave me a tumble, and besides her mother's always there."

"I know you. You'll find a way. You never give up. Just remember: jailbait."

Noah's warning was echoing in Howard's mind as he brought the plane in for a perfect landing on Catalina. It was a tricky little airstrip cut between the highest peaks. Howard loved landing here, because it challenged him. Then he was off to another challenge. He boarded the little bus that took him the three miles or so to the town of Avalon with its magnificent harbor. He had reserved a suite at the Hotel St. Catherine. It was built in 1918 and had a wonderful reputation for its cuisine. One of the oddities of the early days of the hotel was that when the new electric elevator was first put into use, it would dim the lights of the entire town. In 1935 the St. Catherine was considered the finest place to stay on the island, and that was one of the two reasons that Howard had reserved a room there. The other, Ida Lupino, was booked there too.

The last time Howard had seen Ida was in Palm Springs, and through his network of personal friends and spies, he had followed her every move for the past two weeks. He phoned her at least three times daily. He would wake her up at home in the morning, inquire how her lunch was and tuck her in at night; all on the telephone. And, of course, there were dozens of fresh flowers delivered every day, not only to her dressing room, but also to the set, and without fail to her home. Everywhere she went, every place she turned, Ida would be reminded that she was being pursued by the master of pursuit, a man who never, ever took "no" for an answer no matter how much it cost or how long it took.

It was about four hours since Howard had checked into his suite and freshened-up from his flight to Catalina. He had flown down in a tropical-weight, dark blue, double-breasted wool suit with wide peak lapels and his customary white shirt. In his cardboard shirt box, as usual, were an extra white shirt, tie, shaving gear, toothbrush, toothpaste, and after-shave lotion. Howard had put on his clean shirt, fixed his tie, smoothed his suit, combed his hair straight back, as was his style, checked himself in the mirror, thought he looked quite spiffy, and went to the dining room. He was expecting to see Ida Lupino, her mother and one of her friends from Palm Springs eating dinner in accordance with the information he had acquired about her plans for the weekend.

After a good twenty minutes of scanning the lavish dining room, Howard finally asked the maitre d' when Miss Lupino and party would be arriving. When he was told she had canceled her reservation, Howard almost turned pale. The thought of not seeing her after all the waiting and planning left him sick with frustration.

Composing himself, he went to the front desk to find out if Miss Lupino was even a guest at St. Catherine. To his great relief she was. He took a moment to reason that she and her mother and friend had decided—or worse, had been invited—to have dinner elsewhere. Howard decided that, rather than try to find which restaurant, he would proceed to the casino.

There must be a thousand people already here, he thought, surveying the vastness of the famous casino. How the hell am I going to find Ida? The casino had been completed six years before in 1929 and had already acquired a world famous reputation as the place to go on Catalina. It had the largest dance floor west of the Mississippi, and on this weekend Glenn Miller and his band were drawing the tourists, partygoers and especially the dancers. There was excitement going on, and a festive mood was in the air. Howard noticed other young men in groups of two's and three's looking for girls, and he saw equal numbers of girls looking for guys. As he was touring the outside of the dance floor, two rather attractive young women asked him to dance.

Normally Howard would have given serious consideration to an opportunity like this, but not tonight. No, tonight he was the hunter and he was stalking his prey. He was sure she would be there, the hottest spot on the island, and he wouldn't let himself be distracted from the task at hand. He knew he would find her. All he could think about were those violet eyes, those lovely legs, that sensual British accent. Thinking about what was going to happen when he finally got her alone made him dizzy with anticipation.

And then through the din of the crowd and the maze of arms and legs, he spotted her in the middle of the dance floor. She was fabulous as she moved rhythmically to the beat of Glenn Miller's sounds. She was dancing with her girlfriend, a relief to Howard, for he was already imagining that she was off with another suitor. He studied her movements, and with each turn, each step, each twist, he grew more desperate for her. Still there was a voice that rang in his head, the voice of Noah Dietrich repeating just one word—jailbait. Shutting it out, he thought instead about how he was going to get Ida alone.

Waiting until the dance set was over, Howard followed Ida and her friend to the table where Ida's mother was sitting. Then he walked slowly by, making sure Ida's mother would see him. Howard knew Connie Lupino was aware of the calls and the flowers he was lavishing on her daughter. He had played this game before and had made a point of sending flowers for Ida's mother too. Howard knew that Connie, like other mothers, would find it hard to resist trying to put her daughter together with a young multi-millionaire.

"Mr. Hughes, Mr. Hughes!" shouted Connie Lupino, trying to be heard over the vast crowd at the casino. Pretending not to hear, Howard kept walking by, playing the role of coincidentally being in the same place at the same time. Four steps past the table, he felt a tug on his arm and turning he saw the lovely smile of Ida Lupino's mother.

"Why, Mr. Hughes, what good fortune running into you here in Catalina," said Mrs. Lupino in her aristocratic British accent.

"Good fortune for me," said Howard. "I come over quite often to enjoy the big bands here at the casino."

"Well, you must come over and join us at our table," she insisted. "I know Ida will be thrilled to see you and, by the way, thank you for the lovely flowers."

"It was my pleasure. Do you think it would be all right to join you?" said Howard in a voice so shy that Connie Lupino took him by the arm and had to practically drag him to the table.

"Girls, look who I found," she announced. Everything was turning out even better than he had planned.

"Hello, Mr. Hughes," said Ida and her friend almost in unison.

"If I'd known you ladies were going to be on the island," said Howard coyly, "I would have offered to take you to dinner at St. Catherine's." Howard was talking directly to Ida now and couldn't take his eyes off her.

"We were going to eat there," said Ida, "but a friend of Mom's recommended a lovely seafood house on the beach, and we thought we'd give it a try tonight."

Howard hung on every syllable she uttered, watching the way her mouth and lips moved as she spoke. As Ida babbled on about the orchestra, he began to realize how young she really was. Again the voice of Noah Dietrich rang in his head: "Jailbait." But that wasn't going to stop him.

The band started playing once more and Mrs. Lupino suggested that Howard dance with her daughter. Ida had taken dance as part of her training in England, she said. Ida dutifully took Howard by the arm and said, "C'mon, Mr. Hughes, let's take a spin around the ballroom."

They walked arm in arm to the center of the dance floor, and as he took her in his arms, he realized how petite she was. Ida couldn't be more than 5'2". He was more than a foot taller than she. And she didn't weigh an ounce over one hundred pounds. She did the leading and as she pulled him closer, he was afraid she would feel his bulging erection.

"Thank you for the flowers. You made me feel so special," she said as they maneuvered around the floor, "and also for sending them to my mum."

They were dancing their third dance when Ida asked him why the casino was called the casino, since there was never any gambling there. He didn't know, but he saw in her a little-girl curiosity that he found charming—and that gave him an idea about how to get her alone.

"Have you ever heard of the lost treasure of Samuel Prentiss?" Howard asked.

"No, what is it?"

"It's the legend of the vast Indian treasure buried on Catalina Isthmus at Two Harbors," whispered Howard.

"Where did you say?"

"I've said too much already," he answered.

"No, you must tell me the story!" she cried. Howard knew he had her now. He could sense what it would be like undressing her and feeling her beautiful white skin, smelling her sexual vitality, kissing her luscious mouth.

"Okay, I'll go on, but once I've told you about the legend, you'll know the secret too, and then you'll have to come with me."

"What do you mean?" asked Ida doubtfully.

"I mean I've come to Catalina this weekend because I'm going to find the treasure tonight."

"You are? How will you know where to look? How will you get there? How did you find out about it? Tell me the legend, please, please."

Howard was ready to rip her panties off, but he forced himself to pull gently on the line. He had her hooked. All he had to do now was reel her in.

CHAPTER FIFTEEN

LATE SPRING 1935

·

En Route to Two Harbors
At the Catalina Isthmus

The night air was cooler at 1000 feet, and Ida was shivering with excitement as Howard banked the Boeing pursuit plane with its open cockpit on a northwesterly heading toward a small strip of land approximately 3500 feet across that connects the two parts of Santa Catalina Island. He was headed toward the Catalina Isthmus, a tiny strip of land—connecting a pair of coves—that extends from Catalina Harbor to the west and Two Harbors to the east. To sailors out at sea, it would appear as if there were two islands instead of one, that is how small the isthmus is. It was a sparkling night, thankfully with a full moon lighting up the terrain below like a giant searchlight. He guided the craft toward that impossibly small span of ground where Howard had convinced her that the lost treasure lay hidden. He knew that by appealing to the romantic adventurer in Ida, he'd convince her to take the dare and leave with him to uncover the mystery.

The cockpit of the Boeing was designed as a single-seater, but Howard had ordered it enlarged and customized to accommodate his almost 6'4" frame. It was large enough to fit the two of them snugly side by side, so close together that Ida actually had one leg partially over Howard's. The wind blowing through the cockpit was ruffling her blonde curls, and the occasional gusts would lift Ida's dress almost over her head. Howard struggled to keep his eyes on the instruments and not the satiny skin of her inner thighs. He was beside himself: His plan was going like clockwork.

"The legend," he had told her at the casino, "begins with a man named Samuel Prentiss, the first white man ever to make his home on Santa Catalina Island. On Christmas Day in 1824, Prentiss was shipwrecked near L.A. harbor on the rocks just off San Pedro. He almost drowned but was lucky enough to wash ashore unconscious. When he came to and realized he wasn't injured, he thought it was a miracle. He didn't know where he was and started walking inland. He walked for many miles and even though he was exhausted, he felt he was driven to go on. It was as if a strange force was leading him to an unknown destination."

Howard paused, seemingly for dramatic effect but actually because he had to gather his thoughts for a moment. But when he stopped talking, Ida grasped his arm and urged, "Go on, Howard, don't stop, go on."

Howard smiled knowingly to himself and went on: "The place where Samuel Prentiss was drawn to was the old Spanish mission at San Gabriel. There, the legend goes, lived a very old Indian, close to one hundred years, and he was dying. His name was Turie and he was chief of the oldest Indian tribe on Santa Catalina Island. His tribe had seen the comings and goings of the Spanish explorers and of pirates of many nations. For some reason unknown to anyone at the mission, Turie befriended Samuel Prentiss. It was as if he had known Prentiss was coming. The old Indian told him of a huge, fabulously rich treasure which the Indians had buried on Catalina Island. Turie made Prentiss a map, a treasure map that he fashioned on a piece of deerskin. He made Prentiss promise him that he would go to Catalina and dig up the treasure for his people. And then Turie turned his face toward the sun, let out a blood-curdling scream, and died."

Howard paused again for effect, Ida grabbed his arm again, and he went on with the story.

"Prentiss returned to the scene of the wreck near San Pedro. He managed somehow to build a small sailing boat from the wreckage and set sail for Santa Catalina Island. All he had with him were nominal supplies for the voyage, a few meager personal belongings and, of course, the deerskin treasure map that Turie had made for him. But he had been out to sea only a few hours when dark rolling clouds appeared and along with them a vicious sea storm with ten-foot waves. It was all he could do just to hang on for dear life as the tempest raged around him. The waves engulfed the deck of his small craft and took his supplies, his personal belongings and, worst of all, Turie's map of Catalina Island with the location of the treasure.

"But the fury of the storm was spent almost as quickly as it had begun, and Prentiss continued on to Santa Catalina. He had never been on the island before and remembered only that the chief had told him the treasure was hidden somewhere on the smallest part of the island. And so Samuel Prentiss spent the next 30 years digging up all the coves and inlets of Catalina. It will never be known if he intended to give the treasure to the Indians if he found it, but he became the first white man to live on Catalina and the first white man to die there. But before he died, he told the story to the son of one of his shipwrecked companions, Santos Bouchette, who realized that the smallest part of the island had to be the isthmus. But he also never found the treasure."

"Yes, yes, what happened then?" asked Ida, wide-eyed.

"That's it. There is no more," said Howard Hughes, "for all

these years since, no one has found the treasure. Until tonight."

"What do you mean?"

"Well, you see, I figured out where it has to be. I've flown over the isthmus many times, and now I know where Turie's Indians must have buried it. I'm leaving right now to go look for it, and if you want to be in on a find of a lifetime, I'll take you with me. We can fly there tonight in my plane."

"You have your plane here?"

"Yes, of course. What do you say? I can't wait all night," said Howard with mock impatience.

Ida told her mother that they were going to take a walk, they took a cab to the airfield, and soon they were a thousand feet above the isthmus. From about three-fourths of a mile out, Howard could see how treacherous attempting a landing on this tiny strip of land would be. He knew it had been used as an emergency landing strip, but that was solely under extreme crisis conditions, and only during daylight. The trick was to stop once your wheels touched down before running off the end into Catalina Harbor. Howard figured if he could come in low, real low, no more than fifty feet above the ground, he could touch down as close as possible to the beginning of the isthmus. It would be difficult under ideal conditions, but now, at night, with only the moonlight to illuminate his way—and with the sensuous body of Ida Lupino wedged so tightly against him that he could practically feel her heartbeat as well as the heat between them—Howard thought he must be crazy.

"Is that where the treasure is, on that narrow piece of land?" she shouted in his ear. Moving to get a better view, she accidentally brushed her leg across the hard-on that Howard was trying desperately to conceal. Gasping at the touch, he could respond only by nodding his head yes. The electrical shock she had sent through his body made up

Howard's mind for him. He was going to land that damn plane, and he didn't care if the isthmus was only a foot long.

At about one hundred feet, Howard made a pass over the isthmus from the west, put the aircraft into a hard right bank, gaining altitude, and came around again back toward the isthmus heading from the east, then over the moonlit Pacific into another hard right bank and, lowering his altitude, one final pass at what seemed ground level. He looked over at Ida and saw she was spellbound by his maneuvering. Fortunately she had no idea how dangerous it was to even think about a landing on so small a space.

"Hold on, Ida," shouted Howard above the roaring of the 580 horsepower WASP engine. They were 25 feet above the ground speeding eastward at around 100 miles per hour. "I'm going to do a touch and go."

"That's great, Howard!" Ida yelled into Howard's ear. "What's a touch and go?"

Laughing at her naiveté, Howard was excited at her gutsy willingness to try anything, and he shouted back, "A touch and go is when we just touch the wheels to the field as we're moving, and then I pull up on the stick and we're up in the air again. It's like a practice landing." Howard was still shouting as he expertly felt the wheels touch and pulled back on the stick as he gave her full throttle and powered the aircraft back up into the night. Ida was laughing like a delighted child on a roller coaster as she felt the power and exhilaration of the plane lifting them almost straight up toward the stars and into the face of the man in the moon.

He had the biplane lined up on a southeasterly course heading directly into a five or six mile per-hour wind coming from the Catalina Harbor side of the isthmus. His eyes had adjusted well to the light from the moon, which was all the illumination he was going to get on this impossibly tiny strip of land. From the cockpit at about 50 feet above the ocean, he could see the reflection of the moon on the Pacific at the far end of the isthmus. Howard told Ida to hold on tight again: This time it was for keeps. Ida grabbed Howard tightly around the neck and wrapped both her legs over his. He could barely handle the controls, but he wasn't about to discourage her.

Lust was taking his mind off the task at hand, however, and when he turned his attention back to the treacherous landing, he realized that he was already 500 feet inland over the isthmus and maybe five feet off the ground. Dropping the craft to touchdown, he throttled back, moving along the dirt and grass field at about 100 mph.

Ida's dark eyes were beaming in the moonlight and her mouth was wide open, breathless with Howard's daredevil derring-do as the biplane streaked, bumping and creaking, across the tiny strip of earth. Howard hoped he hadn't misjudged the length of field he needed as he saw the glint of the Pacific Ocean fast approaching at Catalina Harbor. The speeding Boeing was fast eating up the 2,500 feet or so that was left of the isthmus. Slowly, slowly he applied the brakes, lowering the flaps, cutting power—and praying. Finally, thankfully, the plane came to a bouncing halt no more than two hundred feet from the shimmering midnight-black sea directly in front of them.

The excitement, the exhilaration of the moment were too much for Ida. She was all over Howard, smothering him with kisses. Her lips and tongue all over his face, his neck, his cheeks, his lips. "Howard, that was wonderful, fantastic, incredible! I never experienced anything like it!" Ida was screaming with delight as she engulfed him. Howard started to kiss her back, slowly at first, on the neck, her ear and then her lips. They were so close together it was almost impossible to move. He was so hard he felt he was going to burst. He had been waiting for this moment, planning for this moment, longing for this moment, and now it was here, she was here, beautiful, sensuous, tantalizing Ida and she was throwing herself at him. He reached around her back and began fondling her breast. She pushed his hand away. He tried again and she told him to stop that. He didn't understand. Ida asked, "Howard, where's the treasure? Aren't we going to get it?"

He couldn't believe what he was hearing. Did she really believe he had taken her here, taken this chance of a night-time landing for an Indian treasure from a legend of dubious authenticity? But he was so hot with desire that he couldn't control himself. The feel of her breast, even for that instant, forced him to go on. Howard leaned close to her ear and took her hand and whispered, "Ida, you are the treasure."

She didn't understand, but she let Howard kiss her ever so gently. He realized that this wasn't going to turn out as he had planned, but he was too excited to stop now. He had her hand in his, and he was grinding himself against it. He kissed her harder as he rubbed her hand over his crotch, and even though he was still in his pants, he came. Howard gasped, feeling lightheaded, and hoped that Ida didn't know what had happened. She pulled her hand away, gave Howard a kiss on the cheek and said, "Are we going to find that treasure now?"

Howard looked straight into her beautiful violet eyes, shook his head sadly no, started the engine, taxied the air-craft down the field and turned into the wind. He pushed in on the throttle, they were rolling down the isthmus, and as they lifted off into the night air, he turned and looked at the radiant young Ida Lupino and thought to himself, the one that got away. What the hell, jailbait.

CHAPTER SIXTEEN

He was standing under the belly of the airplane, running his hand over the underside of the fuselage. This was just the beginning of his inspection. He had gone through a procedure like this more than a thousand times before, but this was special, this was different, this time it was like coming home. Because after an absence of 13 years, the sky was going to welcome him back. He would be free up there, in control up there. He would escape up there.

Howard had begun his examination of the aircraft by walking around it not once, but twice. This was no easy task, since he was still in a very weakened condition from his long confinement in bed at the Inn on the Park, which was really just a continuation of the same confinement in the same kind of suites that had preceded it. Coming down off the codeine had also taken its toll, especially for the first two weeks. He knew he wasn't off the medication by any means, but he was decreasing his dependency. It was hard, much harder than he anticipated. But he was going to do it, he was going to kick it, not the other way around. Yes, his body was frail, but he took solace in the knowledge that his mind was growing stronger, becoming sharper with every passing week, day and minute. It had been about a month since Bob Hunt had reentered his life, and Howard had been leaning on him since that first day, just as he was leaning on him now as Bob escorted him on his inspection tour of the Hawker Siddley 748.

Bob could see the animation and excitement on Howard's face. This was the moment Howard had been waiting for, planning for and, in his own way, working for. But it hadn't come easily, there had been stumbling blocks all along the way, not the least of them thrown in his path by Howard himself.

During the first week, much to the consternation of the aides, Bob had reestablished his special relationship with Howard Hughes. But surprisingly, there was little if any interference. It was during this week that Bob went shopping for clothes for Howard. He thought it would be a one-day affair, two at most. First he went to Harrods in Knightsbridge, known for more than a hundred years as the finest shopping emporium in all of Great Britain. He felt good as he made his way into the multi-storied block-square brick building with the famous forest-green canopy. Heading for the gentleman's department on the first floor, he proceeded to try on two suits, one double-breasted, the other single-breasted. Even though Howard and Bob were about the same height, there was a great weight difference, so Bob had the suits measured for arm and leg length, and then ordered them in smaller sizes to fit his underweight friend.

Bob laughed at the look on the face of the sales clerk when he told him, "I'll take them both, but two sizes smaller." He also bought some ties and socks and a belt for Howard. They were all delivered later in the week. Next, in the exclusive West End, he visited Charing Cross and Savile Row and examined the goods at Tommynutter's and then on to Simpson's, where he purchased shirts, white and light blue, in long and short sleeves for both Howard and himself. When he returned to the suite at Inn on the Park, Howard wanted to know every detail about the shopping spree.

This was a quirky trait of Howard's. He always wanted to know, down to the smallest detail, the events of the day, concerning the people he was most closely involved with, or about the mission they were performing for him. It wasn't so much an interrogation as it was gossip about the events or the people involved. It was a ritual he had put Noah Dietrich through over and over again, and he had done it with every one of his romances. Bob was well aware of Howard's predilection, and it was okay with him. He knew it was a sign that his friend was returning to his old self.

After Bob had relayed the events of the day, Howard asked, "Where's my hat, my snap-brim Stetson?"

Bob explained very patiently that Harrods didn't have one, and that he didn't think one could be found in all of England. Howard insisted that he couldn't fly without that hat. He was in an agitated state: partly from his own self-imposed reduction of codeine, and partly from his anxiety about flying again. Howard wasn't used to being told that something he wanted wasn't available.

"I want that hat, I need that hat," Howard insisted. Not wanting him to slide backward, Bob assured him that he'd find one even if he had to fly to Texas to get one.

The next week, after a lot of searching and some luck, a snap-brim Stetson of the right size was located in the West End and Howard's face lit up like a little kid's when he was presented with it. He put it on immediately and the first thing that any of the aides would see upon entering his room was Howard Hughes sitting up in bed, either in underwear or naked, wearing his snap-brim Stetson. As strange as this behavior might have seemed, Bob knew it was one step closer to having Howard back in control again.

No sooner had the hat problem been solved than Howard decided he also needed a leather pilot's jacket like the kind he used to wear in the 1930s when he was setting his world speed records. As usual, he was explicit as to the style and color it had to be. But this didn't prove to be the problem that the Stetson was. London shops were full of aviator jackets, and one that was just right was bought within a day, much to Howard's great delight and Bob's deep relief. There were no excuses now: All Howard had to do was to get himself fit enough to climb back into the pilot's seat.

Not only did Bob Hunt have to acquire what Howard considered the proper flying attire and concern himself with Howard's mental and physical stability to pilot a plane, he also had to deal with the very genuine fact that Bill Gay and his cohorts wanted things as they were, before Hughes had decided to exert his authority and fly again, and certainly before Bob Hunt had reentered the picture.

Gay held long-distance telephone discussions with McDermott and two or three of the other aides, and the consensus was that there would be no way possible for Mr. Hughes to actually pilot a plane. Their main concern was his new determination to cut down on the medication, and therefore become more aware and much more difficult to manipulate, along with the fact that Bob Hunt was spending so much time alone with the boss. Next Gay set up a conference call with Nadine Henley and Chester Davis. Davis expressed surprise that Mr. Hughes would be contemplating flying again, but Nadine said she could understand his desire and knew he had the stubbornness to at least try. They were all in accord that it wasn't possible, considering his many years on drugs and his present physical condition. Nevertheless, Nadine reminded her two partners of the near miracle that Bob Hunt had brought about in helping Mr. Hughes to recover from his mental breakdown in 1958. They agreed that their main concern was to maintain control. If it kept Mr. Hughes happy to talk about flying and have his friend Hunt with him, they would agree to go along.

They decided to order the aides to keep a closer watch on Hunt, and if Mr. Hughes actually boarded a plane, one or more of the aides would go along and report everything that happened. Gay would personally speak to Hunt and require him to report on Mr. Hughes' condition, and if they ever flew, to give a detailed report of the flight. He would explain that they were in no way interfering and it was just good business to keep the board of directors informed. They concluded it wouldn't be so bad if Mr. Hughes cut back a little on the medication because they didn't think he could ever kick the habit that they had so skillfully, so treacherously, so maliciously nurtured over the years. Let Mr. Hughes think Bob Hunt was his knight in shining armor; let him even take a flight or two. They knew that in the end the real master would be the warmth of the magical medication.

Bob Hunt was well aware of the actual reason he had to give a report of any flights Howard Hughes undertook. Bob was also aware of the motive behind ordering one of the aides to go along on the flights. As much as these restrictions annoyed him, he could live with them. But he remained constantly aware of the animosity the aides bore toward him because he might get Mr. Hughes back on his feet, and therefore, in actual control again. They didn't know where that would leave them, but Bob did, and he knew that Bill Gay did too. So Bob decided he would work with Howard within all the restrictions that Gay and the aides set in his path, because no matter what it took, he had to help his friend Howard to get back where he belonged—in control of his empire as well as himself. For what Bob didn't want to even think about, deep down inside, was that Howard Hughes might be right: He *had* to escape. This was his last chance.

Howard had completed his inspection of the exterior of the Hawker Siddley, a twin-engined turboprop, and they entered the cabin to continue his inspection. When he reached the cockpit, Howard seemed to take on not only a new vitality but a different persona, and Bob realized what it was. It wasn't a transformation into a new man but a metamorphosis back into the man he used to be. In front of his very eyes, he was seeing Howard turn back the years, take the first step toward becoming the Howard Hughes of times past, when he was in command, when he was "the man."

Howard had that glow about him as he stepped onto the flight deck and sat down immediately in the left-hand seat, the pilot's seat. As far as he was concerned he was back in charge. He didn't acknowledge or even notice Tony Blackman, who was awaiting him inside the cockpit. Blackman was the head test pilot for Hawker Siddley as well as one of their best salesmen. It was through Blackman that Bob had arranged to use the aircraft in which Howard Hughes would return to the sky. Hunt had worked out an arrangement for Howard to lease the HS 748, and if he found it satisfactory, to buy it. Part of the deal was for Blackman to act as instructor for Mr. Hughes, to familiarize him with the plane and, of course, to actually fly the plane. What no one realized, what no one understood, was how strong Howard Hughes' resolve was, how tenacious he was, how determined he was to fly again.

"Tony, let me introduce you to Howard Hughes," said Bob Hunt.

"It's a real pleasure to make your acquaintance Mr. Hughes, and as a fellow pilot allow me to congratulate you on all your amazing aviation feats," said Blackman in his most ingratiating manner. "I'm Tony Blackman and I'm here to assist and instruct you on the Hawker Siddley 748."

"I don't need any assistance. Let's go," said Howard as he adjusted the brim of his new Stetson and took hold of the controls.

"Excuse me a moment, Mr. Hughes," said Blackman in a very polite voice. Nodding at Bob, he said, "Bob, will you please step into the cabin with me? I need a word with you." Bob followed him into the cabin, where Glenn Kaiser, the aide selected to accompany Mr. Hughes on this flight and report back on any and all events of the day, was sitting strapped into his seat and perspiring freely. Bill Gay's orders were explicit about keeping him informed, and he especially wanted to know what he suspected Bob Hunt was going to keep out of his reports.

Normally, the aides all clamored to be privy to Mr. Hughes. They had established their own private pecking order in terms of who was closest to him. But to fly with him, now that was far beyond the call of duty. No one knew better than the aides his true physical and mental condition. And knowing that, the last thing anyone in his right mind would want to do would be to go up in a plane piloted by a man who not only hadn't flown in 13 years, but had difficulty going to the bathroom. And worst of all, a man who was addicted to drugs. No, that was too much, but Kaiser had been chosen. Was he the lucky one or the unfortunate one? The sweat in his palms and under his armpits told him the answer as he watched Bob Hunt and Tony Blackman enter the main cabin and begin a heated discussion.

"Hey, Bob, I want to sell a damn airplane, but I don't want to get killed in the process," said Blackman with rising anxiety.

"Take it easy, Tony," soothed Bob. "He's just excited about being back in the pilot's seat again after all these years."

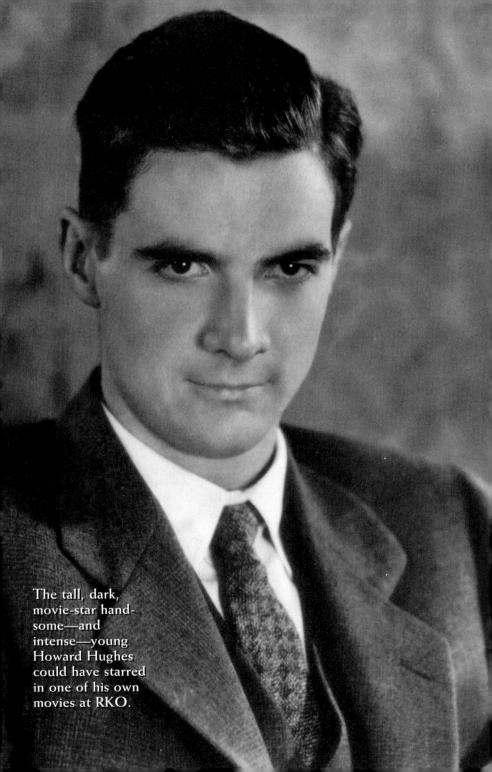

The tall, dark,
movie-star hand-
some—and
intense—young
Howard Hughes
could have starred
in one of his own
movies at RKO.

Blonde, squeaky clean and innocent—that's what appealed to Howard about me in this early studio publicity still.

As a young man, Howard loved golf, but he gave up the game when he couldn't take the time to overcome his one-stroke handicap.

In 1938, after setting a round-the-world speed record in his Lockheed 14, Howard rides through New York City in a motorcade with a waving Grover Whalen, president of the World's Fair. But Howard's mind was on more urgent priorities: a hot date that night with Katharine Hepburn.

After setting a new speed record to his hotel, Howard called Kate and she slipped into his room disguised as a bellboy with a special room service delivery.

Howard's second consuming passion was film-making, and as owner of RKO in the 40s, he became a high-profile movie mogul with a swashbuckling style that soon made him a living legend.

Always a meticulous pilot, he goes over his checklist before test-flying an experimental Hughes airplane in 1948.

In 1946, his XF-11 plane plowed through two houses before bursting into flame. He walked out barely alive, but from then on Howard began wearing a moustache to mask a scar on his upper lip—and he began taking the pain medication that ultimately ruined his life.

Howard behind the controls of his beloved Flying Boat, the giant 300-foot "Spruce Goose," built entirely of wood during an aluminum shortage in the 40s. Critics scoffed, claiming it would never fly, but they were wrong. With him at the controls, it made a triumphant maiden flight that also proved to be its last.

He spent $350,000 to buy a yacht for the sole purpose of seducing movie star Billie Dove on a moonlight cruise. For Howard, it was money well spent.

Howard made a star of his discovery Jean Harlow in his aviation hit *Hell's Angels,* but despite rampant rumors of a torrid affair between them—and an innocent flirtation—their relationship was strictly professional.

One of Howard's
earliest conquests
was a young Bette
Davis, who traded
smouldering glances
with him on the
night they met at
a charity ball,
then invited him
to a late-night
rendezvous in
her Beverly Hills
bathtub.

Howard's relentless
pursuit of 18-year-
old English actress
Ida Lupino began
on the grounds of
the Racquet Club,
a celebrity spa in
Palm Springs, and
ended with an
amorous encounter
in the single seat of
an airborne biplane
over Catalina Island.

Among his most attentive and alluring girlfriends was Ava Gardner, photographed with him at a heavyweight prizefight. She had already played nurse in a hospital room visit during his recovery from a plane crash.

In his familiar snap-brim Stetson and tieless open shirt, Howard cut a dashing figure around Hollywood—and a wide swath among leading ladies of the screen.

In his later years, a drug-addicted victim of his own excesses and eccentricities, Howard allowed himself to become a prisoner of his own palace guard—and a pawn of employees Bill Gay and Chester Davis (center left and right) in a clandestine conspiracy to take over his corporate empire.

"That's what I mean. I'm supposed to be in the left-hand seat, Bob. That was the deal. You know this plane has nose-wheel steering from that seat!" Blackman was practically shouting.

"Don't worry, Tony, you can still fly the plane from the co-pilot's seat. You can still control the throttle, flaps, rudder— just about everything. Take Mr. Hughes through the checklist and you'll see, it'll be all right. He's an accomplished pilot and it'll come back to him once we get going." Bob was using all his persuasive powers to calm Blackman down. He knew he was taking a chance, but he had faith in Blackman's talent as an instructor as well as faith in Howard's skill as a pilot.

"But Bob, I get nervous when I see that goofy smile on his face and the way he keeps touching that snap-brim hat of his."

"Forget it, he's just happy, that's all. And as for the hat, he's always flown with a hat like that one. It's lucky for him."

"Well, it better be lucky for all of us," quipped Blackman. "And what about his license, his pilot's license? You know I'm putting my ass on the line letting him fly without a rating."

"Tony, after he's logged the necessary hours, it'll only be a formality to get him issued one. You know that, you're instructor rated."

"Okay, you seem to have all the answers, but I'm telling you, the first time he doesn't follow one of my orders, I'm taking over and bringing the ship in."

"Okay, Tony, you're the boss."

"And Bob, one more thing."

"Yes."

"He better buy the fucking airplane."

They went back onto the flight deck and Tony ordered the plane towed out of the hangar and onto the field. Howard wanted to know what the hell was taking them so long and kept saying he was ready to get underway. Bob excused himself, wished Howard good luck and returned to the cabin, where he strapped himself in and said a little prayer. Looking over, he saw Glenn Kaiser was pale as a ghost. He was going to say something to assure him, thought about it, and decided: Screw him, the little spy. Then he directed all his thoughts to Howard, hoping he was up to it, and most of all hoping he wouldn't give Tony too hard a time. He knew if Tony canceled the flight, there would be no second chance.

Blackman sat in the right hand seat, the co-pilot's seat, and he stared at the man next to him. He knew Hughes was a legend, he knew he was mysterious, and he knew he was rich, very rich. That was the reason Tony was there, to sell this guy an airplane or two. Also, Tony couldn't kid himself about the thrill of actually meeting Howard Hughes. All he had heard, all he had read was shrouded in a veil of mystery, and above all secrecy, concerning the man who now sat in the pilot's seat of the Hawker Siddley 748.

Blackman had to admit he was intrigued and flattered that Bob Hunt had come to him with this opportunity. He remembered the most important element that Bob had stressed was confidentiality. Mr. Hughes didn't want anyone knowing about the flight; he wouldn't tolerate any leaks, and most importantly, he had a fear, yes a fear, of the press finding out about it. He would notify the press in his own good time, when he could control it, and announce his triumph then. Tony didn't quite understand the need for all the cloak-and-dagger nonsense, but he would be a good soldier and follow orders. What the hell, there was adventure about this game and maybe, just maybe, a pot of gold as well.

The first thing Tony noticed was that Hughes looked old. Much older than he knew he was. And the man was under-weight, actually emaciated. Then he took notice of his hands: They were large hands, with spots on them, long fingers, but bony; the skin seemed to be pulled very tight around the entire hand. But he could see the strength in them as they gripped the controls, ready to put the plane in flight. Hughes had on slacks in what appeared to be a fine grade of wool, pants from a suit, he guessed; a light blue dress shirt; a leather pilot's jacket and that damn snap-brim Stetson. But what was strange was that Hughes had the jacket open, the shirt unbuttoned, the slacks open and unzipped. Tony felt he had to say something.

"Mr. Hughes, pardon me, but you're practically undressed." There was a moment of nervous silence. Then Blackman started to speak once more, but Howard cut him off:

"I know. It's hard getting used to wearing clothes again. It'll take a little time. Bear with me, okay? It'll be our little secret." Tony didn't understand. He had heard all sorts of strange stories, as had everyone, about Howard Hughes. But if he wanted to fly with his trousers and his shirt open, there was no law against it. As long as he wasn't a danger and he followed orders. Besides, he was thinking of the sale.

"Okay, Mr. Hughes, we'll keep it our secret."

"Fine, Tony. Fine."

What Blackman noticed next were Hughes' eyes. They were sad eyes, sorrowful eyes, eyes that had seen everything—but there was a glint in them. Tony looked closer and saw it—yes, there was a fire in his eyes, the fire of determination. That was enough for Tony Blackman. He knew about that fire from his own experience, and he respected it. He was determined now to help Howard Hughes to fly again. He had heard all the stories, the rumors of hair down the back, fingernails curling under the hands, toenails six inches long. But what he saw in the left-hand seat was just a well groomed old man, his nails cropped, his hair a proper length, and his attitude seemed just fine. So damn all the bloody rumors, Hughes was his co-pilot and they were about to take off.

"Okay, sir, we're going to go down the pre-flight checklist."

"Roger," Howard answered. Blackman started counting down all the duties of the co-pilot as his pilot checked off each one. Tony was impressed. Very impressed.

"Mr. Hughes, tell me, how are you so well-versed on the flight-deck checklist of the Hawker Siddley 748?"

"For the past month I've been reading every magazine on flying that my aides could get me. *Aviation, The Pilot, Aircraft Journal* and many others. When Bob Hunt told me we would be flying the HS 748, I had him get me the specs on the plane and I made sure to familiarize myself with them." Tony was speechless. He didn't think it was possible for anyone to learn the intricate workings of the twin-engined turboprop just from the engineering specifications. Then he realized, this wasn't just anyone, this was an aviation legend. This was Howard Hughes.

"Okay, Mr. Hughes. I'm starting the engines."

"Check," said Howard. After both turboprops had warmed up, Blackman gave him the okay to taxi out and down the runway. Blackman was reluctant to let him do it, but the last few minutes had bolstered his confidence in the man. He told Hughes to take it slow and easy until he got the feel of it. Howard started the craft down the runway on an erratic course. He wasn't used to the feel, and the plane was straying from its course down the center, along the yellow line. But by the time it neared its spot at the end of the runway, the 67-year-old pilot has mastered the nose-wheel steering system and had the HS 748 directly down the center of the runway. Without instruction from Blackman he turned the craft around and into the wind, awaiting clearance from the tower.

Clearance came through, and Tony and Howard both pushed forward on the throttles. The 748 roared down the runway, reached takeoff speed, and the moment Howard had dreamed about, planned for, worked for and even prayed for had finally arrived. Howard pulled back on the controls and in an instant he was airborne. Howard Hughes was flying again!

He told Blackman that he most wanted to practice his touch and gos. That was the way he first learned how to fly, and that was the way he felt he would restore his confidence back in the pilot's seat. Tony didn't want to proceed with a series of touch and gos, since that was the most dangerous part of flying: takeoffs and especially landings. But Howard was most persuasive, and he allowed Blackman to control most of the maneuvers. There were some close calls, but Tony's expertise bailed them out. Howard had a lot of catching up to do, but he was determined to do it. Glenn Kaiser as well as Bob Hunt were sure they were goners on one pass in particular, when Howard totally misjudged the landing, but it was Blackman to the rescue once again. There were some harsh words between the two of them in the cockpit, but Tony came away rather liking the old man. Above all, he truly gained respect for Howard's grit and determination, and he made a decision that day. If Hughes was determined to fly, he was going to be the man to fly with him.

After the plane was brought in for the final landing of the day, Bob Hunt congratulated his friend, and they both knew it would just be a matter of time until the man was back in charge again. This was a different Howard Hughes than the one who boarded the Hawker Siddley a few hours earlier. Howard knew he could do it now. He knew it, and he wanted more than ever to keep it a secret, because he also knew that if the other side knew, they would do anything to keep him from being in control again.

CHAPTER SEVENTEEN

MID-JULY 1973

·

*In the Air
Over Northern England*

"This is more like it," said Howard Hughes as he put the de Havilland 125 into a right bank at about 1,000 feet to come around and make another touch and go at Stansted Airport. Tony Blackman saw the grin on Hughes' face and the new fire in his sad eyes. Howard sat in the pilot's seat as Blackman monitored all of his maneuvers from the co-pilot's seat. "That's good, very good," he said as Howard gave more throttle to power the jet through the turn.

This was a big step up for Howard, for today marked the third time he was flying, actually piloting, since he had made his decision to fly again. And today he was back in jets. At the controls of a de Havilland 125–400 series twin engine executive jet, he was more at ease than he was in the Hawker Siddley. He felt the HS was too bulky, too slow, too much like the DC-3 and just too damn old. He had made up his mind to change, to go forward, to begin something new, and now that he was back in the pilot's seat, new meant the plane he was flying.

It had been more than a month and a half since he had taken to the air again. He didn't sleep for the first two nights after that first flight, he was too damn high, not on the medication but on the excitement, on life itself. He tried to keep Bob Hunt up with him both nights, reliving every moment of the flight. As was his custom, he recalled every detail, from the moment they stepped out of the Daimler limousine, through every word said between Tony Blackman and himself, to the final touchdown and landing.

To hear Howard tell it, Blackman was the student and Howard the instructor. That was all right with Bob. He wanted to keep him high; he wanted his spirits up; he wanted him to continue believing he was going to go all the way, so Bob brought him back to earth very gently over the next few weeks. They discussed the problem of keeping the aides off balance. Bob and Howard didn't want them and, by extension, Bill Gay to find out the real purpose of his return to flight. This was one time when Bob believed wholeheartedly in Howard's penchant for secrecy, so in his first report he didn't let them know how well he really did. He informed them only of the time of the takeoff and final landing and the name of the airfield. He also included some details about the aircraft, and they both agreed to keep the reports strictly business. Since the accompanying aide couldn't go into the cockpit, he could only speculate as to who was actually doing the piloting, and therefore what progress Mr. Hughes was really making.

Howard knew he had done well on his first flight in 13 years, but not as well as he had wanted or envisioned. Bob and Stan Dean kept on him about building his weight up, but it was very difficult for him. Even though he had reduced his medication, he still needed and—he hated to admit it—he still *wanted* that damn codeine. The problem was that for his whole life, he'd had trouble with his colon and the medication only caused worse constipation than ever. Knowing that he'd be sitting on that damn toilet for hours at a time, it was hard to try to put on weight and difficult to build any strength. He had to get sleep to get stronger, and he was determined to do it. God, he loved being in the left-hand seat again, and nothing was going to keep him from it. He made a decision to tell the boys to give him something strong to help him sleep. And he was going to try to cut down even more on the codeine. "Don't worry, Bob," he told him, "I'm going to do it. Just remember: secrecy."

Howard's second flight came near the end of June. He wanted a flight plan that would take them over the English Channel to Ostend, Belgium and back. He reasoned that a short flight over water would help him redevelop all the pilot skills he would need: He had to fly; he had to navigate; he had to get tower clearances; he would have to do it all. Of course, he would count heavily on Tony Blackman, but that would be another step forward. Bob Hunt fought Howard over this decision. He felt it was too soon and that Howard should stick to the basics. Blackman agreed, but Howard won out in the end. After all, he was the man with the money, and like it or not, money talks.

As far as the aides were concerned, Bob had changed one important procedure about Mr. Hughes' flights. The first flight had been announced beforehand, but starting with this second flight, there had been no advance notice. Only Hughes, Blackman and Bob Hunt knew when they were taking off. So when Bob told the boys to get the Daimler limo ready because Mr. Hughes was leaving for the airport, it threw the aides into a panic. They were actually in fear for two reasons: One, they were ordered to give notice in advance to Bill Gay's office, and number two, none of the aides wanted to accompany Mr. Hughes on his flying. Glenn Kaiser had told them all of the close call that he'd put the Hawker Siddley through in attempting a touch-and-go landing. Kaiser said he had actually kissed the ground when they landed, and this didn't exactly build confidence among the others. If the aides had been betting men, the odds would have been more than 100 to one against the boss trying to fly again. They were aware that he'd been weaning himself off the drugs, but they felt he still wasn't in full possession of his faculties. And the consensus was that he never would be. That's why there was shock and panic. They tried to stall so they could get a call into the States, and decide who was going to draw short straw for the latest flight. But stalling tactics didn't work, and within a few minutes Mr. Hughes himself came out dressed in his leather flying jacket and snap-brim Stetson with Bob Hunt at his side.

"Where the hell is my goddamned car?" asked Howard.

When he didn't get a quick enough answer, he said, "Bob, you drive us in your car." McDermott almost choked. He told Mr. Hughes the car would be at the service entrance in just one minute.

Then Howard looked around the interior of the suite and said laughingly, while he winked at Bob, "Which one of you lucky fellas is going to come along with me today?" An eerie silence descended on the room, and Howard watched with amusement as the aides tried to merge into pieces of furniture.

Hughes broke the silence by pointing his finger at Leland Dickinson and said sarcastically, "Leland , I always knew you wanted to stay close to me. Let's go."

The weather was lousy, but the flight was uneventful. There were no practice landings, no touch and gos. From Hatfield, they had to stop at Stansted Airport for fuel. The weather was so terrible that Tony Blackman practically begged Hughes to cancel the flight. Bob agreed, but Howard won out as usual. It was approximately 150 miles to Ostend from Stansted, 300 miles round trip. The visibility was so poor that no landing was attempted in Belgium. Howard spent some of the time in the cabin in discussions with Bob while Blackman handled the mundane chore of keeping the Hawker Siddley on course.

Leland Dickinson tried to eavesdrop on their conversation, but they were careful not to be overheard, and besides, Hughes had fallen into the habit of wearing his hearing aids. What shocked Bob was what Dickinson couldn't hear. Howard had made another major decision. He didn't want to fly a turboprop any longer. What he had in mind required more, much more. He told Bob to acquire a private jet for all future flights. The Hawker Siddley 748 returned to Hatfield without incident. Even though it was nighttime, Hughes brought in the twin-engined turboprop for a perfect landing. It would be the last time he would ever pilot a propeller plane.

In his corporate office in Encino, Bill Gay had just finished reading the second report from Bob Hunt. It read much like the first one, listing nothing more than the facts, dates, times, names of airfields, serial number of the aircraft. What interested Gay was the first report of Glenn Kaiser. Even he had to chuckle as he read that Kaiser thought he was going to get killed when the plane missed the runway, time after time, on its landing approaches. Kaiser was certain that Mr. Hughes couldn't handle an aircraft any longer, and to want to fly with him would be the equivalent of a death wish. Dickinson's report was different, stating that on Mr. Hughes' second flight, the takeoffs and landings were all right, but that Mr. Hughes, in his flying jacket and snap-brim Stetson, had spent a good deal of time in the cabin with Mr. Hunt, but that he hadn't been able to overhear their conversation. Furthermore, he couldn't determine who had actually been controlling the plane in takeoffs and landings, but he assumed, hopefully, that it was Tony Blackman.

It was also his opinion that Mr. Hughes was incapable of piloting the aircraft, especially considering the weather conditions, and that he too would have feared for his life had he thought that Mr. Hughes was really in control.

"What the hell do you mean he went flying again?" shouted Chester Davis on the telephone to Nadine Henley and Bill Gay. "I thought it was a one-time shot."

"I knew he would persevere," answered Nadine in her sweet, steady voice, "but it isn't the flying that concerns me. It was the surprise of the second flight itself."

"That is exactly what disturbs me also," Gay interjected. "Apparently Mr. Hunt felt it wasn't to Mr. Hughes' advantage to notify us in advance. Still, from the reports I've received from Kaiser and Dickinson, there seems to be nothing for us to be overly concerned about. Kaiser's biggest anxiety was that he was going to crash and burn with Mr. Hughes at the controls. And Dickinson doesn't even know if he was actually piloting during critical maneuvers at all."

"I still don't like it," said Davis.

"Take it easy, Chester," assured Gay, "I'll have the situation more closely monitored. Don't forget he's still on the medication, and he's not going anywhere without one of our people along with him."

"I still don't like it. Let's start thinking about a way to get Hunt out of the picture. That's when this whole situation started," said Davis.

"Chester has a good point," added Nadine, "I don't think Mr. Hughes is really piloting either, but Bob Hunt could still become a problem. Is there any way we can get to Tony Blackman?"

"No, we've tried," said Gay. "He's a long-time friend of Hunt's. Let me think of a way to get Hunt on our side. You can catch more flies with honey."

"All right, but remember what I told you last time," said Nadine. "Bob Hunt worked a miracle with Mr. Hughes in '58."

Howard had just completed the turn and was lowering the flaps in preparation for the touch and go. He was throttling back and preparing to bring his air speed down to 110 knots for landing.

"Flaps down to forty degrees," Howard commanded Tony Blackman.

"Mr. Hughes, are we coming in for a landing, or a touch and go?" asked Blackman.

"You know I want to do touch and gos," said Howard.

"Then don't take offense and let me give you some instruction," said Blackman diplomatically, since he didn't want to lose his potential customer—and he didn't want to lose his life. "Mr. Hughes, if we were landing, we would go to 40- or even 50-degree flaps, but in a touch and go, we'll only go to partial flaps, 15 or 20 degrees at most. I also want to keep our air speed up to between 125 and 130 knots. 110 knots is actually landing speed in this aircraft. Once we feel the wheels touch, I'd like you to give more throttle and pull up on the stick. Put the nose of the ship straight up and then give full power. Don't worry, we have plenty of runway."

"I know all that!" said Howard belligerently. "It's just that I'm not used to this plane yet."

"Yes, sir. I understand that. I'm only here to assist you. You're the captain." Howard liked the way that sounded. He had to admit that he actually liked this Britisher. Howard knew he was being difficult at times, but hell, he had a lot to accomplish, and he wanted to do it before anyone realized what was happening. Blackman would just have to put up with him. Bob had assured him that Tony could be counted on, and Howard had promised that the rewards to both of them would be great.

"All right, Mr. Hughes, you're doing fine. We're at 20 degrees flaps and airspeed is 128 knots. We're 20 feet above the runway. Soon as you feel the wheels touch, power up and pull the stick back. I want to see the nose go straight up."

"Roger," was all Howard said as they felt the bump of the wheels hitting the tarmac at 130 knots. Howard expertly pulled back on the controls and the nose of the de Havilland started coming up—but he forgot to give more throttle. But Blackman didn't want to override Hughes, so he decided to give him a little more time. The nose started dipping as the jet lost speed. Blackman knew he would have to act fast. He didn't want the DH 125 to even approach stall speed of 77 knots.

"Mr. Hughes, you forgot to throttle up. I'll take over."

"Oh damn, son of a bitch!" said Howard as he watched Blackman give full throttle and pull back on the stick. As the high-grade jet fuel reached the twin Rolls Royce Viper 522 engines that powered the 47 1/2 foot long private jet, the sleek nine-passenger executive jet cleared the tarmac of Stansted field.

No sooner had this maneuver been completed than Howard said, in a most unusual gesture, "Tony, I'm sorry. I just forgot to give throttle. I guess I was too excited about being in the jet. Let's try it again and this time I'll get it right."

"No problem, Mr. Hughes, the stick is yours." Howard checked the altimeter and saw they were fast approaching 1,000 feet. He started the bank that would bring them around to attempt another touch and go. He couldn't understand how he had forgotten to give more throttle. He had practiced this a million times before, both in real life and in his head. It was as easy as 1-2-3.

"No problem, Tony, here we go again."

Blackman watched as Howard slowly took the plane out

of the bank and lined up the de Havilland for approach, then brought the flaps down correctly to 20 degrees, partial flaps. He watched at Howard reduced speed to 130 knots, marveling at how quickly he had made the necessary adjustments—this man who didn't have a current pilot's license, whose physical appearance misrepresented his true will and determination. This aviation legend was putting the executive jet through its paces.

"All right, Tony, watch me," shouted Howard as he ran his fingers along the brim of his Stetson and then gently and expertly, as in days long past, watched the yellow-spaced lines marking the middle of the runway approach at 130 knots. He felt the wheels touch tarmac. In one fluid easy movement, he pulled back on the controls with his left hand, and with his right pushed forward on the throttle. Howard felt the slight vibration and heard the roar of the Vipers as they gulped in fuel and surged with the power he needed to bring the nose of the de Havilland 125 back up and into the sky.

"Perfect, Mr. Hughes. Perfect," said Blackman.

All Howard said in reply was, "Let's do it again."

Writing his report in one of the passenger seats, Bob Hunt would record only the time that the plane took off from Hatfield, the landing at Stansted and the return to Hatfield. There would be no mention of the dramatic progress Howard Hughes was making.

On the drive back to the suite at the Inn on the Park, Howard was very quiet as he sat in the back of the Daimler. Glenn Kaiser, the aide who was accompanying them that day, took Mr. Hughes' mood to be melancholy. What he didn't know was that Howard was ecstatically reliving every moment of his first flight back in jets, fighting to contain himself from discussing out loud every moment of the entire day.

Secrecy was still essential, first and foremost. He wasn't ready yet, but he was getting closer, much closer. He knew he still had obstacles, not the least of which was his continuing battle with the medication. But for the moment he wanted to focus only on today's triumph. He closed his eyes and sat back deep into the comfort of the big leather seat, congratulating himself on his planning and resolve to have come even this far. In his mind he rolled back the years to a time when he had planned for a different kind of triumph, and a smile appeared on his sleeping face as his dreaming mind focused on the big blue eyes of Bette Davis.

CHAPTER EIGHTEEN

THIRD WEEK OF AUGUST 1938

·

*Coldwater Canyon
Beverly Hills, California*

He'd had his eye on her for some time. In fact, it was a little more than four years since he'd first seen her in *Of Human Bondage*, and she was electrifying. He thought she should have won the Oscar, or at least been nominated for her performance. A lot of others in Hollywood thought so, too. It took almost two more years to prove him right. That was when she accepted the Academy Award from the legendary D.W. Griffith on stage at the Biltmore Hotel in Los Angeles for her portrayal of a faded actress in *Dangerous*. He loved the gossip that he heard about the events that led up to her award. She had been unhappy with her relatively small salary, compared to other stars at her studio, Warner Brothers. She was disgusted with most of the roles her boss, studio head Jack Warner, had offered her, especially after *Of Human Bondage*. She had been in a year-and-a-half conflict with him trying to raise her salary and get him to lend her out to the other studios that were sending wonderful scripts her way. She hadn't gotten Jack Warner to budge on either count. And then she won her Oscar. Warners had never had an Academy Award-winning actress. The studio had gone six years without even a single actor winning one. And they'd had some good actors in great performances: Paul Muni, Edward G. Robinson and James Cagney, to name a few. And name a few she did. In fact she didn't stop naming and calling and arguing to the point that she was threatened with suspension by the studio. That's the worst thing a studio could do to one of its actors, suspend them without pay.

She gave in a little to avoid outright suspension, but it had become a feud. Then it was 1938 and she was going to be nominated again. Howard and the rest of the town were sure of it. Warners had released her movie *Jezebel*, in which her co-star was Henry Fonda. The word was out that this was her greatest performance ever. But she was still feuding, and Howard loved it. He wondered what tactics she would employ if she won her second Oscar. This was an exciting woman, and everything he learned about her only made his passion for her grow. So he made plans for the conquest of Bette Davis. Only what Howard didn't know was that Bette had plans of her own: the capture of Howard Hughes.

He had put his plan in motion about two weeks before he left for the east coast for his attempt at breaking the around-the-world speed record. He was hoping to see her sometime during the month of August, since he knew his current love, Katharine Hepburn, was planning to stay in New York and New England through the end of summer. It was typical of Howard to try balancing two romances at once. Sometimes even three. He needed to know everything he could about Bette, more than just the gossip, something to give him the advantage. As usual, he turned to Noah Dietrich, Howard's right-hand man and, as always, Noah came through. He had been through this many times before, and no matter how often he lectured his employer about Howard's handling or mishandling of his love affairs, he always got the same answer.

"Why not, Noah? I'm young, I've got money, I'll make the time, and what the hell, you only live once, right?!"

And Noah, in exasperation, would reply, "Howard, with all that you're trying to pack into your life, you'll have to live twice."

Two days later Howard had the report he had ordered. He was reading through the basics like her date of birth, April 5th, 1908; place of birth, Lowell, Massachusetts; mother's name, Ruth. She had a younger sister, born on October 25, 1909, who was named Barbara Harriet Davis, but everyone knew her as Bobby. Bette's real name was Ruth Elizabeth Davis. He read that her parents had been divorced when she was seven years old. Even though her mother was still alive, Howard felt a kinship with Bette, because his parents had died while he was still in his teens and he had always considered himself an orphan.

He read about her stage debut in productions in Massachusetts and upstate New York. He read about her beginning in movies, including her first film role in *Bad Sister*, and was surprised at how many she had made, and starred in, up to this time: *Seed*, *The Man Who Played God*, which got her noticed, *The Rich Are Always With Us*, *Fashions of 1934* and *Of Human Bondage*, her big break. *Dangerous* won her an Academy Award and made her a full-fledged star. Then came *The Petrified Forest*, *That Certain Woman* and the recently released *Jezebel*, which made her the talk of the movie industry. Oh yes, thought Howard, he had to have her. But none of what he read gave him the edge he needed. Impatiently, he read the note Noah Dietrich had paper-clipped to the next page. It read simply, "Howard, knowing you, you're bored to this point; but these next pages should be what you're looking for."

The report went on to reveal that Bette Davis was a married woman. This was not a secret, so Howard read on rapidly to get to the parts Noah had alluded to in his note. Bette was married to Harmon Oscar Nelson, known as Ham Nelson. They had been high-school classmates. He was a graduate of Massachusetts Agricultural College and a singer and musician by trade. He was not successful in his career. They had been married on August 18, 1932 in Arizona. The word was that the marriage was on the rocks and had been for some time.

Howard smiled as he read the last sentence, and he read even faster now. Bette Davis was generally not known to have had any extramarital affairs. A frown appeared on his brow, and then the smile returned as he read, "Her first and only extramarital liaison, that we uncovered, occurred on her latest movie *Jezebel*. It was with her director, William Wyler. Miss Davis also became pregnant and had an abortion soon after the film wrapped. From all accounts, the affair is over, and it was Wyler who broke it off. Additional information on Bette Davis: She is the president of the Tailwaggers Club." Howard had a chuckle over the name of the club, and with his curiosity peaked, read on. "The Tailwaggers Club is an organization pledged to raising money for the care of stray, lost or abused dogs and also for the training of seeing-eye dogs. Miss Davis is very active in this club. A major fund-raiser is planned for August 11th of this year at the Beverly Hills Hotel."

Howard put the report down and started to formulate a plan. He had always been shy about making introductions on his own, but he also knew that nothing could arrange an introduction as quickly or as correctly as money. Thank God for Hughes Tool, he thought again for the thousandth time. His mind was made up. He wanted her, he had to have her, he was going to get her, and what the hell, if it cost some money, that's what it was for.

Thirty-two year-old Howard Hughes picked up the telephone and dialed Noah at his home. Usually, Howard would call in the middle of the night, since he would lose all concept of time when he was working on whatever he considered the priority at the moment. Even with last-minute arrangements still to be made concerning his flight around the world, and people standing by waiting for his orders, there was no more urgent priority for Howard than setting into motion his plan for the seduction of Bette Davis.

"Hello, Noah, I've got something I want you to do for me."

Noah knew there would be no thanks forthcoming for the swiftness and accuracy of his recent report on Bette Davis. In fact, Noah was thankful that this phone call came at ten p.m. rather than the customary two or three a.m.

"Okay, Howard, what do you need me to do?"

"Well, I read here that Bette is real interested in dogs. She has this crazy-named club, and they're going to throw some big dinner."

"And you want me to get you an invitation, is that it, Howard?"

"Well, I was thinking," he said, and Noah thought he sounded like a little boy who had just done something naughty. "I was thinking: more than ask for an invitation. I'd sort of like it if they would want to invite me. So I figured if you send them a nice letter explaining how interested I am in stray dogs and such, and also enclose a little check made out to their organization, they might ask me to come to their dinner."

"Howard, you couldn't care less about stray dogs. You've never even had a pet."

"If they ask, tell them I'm thinking of getting one." Both men started laughing at the same time.

"Okay, how much should I send, five thousand?"

"Are you nuts, Noah?" shouted Howard. "I was thinking more like five hundred. What do you think?"

"Howard, the whole reason you're doing this is to get close to Bette Davis. You want to make sure that you are not only invited, you want to be sitting next to her. Right?"

"Yeah, so?"

"So make sure she knows you sent a good amount. You have a reputation to keep up, and it's a nice cause. Give them at least twenty-five hundred."

"You think so, huh?"

"What I think is that you should be keeping your mind on the flight coming up and not chasing women."

"Okay, Noah, send the twenty-five," and without another word Howard broke the connection.

With Howard back in Southern California, his first official piece of business, a few weeks later, was to sit down in person with Noah and catch up on his various operations. So they met at Hughes Aircraft in Burbank. Howard loved it there with the planes, the machinery, and the camaraderie of the mechanics and pilots who shared with him his first great love, flying. His second greatest love was movies, watching them and making them. But the best part of all were the movie stars. He had just left one behind in New York, Kate Hepburn, and now he wanted to know about his next one, Bette Davis. Noah had hardly begun to bring him up to date on business affairs when Howard cut him off: He only had one kind of affair on his mind.

"Noah, did we hear from Bette? I mean did we get an invitation?" Noah couldn't believe it. After just returning from flying around the world and being the sole owner of so many varied multi-million-dollar interests, all he had on his mind was getting laid. Sometimes Noah wished *he* was more like Howard: All that money always pouring in from Hughes Tool, and to be in total control of it and the freedom that it allowed. Yeah, damn it, to be free, free to think of nothing but getting laid.

"Noah, I'm asking you a question. Did we get an invitation?"

"You know, it's funny," said Noah, "but the day after I sent the letter and check, we received not just an invitation but a special invitation for you to be the guest of honor at the Tailwaggers Ball."

"Well, what do you think of that? You see, my plan worked, even better than I thought."

"Well, you see, that's what's so strange, Howard."

"What do you mean?"

"The invitation for you to be the guest of honor was mailed before they had a chance to receive my letter."

"So you mean they were inviting me anyway?"

"Sure looks that way."

"Noah, get my check back. Stop payment."

Noah's mouth opened wide. Howard Hughes never failed to astonish him.

"Howard, what's wrong with you? That check must have cleared at least three weeks ago. If I tried to get the money back now, you would be known as the biggest cheapskate in town."

"Damn it, if I'd known Bette was going to invite me, I could have saved the money."

Noah had the last laugh. "Yeah, Howard, and now you'll probably have to get a dog, too."

It was the evening of August 11, the night of the Tailwagger's Ball. Howard was in the main ballroom of the Beverly Hills Hotel, he was dressed in his black double-breasted tuxedo, Bette Davis was holding his hand, and he had the biggest hard-on he could ever remember.

It was a real Hollywood event, the kind that fans read about in the movie magazines. And the movie people who weren't in the "in crowd" read about it in the *Hollywood Reporter* and *Variety* and wished they were there. Howard felt the electricity all around him. The glamour of the people who were in attendance seemed to bring their own special brand of excitement, an excitement Howard found contagious. What he didn't realize was that he was adding to the fervor of the evening just by being there. Not only was he known as a wealthy young oilman; he had a reputation as a mysterious but successful motion picture producer, as a daring aviator who had just broken the around-the-world speed record, as the most eligible bachelor in town, who was carrying on a much publicized romance with Katie Hepburn, and here he was with the hottest actress in the movies holding tightly to his arm. Being as shy as he was, Howard was oblivious to all the eyes that followed him. He was aware only of the deep cleavage that he hoped no one noticed him staring at every time Bette squeezed up against him or bent down.

Everyone was dressed in their best, but Bette stood out from the crowd in a long gown with a deep V-cut bodice in lace styled from the dress she wore in *Jezebel*. She was radiant with her hair parted to the side and curling to shoulder length. She had on bright, ruby-red lipstick, and her eyes were a fabulous shade of blue. She was known for her eyes, which seemed to stand out just a bit, and she didn't take them off Howard for a moment. And her voice, that voice. Howard had wondered if it only sounded like that on the screen. But when she greeted him, "Hello Mr. Hughes, our guest of honor. May I call you Howard?" he knew the voice was for real. And then she kissed him full on the mouth. Howard didn't know how to react. He was always the pursuer, always the aggressor. He was always the one to initiate the chase. He knew at once that this was going to be an interesting evening.

People streamed forward to meet this glamorous couple, the president of the Tailwaggers Club and her distinguished guest, to wish Bette well on her goal of a second Oscar, and to congratulate Howard on his recent achievement. Howard wasn't one who liked to shake many hands, especially if they were people he didn't know. Bette saw that everyone in the room wanted to meet the mysterious Mr. Hughes, and she knew what a coup it was for the Tailwaggers to land him as guest of honor. But she could see he was uncomfortable greeting the other notables, so she led him to their seats, where they at least would no longer be in the middle of the room as the center of attraction. When she pointed out to Howard some of the more famous people in attendance, he said he either knew them personally, or was a fan.

Bette asked if he really meant that, and Howard won her over by replying, "I didn't know you until tonight, but I can assure you I was a fan of yours from the first time I saw you in *Of Human Bondage*. And I hope I can become more than just a fan." Bette looked at him with those big blue eyes of hers, said nothing, and then Howard felt her hand under the table gently touch and squeeze his crotch. Just as quickly and silently, she took her hand away and continued talking about some of the other stars at the gala. Howard had lost his breath and almost his equilibrium and didn't know if what just happened had really happened or if it was just a fantasy. All he knew, at that moment, was whether he had to make another donation or get ten dogs as pets, he was going to have Bette Davis.

From their vantage point on the dais, the whole room spread before them.

"There's Mary Pickford," Bette pointed out, and Howard mentioned that he had met her a few years before at one of Marion Davies' and William Randolph Hearst's parties at San Simeon. Howard spotted Norma Shearer and said that he had also been introduced to her at one of the parties at

Hearst Castle. Bette told him she had never been there but had heard all about it from friends. Howard was enchanted by all the questions she was asking him about the goings-on at San Simeon. It always perplexed him why famous people wanted to know about other famous people, but then he realized he might be the biggest gossip of them all. Howard acknowledged that the Hearst parties were the most fantastic he had ever attended, and unwittingly he found himself talking directly into Bette's bosom. He was beginning to feel an ache in his groin as his longing for her intensified, and he began to envision her naked. He could see that her breasts were larger than he had thought. It hadn't come across on screen that she was rather large on top, and this new discovery aroused him even more unbearably.

"Look, Howard, there's George Brent, and Reginald Denny. You know I've worked with both of them. And there's Lupe Velez!" At that moment Doug Fairbanks came over to their table and stuck out his hand to congratulate Howard on his flight, then gave Bette the customary kiss on the cheek.

"I didn't know you knew Doug Fairbanks," she said.

"San Simeon, that's where I met just about everyone."

"Howard, you have to arrange for me to visit there. Will you?"

"Let me see what I can do. I'm sure they'd love to have you."

"But I don't want to go without you, Howard, understand." Howard understood. He was getting the picture. Now all he wanted was to get her into bed.

For her part, Bette wanted more from Howard than just a trip to Hearst Castle. She had been on the lookout for someone to replace William Wyler. She didn't want to admit even to herself that he had broken it off with her. Her marriage to Ham had been over long before it began. Wyler had been her only extramarital affair up to this point in her life, and she thought if she was going to have another one, it better be with someone who was worth it. And Howard Hughes was worth it in more ways than one.

Like everyone else in town, she had been very much aware of Hughes' presence on the scene. It had been a couple of years since his affair with Katie Hepburn had become public, and he had heard that he had romanced many of the beautiful young actresses in Hollywood. But she knew she was different. He had never met a girl like her. She would turn the tables on the handsome young Mr. Hughes. *She* was going to romance *him*. That's when she got the idea to make him the guest of honor at the Tailwaggers event. She'd bet he'd never been on the other end of the chase before.

The party was winding down and Howard wanted to leave with her. She told him that tonight would be impossible, since she had her sister and mother staying with her. Her sister had helped with the Tailwaggers affair and she knew they would be up half the night discussing it. Howard confessed that the only reason he had attended was to be with her, and she admitted that the only reason she invited him to be guest of honor was to be with him.

"When am I going to see you," he pleaded.

"Give me your number and I'll call."

"What if I'm not there?"

"Then give me a number where I can leave a message."

Howard wrote out Noah Dietrich's office number as well as his own home numbers. Bending to kiss her good night, he felt her tongue dart in his mouth and out again. His knees went weak. All he could think of on the drive home were her large white breasts and the feel of her touch.

Howard had been calling Noah's office and house almost every hour for the past three days. Noah was going crazy and told Howard that he had to stop calling him at home in the middle of the night. Howard thought he should have given Bette his damn number at Hughes Aircraft. Why wasn't he thinking straight? He had been flooding her with flowers, as was his custom. And he had been calling incessantly, but getting no answer. He was ready to hire a private detective to track her down. She was all he could think about. All he could remember was her tongue, her breasts, her hand on his crotch. He was driving himself mad. And then on the fourth day he got a call from Noah.

"Howard, a messenger just dropped off an envelope addressed to you marked private and confidential."

"Yes, yes, go on."

"Well, do you want me to open it and read it to you, or do you want me to send it over to you in Burbank?"

"Open it, damn it, Noah, open it now. I'm going nuts."

"'It says '1700 Coldwater Canyon. Eight p.m. Tonight. Let yourself in. B.D.' That's all it says."

"That's enough," said Howard, hanging up.

Howard was driving alone in his Duesenberg up the winding road known as Coldwater Canyon that snaked its way through the very middle of Beverly Hills. The sun had just gone down and Howard was driving slowly and carefully looking for the 1700 address. He felt if he could make his way around the world and back, he should have no trouble finding a house, especially a house that he hoped contained a very special reward.

Ever since Noah had read him the message, his mind had been a blank. All he could focus on was fantasies of Bette. He was planning what to say and how to say it. He wanted to be cool, calm and collected, but he was afraid he would blow it. He had his plane on standby at Hughes Aircraft so he could fly them to Palm Springs or Catalina or anywhere she wanted if it would help him get her into bed. There was something different about this blue-eyed gal, and it was more than that sexy, raspy voice. She had an edge. There was something simmering underneath, and he was going to discover what it was.

Coming up on the right, yes, there it was, 1700 Coldwater. Howard pulled the Duesenberg into the driveway and cut the engine. He could see it was a spacious house in the hacienda style that was a trademark of Southern California. He walked to the front door and instead of just letting himself in as she had instructed, he rang the bell. He knew she was still married. Even if she was getting a divorce, Howard didn't want or need any surprises. He rang again, but still no answer. He felt the adrenaline start to pump through him. There was a moment of hesitation, then a feeling of adventure, then a twinge of arousal and finally a bit of fear. There was always fear of the unknown, but also there was promise, and Howard hoped to fulfill that promise as he turned the door handle and slowly pushed open, hoping to find a waiting and willing Bette Davis. What he found was a large, dimly-lit foyer with only one lamp burning. He had to strain his eyes to see. Then he saw another light at the end of a hallway. It was also very dim. He made his way to the end of the hall and saw that it led to what appeared to be the master bedroom. It was very large and beautifully furnished, but there was no one there. His heart was beating furiously from both anxiety and desire. This was a new game to Howard, and he didn't know if he liked it.

Then he noticed a flickering light in the corner of the bedroom. And from the light he could make out a doorway. He followed the light and saw that it led to the bathroom connected to the master bedroom. The shimmering was caused by three candles set around the oversized bathroom, which was the color of eggshell. Halfway down the walls were in stucco, the rest of the walls and the floor in tile.

There were heavy wood beams in the ceiling, hacienda style. He saw that the glass-enclosed shower was very large. There were huge double sinks in a counter that ran almost the entire length of one of the walls, and mirrors that went to the ceiling, giving the room the illusion of even more spaciousness. Reflected in them, as he moved his gaze around the room, was a giant bathtub, and in the middle of the tub, two-thirds full, with steam rising from the water, her back turned toward him, a cigarette in her hand and her hair piled high on her head, sat Bette Davis, naked as the day she was born. Howard could swear she must have heard his heart beating. He thought he was going to have a heart attack and if not, then he had to be in heaven. He had been dreaming of this, but the reality was turning out even better than the dream.

"You know I've been planning this night for quite some time," said Bette in her raspy voice, keeping her back to Howard. "And I've been wanting you even longer." Howard was mystified, because this was the kind of line he usually gave the women he was after.

Recovering, he said, "And I've been dreaming of you from the moment I first saw you on the screen."

"Tell me, what were you dreaming about, Howard? Were you dreaming about my eyes, my big blue eyes? Or were you dreaming about my breasts and how they would feel in your hands?" Bette started rising from the tub, keeping her back toward Howard. He was perspiring freely now, and had taken off his hat and jacket and thrown them on the tile floor.

"Or were you dreaming about my tummy and how smooth it would be, and how it would feel when you ran your hand over my stomach down to my pussy and how silky the hair would feel?" She was standing in the tub, the water just below her knees, and she slowly turned to face him. The shimmering light of the candles was reflecting off the wetness of her arms and breasts and legs and torso. She began to run her hands over her breasts and nipples, squeezing them as she looked directly at Howard. Then she ran her hands over her stomach and down between her legs, and Howard could see she was putting a finger inside herself.

Howard was wild with lust. His mouth had gone dry. His tongue felt like sandpaper, his heart was beating so fast he was afraid he was going to hyperventilate. And worst of all, his cock was ready to burst from his pants. He had to have Bette *now*. He unbuttoned his shirt and started to take it off.

Bette stepped from the tub, walked over to where he was standing, took his hand, placed it on her breast and said, "Don't get undressed yet." Howard didn't want to stop. He started grinding into her wet belly and kissing her on the neck.

She pulled away and as she ran her hands from her shoulders to her knees, said, "Can Katie Hepburn offer you this?"

Howard was dumbstruck. "Well, can she?" demanded Bette.

"I don't know what you mean," said Howard.

"Don't play coy with me. You know exactly what I mean," she purred as she moved back to Howard's arms, and as he felt her breasts and backside, she reached inside his pants and began kneading him and whispered, "I'm going to show you what it's like to fuck a real woman." This was the moment Howard had been waiting for, only he had thought he would be the one to do the leading. He ripped off his shirt and kicked off his shoes as Bette undid his belt and pulled his pants down. He had no underwear on, and Bette was beginning to stroke him as she led him the few steps into the bedroom and onto her bed. He was lying on his back as she ran her tongue up his chest, over his neck and into his mouth. Then she sat on top of his chest, grinding herself into him, moving higher until she was over his face and mouth, and he could taste how wet she was. Almost immediately, she climbed off him and sat on her knees between his legs, facing him. One by one she placed his long legs over her shoulders and guiding her breasts, rubbed them into him. Howard was moaning and told her he fantasized about this with her.

All Bette said was, "I know," as she put her head down and took his throbbing erection in her mouth. Howard wanted it to last, but he had been anticipating it too long, he had been aroused too long. In what must have taken a while, but seemed only a second, Howard came from deep inside himself as Bette smiled up at him, continuing to stroke him.

After a while his pulse and blood pressure began returning to normal, and he asked Bette, "What did you mean by that crack about Katie?"

Bette didn't answer at first. She lit a cigarette, took a deep puff and he watched as she blew the smoke out. Bette crawled up into the bed, laid her head down over Howard's outstretched arm, turned her face up to his and said, "I meant exactly what I said: Can she offer you this?" Before Howard could say anything Bette went on. "We're both New Englanders. Kate's from Connecticut and I'm from Massachusetts. But she was lucky enough to be born into money. I've followed her career from the beginning. I worked hard to get to Broadway and then it took a while until I got noticed; whereas Kate was a big success on Broadway almost from the beginning in *The Warrior's Husband*. I made many films before I got one I could sink my teeth into, and I had to fight for that. While Kate was lauded and praised for a so-so performance in her film debut, *A Bill of Divorcement*. And then she got the Oscar for *A Morning Glory* and I wasn't even nominated for *Of Human Bondage* because of that rat Jack Warner."

Howard didn't say anything. He had been totally unaware of these pent-up feelings of Bette's. He had no idea of her resentment and jealousy. He was still crazy about Katie, but he didn't want to say anything that would upset Bette. Especially not now. This was a new kind of sex for him, with the woman taking charge. He would just let her talk herself out—and besides, he wanted more of her.

"But then it started going my way," she went on, "when a couple of years ago we were both nominated, she for *Alice Adams* and me for *Dangerous*. I figured it was my turn and I was right. Now I think I'm going to be nominated for *Jezebel*, don't you, Howard?"

"They'd be crazy not to nominate you, and I'll tell you one more thing—you're going to win."

Bette crushed out her cigarette and gave him a wet kiss on the lips. "Thanks for your encouragement, Howard, I knew you'd be in my corner. When I read that Kate was staying in the East for the summer, I got the idea to make you guest of honor at the Tailwaggers. You don't know how thrilled I was when you accepted. And your generosity, what a check. There're a lot of puppies thanking you."

"It was nothing, you don't have to mention it. I really love dogs." Howard almost choked.

"But I wanted to mention it, and I also want to tell you that you're too good for Kate Hepburn. That's enough talk. Now I'm going to show you what the word fuck really means."

Howard Hughes was smiling widely as Bette Davis climbed on top.

CHAPTER NINETEEN

AUGUST 9, 1973

.

Howard Hughes' Bedroom
London, England

There was a movie showing on the screen, but he didn't even know what it was because he wasn't paying attention. His mind was on much more serious matters. Howard was lying on his bed in his bedroom at the suite at the Inn on the Park. He could have switched to a much larger and more luxurious room anytime he wished, but he decided to stay in this one. Let the aides have all the ambiance and luxury, let Gay and Davis and Nadine keep playing with all their perks and privileges. While they still can. Because sometime after tomorrow, it's all going to change. Tomorrow is the day. The first day of escape from this fucked-up world I've created for myself and back into taking control.

But something was bothering him, and it worried Bob Hunt too. They had both noticed that since his last flight, the second flight in the de Havilland almost two weeks ago, there was something strange going on. It seemed as if the aides were nervous and jumpy. They seemed to be sticking closer to Howard than ever before. Bob even told Howard he was beginning to feel paranoid. It always seemed that the aides were whispering, and he knew they were talking about him.

Bob said they were actually trying to ingratiate themselves with him. Asking him how he was, what he was doing, what his plans were. Bob said it made him suspicious. He liked it better when they acted like antagonists. He and Howard agreed something was up, but they just couldn't figure out what the hell it was. They'd been over the last flight and the last few weeks a couple of times, looking for something that might have been missed, that might have been said, that they might have overlooked. But they came up empty.

It was getting Howard upset, but not as upset as his damn constipation. He was in the middle of one of his severest bouts yet. Why did it have to come now on the eve of such a crucial day? He still hadn't come all the way off the codeine, but he was working toward it, and he was using less than half of what he'd been taking. He knew the medication clogged him up, but the main culprit was his rotten colon. At least that's what his doctors and the aides told him. He was going to lie here and wait for the pain to subside so he could, hopefully, take a crap. Meanwhile he put his head on the pillow and, rubbing his stomach, went over the last flight and the last few weeks in his mind for the umpteenth time. He couldn't quite put his finger on it, but he knew there was something going on. He was resolved to find out what it was because he couldn't, he wouldn't let anything stop him from taking over again, from being free again.

It was almost two weeks since Howard had piloted the de Havilland 125 for the second time, the fourth time he had flown since his decision to fly again. Tony Blackman had commented that his progress was remarkable, but there was still a way to go for Mr. Hughes to be rated as a pilot for the de Havilland. Bob concurred, and this encouragement only made Howard more determined than ever. He knew he could do it, he knew it was all within his grasp. He'd have to be patient, he'd have to concentrate, and above all he had to keep his real purpose absolutely secret.

The flight started that day just like the one before it. With no notice given, he and Bob emerged from Howard's bedroom and ordered the Daimler limo to the rear entrance of the hotel. The aides on duty knew immediately what was going on, because Mr. Hughes was already dressed in his leather flight jacket and snap-brim Stetson. McDermott and the other aides had been beseeching Mr. Hunt to please give them prior notice of the boss' flight plans, but this only led to Bob implementing even tighter security. With no warning when Mr. Hughes would be flying, the job of accompanying him fell to whichever aide happened to be on duty, which in this case was Leland Dickinson. The ride to Hatfield Airport was uneventful and there was nothing said in the limousine that was out of the ordinary. Bob and Dickinson were the only passengers on board as Tony Blackman took the right-hand seat and Howard Hughes the pilot's seat in the cockpit of the jet.

The de Havilland roared down the runway, and as Howard watched the indicator reach 110 knots, he gently pulled back on the controls and the feeling of euphoria flowed through him as he watched the nose of the jet lift almost straight up and he heard the scream of the twin Viper engines powering the craft skyward. Their destination was to the northeast, to Woodford, where Tony Blackman's club and lodgings were. He lived adjacent to the airfield there, and that was where Howard was going to practice his customary touch and gos today. Tony also wanted to see how Howard could lay out a navigational plot. To Tony's surprise and with his help, Howard did quite well. In fact this was the most that he had accomplished since the first flight in May. Howard was more alert, his reaction time quicker and his mind sharper than on any of the previous flights.

The only negative was his physical appearance. Since his third flight earlier in July, he had not allowed Stan Dean to barber him. His hair and beard were getting that scraggly look again. He wasn't allowing his nails to be trimmed. And he hadn't succeeded in cutting back any further on the medication. He reached a point and seemed incapable of making the last final steps toward kicking it. Bob argued with him about his appearance saying that he was playing into Bill Gay's hands by not taking a firmer stand concerning the goddamned codeine. Howard refused to discuss it, saying he knew what he was doing and that the only priority was the secret true mission of the flights. But despite Howard's failure to further decrease his reliance on the medication, this was by far his finest hour since he had climbed back into the pilot's seat.

During the course of the flight, Blackman told Howard about his lodgings at Woodford, explaining that many in the aviation community lived there, close to their work and to their first love: flying. Howard thought it might be a good idea for him to spend some time at Woodford and asked Blackman to show him around the facility when they arrived. Then, with Blackman at the controls for the final approach, Howard went back into the cabin and told Bob about the possibility of moving to Woodford as the first part of his plan.

While Blackman led him and Bob on a short tour of the facilities, Howard wore his leather jacket and Stetson, along with a pair of dark aviator glasses, asking Blackman not to introduce him, if possible, to anyone at all. If it became necessary, he told Blackman to use the name "Mr. Alexander," an alias Howard had used in the past for a number of his many secret trysts. He hadn't thought of that name in such a long time, and for a second or two it brought back memories of an easier, gentler, happier time. Dismissing those thoughts, he tried to concentrate on the mission at hand, but it soon became obvious to Bob that Howard was tiring. It had been a long day. Many practice touch and gos, and now this tour of Woodford. He was also feeling the mental pressure of making his plans and the stress of keeping them secret. Howard was leaning heavily on Bob Hunt as they made their way back to the plane for the flight back to Hatfield.

Leland Dickinson came to Mr. Hughes' side to be of assistance, but Howard waved him away and continued walking on, relying on the support of Bob. Tony Blackman was already on board the de Havilland, and both Howard and Bob were in deep conversation as they walked slowly toward the aircraft. Both men were focused on their conversation, not paying attention as Dickinson moved closer and closer to them, dogging their steps. Following his orders to find out whatever he could, he was just about in hearing range and straining to pick up anything. But he was only making out bits and pieces. He heard Bob Hunt raising his voice and he could make out, "Why don't you just fire these assholes?" and Mr. Hughes mumbling something like, "It'll wait, this is more important." And then he heard Mr. Hughes say something about "priority." Dickinson carefully moved even closer as they approached the steps to the jet. He knew he would be required to help Mr. Hughes up the stairs, because Howard was still not a well man, and dead tired after this exciting but exhausting day.

His guard was down and he was in mid-sentence saying, "I'll be ready for the escape," as Leland Dickinson came to his side to help escort him into the de Havilland.

Even above the whine of the engines, even with the wind blowing, Leland Dickinson heard. He knew he wasn't supposed to hear; he wished he hadn't heard. He didn't even really know what he heard or what it meant, but he had heard. The only thing he could do was to report it and let the others make decisions about what it meant. Let them figure it out.

That evening Howard had one of his best night's sleep in many years. Whether it was from the exhilaration of knowing his plan for escape and control were to be implemented shortly or, if it was simple exhaustion, he slept well. And without the help of any medication. That same evening Bob looked in on his friend, saw that he was sleeping and retired to his rooms to start work on the logistics involved in getting Howard moved to Woodford, or wherever else he decided. That was what they'd been waiting and planning for, that was going to put Howard Hughes back in control again.

But on that same evening, Leland Dickinson was in a near panic. He felt most comfortable talking to McDermott, but he wasn't on duty and he wasn't in his room. Dickinson didn't know how important what he had overheard really was and he didn't want to discuss it with the other aides and start the gossip mill rolling. So he waited in the lobby of the hotel for McDermott to return from a late supper. When he finally saw him walking in, Dickinson ran over and, almost trembling, said they had to talk in private—*now*. McDermott told him to calm down. Then they went up to his suite on the penthouse level. Once there, Dickinson related in detail the events of the day, blow by blow, from how it started to how it ended, complete with the ominous dialogue between Mr. Hughes and Mr. Hunt on their way back to the plane. Listening intently, McDermott had him repeat three times exactly what he heard Mr. Hughes and Hunt say to each other, but when he offered no explanation for it, Dickinson finally asked, "Well, what do you think Mr. Hughes meant by that?"

"How the hell should I know," replied McDermott angrily. "Who knows what's going on inside his head? I swear, he must be half crazy with all the medication we've given him over the years. But I can tell you one thing for certain."

"What's that?"

"I sure know what Bob Hunt meant when he told Mr. Hughes to fire us. Let's get Gay on the phone."

"Are you sure that's what he said?" asked Bill Gay for the second time. Gay had Dickinson go through the story all over again. When he was sure he got it right, with every word and every nuance, Gay ordered the aides not to let Mr. Hughes out of the penthouse and hung up.

"What kind of bullshit is that, 'Why doesn't he fire those assholes?' Who the hell does Bob Hunt think he is?" shouted Chester Davis into his telephone, which was connected to the speakerphone in Nadine Henley's office. Sitting across from her was Bill Gay, who had just finished relaying the Dickinson story.

"Chester, I know you're agitated, but control your language. Miss Henley is present," said Gay.

"I've heard worse language in my life, Bill, and frankly I'd like to know who the hell he thinks he is too," said Nadine.

"Thank you, Miss Henley," said Davis.

"But I'm much more concerned over the meaning of Mr. Hughes' remark, 'I'll be ready for the escape,'" she said pointedly.

"It sounds to me like he's hallucinating," said Davis.

"Don't kid yourself, Chester," Gay interjected. "Remember how surprised we were to see how well Mr. Hughes handled himself with the governor? He was in control of himself, if only for a little while. That meeting worked out well for us, but it marked the start of the problems we're experiencing now."

"You've got a point, Bill, that's when he demanded—actually ordered—you to get him Bob Hunt?"

"Yes. I stalled as long as I could, but Mr. Hughes was giving the boys too much trouble. Besides I didn't figure Hunt could hurt us."

Nadine decided it was time to take charge of the situation. She knew she'd have to. "I told you both last time, do not underestimate Bob Hunt. I don't know exactly what's going on, but ever since he arrived, the facts are that Mr. Hughes has been leaving the penthouse more often in the last few months than he has in the last ten years. Whether he's actually piloting or not, we still don't know for sure, since we have to depend on Mr. Hunt's reports. Another fact is that Mr. Hughes is cutting back on his medication, both codeine and Valium. Even though he's still addicted, I'm concerned that he, at the very least, has the willpower to try to stop. We can be sure Mr. Hunt is helping Mr. Hughes in whatever it is that's going on." Before Nadine spoke again, she took a moment to think back to the time when she had been humiliated at the hands of Howard Hughes. She remembered that night at his house, and she shuddered at the thought of Ava Gardner with Howard, her Howard, at the hospital. Well, she had fixed him, fixed him good. If she couldn't have him, nobody ever would, even now.

Her voice icy calm, Nadine spoke again. "Gentlemen, I propose that, until we know exactly what is going on, we do not allow Mr. Hughes out of the suite without our permission. Agreed?"

"Agreed," said Gay.

"Agreed," said Davis.

Later, Nadine Henley and Bill Gay got on the phone with all the aides at the same time. Glenn Kaiser asked, "What should we do? We never know when they plan to go flying."

"Make it your business to find out," said Nadine.

"What should we do about Bob Hunt?" asked Smith.

"We don't care about Mr. Hunt," she told him. "We only care about Mr. Hughes." Nadine was well aware of the aides' loyalty to Bill Gay, and that's why she made sure he was on the line with her. It was left unspoken between them, but the fact that Gay was there with her meant she had the authority to speak for them. It meant she was in charge now. She was in command, and that not only included the aides, it also included Gay and Davis.

"What do we do when Mr. Hughes is starting to leave?" pleaded Dickinson.

And McDermott chimed in, "How do we tell the boss he can't do what he wants to do?"

There was a moment of silence, and Nadine Henley said in a slow, even tone, edged in ice, "If you want to keep your jobs, you'll stop him. Don't ask me how. I don't want to know how!" The last words the aides heard before the line went dead was Miss Henley repeating, "Just stop him!"

CHAPTER TWENTY

AUGUST 9, 1973

.

Late at Night
Howard Hughes' Bedroom

The screen was reflecting only the white light from the
projector. The unwatched movie had long since been
over, and the only sounds in the room were the tic-tic-tic of
the film as it slapped against itself endlessly at the end of the
reel, and the hollow groans and gurgles that came from deep
within the stomach, intestines and colon of Howard Hughes. This might be the worst constipation he had ever experienced. It was more like an attack, and he knew he didn't help
his cause by taking more of that damn medication. He was
dozing in and out of a frightful sleep. He was still reviewing
the last two weeks in his mind. And he still couldn't come up
with the answer to what the hell was going on.

The incident when Dickinson helped him up the stairs to the
de Havilland came back under scrutiny. He had been over that
with Bob Hunt, and they had both concluded that with all the
noise of the engines, he couldn't have heard anything. And
even if he had, it was only pieces of a puzzle, and it wouldn't
make sense to him or anyone else. As far as they could make
out, they had maintained security. And a good thing, too,
because tomorrow at 10 a.m., Howard was scheduled to be

back at the controls of the de Havilland 125 with Tony Black-man in the co-pilot's seat and Bob Hunt as the only passenger. When they took off this time, it would be Howard Hughes' escape, his flight to freedom, his return to control of his own life.

The plan called for Blackman to have the jet fueled and ready, waiting on the tarmac at Hatfield by 9:45 a.m. Howard and Bob would be on board sometime before 10 a.m. They were going to leave the hotel as usual without any prior notice. Only they weren't coming back. They would fly to Woodford, and Howard would stay at one of the guest cottages there while he continued flying on an almost daily basis. Bob Hunt was to act as liaison between Howard and the Summa group, and he had hired special security to meet the de Havilland when it landed at Woodford. The security teams would be on duty 24 hours around the clock, body-guarding Mr. Hughes in his new temporary residence as well as on whatever travels he might undertake. And the best part was they would report only to Mr. Hughes and Bob Hunt.

They knew they still had the problem of the aide who would accompany them for the day, and Hunt decided it would be wise to let him get as far as the aircraft without alerting him. At that juncture, Mr. Hughes would tell him he didn't need him coming along on the flight. They knew the aide would be shocked and, if he didn't obey Mr. Hugh-es' orders, then Bob and Tony Blackman would physically block him from coming aboard. The aides didn't carry firearms and Hunt saw no problem in stopping whoever the aide was. The only problem was maintaining secrecy. Once they were safely ensconced at Woodford, Howard could start the long process of extricating himself from the prison he had built around himself and take the necessary steps toward taking over his life once again.

Bob and Howard had gone over the plan during the last

week. They agreed that even though it was simplistic, it could work. The major objective was to get Howard out of reach of the aides and therefore out of their control. That would be achieved just by reaching Woodford and his new security team. But the key was not the timing of the operation, nor the speed of the plane, nor the size of the new security force. The key was secrecy. It was a lesson Howard had learned from his father. He told him over and over, in all his affairs, both business and private, to remember that secrecy would be his most powerful weapon. Howard found himself reminiscing about the story that his father had told him long ago.

Howard Robard Hughes, Sr. had started the tool-bit business by partnering with Walter Sharp in 1909. They called it the Sharp-Hughes Tool Company and opened a small manufacturing plant and office in Houston. Howard Sr. had patented his revolutionary 166 cutting-edge drill bit earlier that year. It took a year or so, but the new business finally got off the ground. Before long the Sharp-Hughes Tool Company became the leading supplier of drill bits to the oil industry. Sharp and Hughes were always looking for ways to improve their bits. They set up a shed by their plant for the exclusive purpose of building and testing new and improved drill heads. If one worked well in the fields, they would get a new patent for it. Howard Hughes Sr. was a great man for detail and kept complete records of every model they invented, whether manufactured or not. Then, tragically, in 1912 at the age of 42, Hughes' partner died. By 1918, Big Howard—as he was called—had 100% control of the now re-named Hughes Tool Company by buying out Ed Prather, who had bought the interest of Walter Sharp's widow. For the next few years the Hughes Tool Company continued to grow and it looked like there was no end in sight.

Then tragedy almost struck again, but in a very different

form. His name was Clarence Reed and he was a valued and trusted employee of Big Howard's. As his father told the story, one day, Reed up and quit Hughes Tool, started the Reed Roller Bit Company and tried to acquire patents very similar to the original Hughes Drill Bit. By the time a lawsuit got to the courts, Reed was doing big business. Under penalty of perjury, he admitted that he had stolen the blueprints, adding only enough to make sure that his new drill bit wouldn't copy the Hughes model. Thankfully, for the Hughes family, the court decided against Reed and awarded a $500,000 judgment and a 15% royalty on the gross sales of Reed Roller Company to Big Howard.

In recalling the story, Howard remembered his father stressing how lucky he was at the time, and from that moment on how everything he did at Hughes Tool was shrouded in the strictest secrecy. He impressed on young Howard how important it was to keep things quiet, to keep things hidden, to keep things secret. He stamped into young Howard's conscious and subconscious mind the reality that there would always be someone trying to steal something from him. So he should never forget that the best defense was secrecy. Howard would never forget. He conducted his business in secret, his love affairs were secret, he even lived his life in secret. His only hope now was that the veil of secrecy that he kept over his plan for escape would hold.

Bob Hunt had taken care of all the last-minute details. He had made sure the house at Woodford was ready for Mr. Hughes. He had made sure there was a projector and movie screen waiting in readiness. And a large supply of Poland water. The house was located out of the way of foot traffic, so there need be no blacked-out, taped-up windows. This residence—no matter how temporary—had a wonderful view of the airfield. He had made sure the new security people knew how to act around Mr. Hughes, how to address him and most importantly, not to allow any unauthorized medication to get through to him. He made arrangements for a new doctor to take charge and to be temporarily quartered at Woodford. He made sure to buy new clothes for Howard, since they would be leaving his other belongings behind. He even took the precaution of buying an extra snap-brim Stetson, just in case. He went over the final details about take-off time with Tony Blackman and the possibility—more the probability—of needing his help in getting rid of Gay's aide. He had Blackman go over the plan with only the chief of his maintenance crew to make sure the plane was ready. No one on the maintenance crew itself knew about the flight, only that the plane had to be ready. The chief had orders to speak only to Blackman concerning the readiness of the de Havilland, and he too had been sworn to secrecy. Bob checked and re-checked all the arrangements until he was satisfied that all that could be done had been done. He was convinced that the plan was known only to those who had a need to know and with a little bit of luck—you always need luck—everything should go off smooth as silk.

It was the middle of the night. Approximately seven hours before Howard Hughes was to begin the new chapter in his life. Howard had been sleeping, intermittently, between the pains of the acute constipation, but for the last hour or so he had achieved a relatively decent sleep. With the exception of some of the sounds of London traffic that reached the penthouse level, all was silent and serene in the series of suites. The two aides on duty at this late hour had long since performed their last task—bringing Mr. Hughes a bottle of ice-cold Poland water.

It was around three in the morning when the calm of the night was broken by the ringing of the telephone in the main salon. It seemed to be louder than usual, and neither aide wanted to answer it, but the one on the couch closest to the phone finally picked up the receiver. The other aide heard him say "who" and then "he's not here" and then "I don't take messages for him" and finally, "okay, okay." When he replaced the receiver, his colleague saw even by the dimmed nighttime light in the living room that the man had turned ashen pale from what he had just heard.

He asked his companion what was wrong, and his answer was to get the aides assembled at once. They set about dialing the rooms of the other aides and waking them with the news of a potential emergency. In less than 15 minutes, all the aides were gathered in the salon, and the one who answered the telephone repeated what he had been told.

"The caller asked for Bob Hunt, and I told him he wasn't here and I don't take messages for him. Well, this fellow had a strong English accent and told me he was head mechanic for Tony Blackman. That got my attention. He said he couldn't locate Mr. Blackman and that in an emergency he was to contact Mr. Hunt. He apologized for calling at this hour, but if I see Mr. Hunt to tell him that the de Havilland had developed a minor problem with the nose wheel. Not to worry, he'll have it repaired, but they should move back their schedule by two hours." It seemed as if not one of the aides had taken a breath, and then they all started talking at once.

John McDermott waved his hands above his head to get everybody's attention and put a finger to his lips. "Shut up, everyone shut up," he whispered as loudly as he dared. "We don't want to wake the boss. I've got to hear myself think." After a moment he walked over to the phone and placed a call to Bill Gay's office in California. It was 7:25 p.m. on the West Coast and Gay could not be reached. McDermott tried his home and there was no answer there, either. He had left a message with Gay's office that it was an emergency, that they should find Mr. Gay and have him call London at once.

An hour or so had passed and still no call from Gay. The aides were all nervous and the talk among them was about their last conversation with Mr. Gay and Miss Henley and her last words, "Just stop him." What did she mean, how far were they to go, what should they do? They were thinking about their jobs and the easy lifestyle they had become accustomed to. None of them kidded themselves. They knew they couldn't make the kind of money, in the real world, that they were pulling down here in their own perverse, corrupt but very private world. They all agreed that they couldn't allow Mr. Hughes to fly that morning. But none of them had any idea how important this flight, of all his flights, really was. They had no inkling how much this particular flight meant to Howard Hughes. They had no conception of the planning that had gone into that morning's flight. They had simply stumbled onto it accidentally, and now they were stuck about what to do. Their jobs were on the line, their lives were on the line. The pressure was building. It would be morning soon, and that meant Mr. Hughes would be leaving to go flying. Nadine Henley had ordered them to stop him. So they had to make a decision, and fast. Time was running out.

Howard Hughes was waking from the sleep he so badly needed. He had dozed a little more than two and a half hours, and his intestinal pains had eased somewhat. He felt he could finally go to the bathroom and get some relief. He started to get up from the bed and felt himself sliding back down. He was weaker than he thought. He lay there a moment and thought about what this new day would bring and summoned the strength to rise up and make his way toward the toilet. He had gotten two or three steps from his bed when he felt his knees start to give out. Reaching out, he grabbed the wall, leaned against it, and held himself up.

After a minute or so he went on, resting against the wall and using the light from the movie projector to see his way to the bathroom. He made it another few steps to the door of his bedroom and realized he wasn't going to be able to go on without help. The pains returned, shooting through his intestines and clenching them into a tight knot. Howard started to double over from the searing daggers of agony that ran through his entire midsection. He seized the doorknob and with what little strength and will power he could muster, turned the knob and slowly opened the door. He looked out into the vast suite, and as his eyes began adjusting to the light, he called out for the aides. His hearing aids weren't in and he didn't realize his voice was weak. Just above a whisper.

He tried again, "Who the hell's there? I need help. Help!" This time it was much louder. Howard still didn't see the aides. He turned back into his bedroom and took one step toward his toilet.

They were all sitting around the living room, discussing their options, when one of them thought he heard something from the direction of Mr. Hughes' bedroom. And then a moment later they knew it was him when they heard him call for help. The two aides closest to his bedroom jumped out of their seats and bolted to the boss' room, smashing open his bedroom door, only to hear a dull thud and a scream of agony as the door whipped open, crashing into Howard, sending him hurtling into the table by the side of the bed and falling onto his hip. He fell to the floor like a broken rag doll. He lay there silent, breathless, and they thought he was dead.

The other aides came running to the bedroom. All of them were standing over Mr. Hughes, and there was practically no room to breathe, let alone move. McDermott bent down to see if he could feel a pulse or hear a breath. He was about to feel for the carotid artery in Mr. Hughes' neck when he heard a moan and shouted, "He's alive!" There was a collective sigh of relief, quickly followed by arguments and accusations as to who was at fault. It was Mr. Hughes himself who stopped the conversation by complaining about a sharp pain in the region of his left hip. He ordered them to get him off the damn floor and give him something for the pain. They brought him four of his blue bombers, ten-milligram Valiums, and administered a hypo of codeine. At the instant that Howard Hughes felt the warmth of the medication begin flowing through him, he realized that his dreams of escape would have to be put off to another day—but he prayed not forever.

The aides decided that rather than fight with one another over Mr. Hughes' fall, they would be better off sticking together. That meant all telling the same story. They had too much to lose, and it really was an accident anyway, wasn't it?

About one hour later after they had sedated Mr. Hughes, the telephone rang in the suite, and Chris Mays answered it.

"Yes, Mr. Gay. Yes, Mr. Gay," he said, handling the phone like it was a hot iron and giving it to McDermott.

"Yes, Mr. Gay."

"They got hold of me. What's the emergency?"

"Well, the situation has changed since we first put in the call to you."

"What are you talking about? What situation?"

McDermott could hear the exasperation in Gay's voice. "You see, Mr. Gay, we found out the boss was going to go flying this morning and . . ."

Gay cut him off, "You can't let him do that! How did you find out?"

"Well, that's why I said the situation has changed, Mr. Gay." McDermott took a moment and continued, "You see,

Mr. Hughes has had an accident."

"What!" screamed Gay. "What kind of accident? How is he?"

"Mr. Hughes fell. It seems he may have broken his hip. No one knows for sure how it happened. I think he tripped going to the bathroom. Harley Smith thinks he must have lost his balance, Dickinson thinks he probably fell down coming out of the bathroom. Everyone has a different theory."

"You mean he was alone?" asked Gay.

"Yes, sir."

"How do you know his hip is broken?"

"We don't know for sure, but Mr. Hughes is complaining of a severe pain in that area. The doctor will be here soon."

"Have you given him his medication?"

"Yes, sir." McDermott could tell that Gay was worried, but even angrier than he was concerned. But what he heard next would make him and the rest of the aides deeply fearful. Fearful of what Bill Gay would do with the knowledge that McDermott suspected he had figured out.

"Listen, you bunch of morons," screamed Bill Gay, "your orders were to stop him, not to hurt him. Why did you have to break his damn hip?" and Bill Gay slammed the receiver as hard as he could.

CHAPTER TWENTY-ONE

AUGUST 12, 1973

.

Operating Room
London Clinic, England

I t was like looking directly into the sun, only a hundred times brighter. The lights were from the overhead surgical lamps, and they made him close his eyes; he could only squint as he tried to rise up and see his surroundings. He heard reassurances and felt a gentle but firm push on his shoulders as he was made to lie back down on the table that stood in the middle of operating theatre number one of the famed London Clinic.

What the hell am I doing here? thought Howard Hughes. I'm supposed to be at Woodford, I'm supposed to be flying. I should have escaped. And then it hit him, then he remembered. The terrible constipation, his cries for help, the door bursting open and knocking him into the table. And then the awful cracking sound that he heard from inside his own body, telling him that something horrible had happened. And the excruciating pain.

He remembered hitting the floor and his world going black. The aides told him he had been out for over an hour. The severity of the pain on his left side had made him demand his medication even though he wanted to stay away from it. His only thoughts were, please don't let anything be broken. I can't afford the time, I can't have a setback, my plans are all set, I have to get away. I *have* to.

"Get me my own doctors," were the orders he had barked from his bed. "Where the hell are they? I don't trust these British quacks." The aides in London as well as Bill Gay in the States were frantic. They were trying to get the regular team of Howard Hughes' physicians up to the suite at the Inn on the Park. Howard felt more comfortable with them, since they always acceded to his wishes and never demanded that he follow their medical advice. They were also the main suppliers of his medication, through prescriptions made out to the names of various aides. The Gay/Henley/Davis triumvirate, as well as the aides, wanted Hughes' doctors as much as he did. If for no other reason than the fact that his own physicians were well aware of Mr. Hughes' true physical as well as mental condition. Even though he had been making remarkable progress these last couple of months, his physical appearance and condition, in the last day or so since the fall, had deteriorated so greatly that he looked in even worse shape than before.

His dread of doctors had resurfaced, and so had his phobia about germs. Howard knew he was losing control, control of all that he had regained these past few months. He felt himself slipping backward, and he tried to fight, he wanted to fight, but the pain was too great, and the warm magic of the medication would make everything seem all right again. The aides were forced to bring in a radiologist to take X-rays of Mr. Hughes, and as gentle and reassuring as the technician tried to be, Howard still fought him, not wanting to be touched, and even more fearful of what the pictures would show. The X-rays did show what everyone feared the most—that Mr. Hughes' left hip was indeed fractured. As bad as the news was for the aides, who now had to make arrangements for an operation, it was devastating for Howard Hughes.

He felt that his last chance had been taken from him. He felt so alone, so terribly alone. And worst of all, he felt that the demons that had always plagued him were returning. His fear of doctors, his fear of germs, his craving for secrecy, they were all coming back to haunt him, just like before. Worse than before. The aides made arrangements for the most eminent orthopedic surgeon in London, Dr. Walter C. Robinson, to perform the operation. When Howard was informed of this good news, he insisted that the operation be performed in his suite at the hotel. As ludicrous as this sounded, the aides tried to persuade the doctor to do just that. Mr. Hughes had his own reasons and his own fears, known only to him, but the aides also would have preferred it done at the hotel so that they could maintain their control of the situation, and see that no outsiders at the hospital would get the opportunity to look at, or worse, speak to Mr. Hughes. But the point was moot. Dr. Robinson, of course, wouldn't hear of it. He would only perform the procedure under the most clinical and antiseptic conditions. And that meant in the operating theatre of the prestigious London Clinic.

Lying on his back, Howard had his eyes shut to shut out the piercing light from the overhead lamps. He was in the twilight sleep that had been induced by the large dose of Valium that had been administered to ease his anxiety prior to the operation. He could sense the activity going on all around him and his nostrils picked up the medicinal smell of the antiseptics in the operating room. It brought back memories of his terrible plane crash of 1946 in Beverly Hills. There was the same smell in the operating room then. What the hell, he had been much more severely injured then, and he recovered. This is just one goddamn broken bone. I can do it, I can fight it. I have to.

"Mr. Hughes, Mr. Hughes, I want you to know you're going to be fine." Dr. Robinson was bending over Howard and speaking directly into his ear. "Dr. Johnson is going to put you to sleep now, and when you wake up, your hip will be good as new."

The anaesthesiologist, Dr. E. Freeman Johnson, was leaning over him and saying, "Mr. Hughes, I understand you enjoy watching motion pictures, and that you've even made some. Well, we're not going to bother with counting backward from 100. Instead, I want you to think of the best moment you ever spent watching a film. That's it, go back and enjoy it." Howard heard the soothing voice of Dr. Johnson as he was just slightly aware of the mask being applied over his nose and mouth. While the anaesthetic started to take effect, Howard decided to take the doctor's advice, and the movie he chose was *Gilda* starring Rita Hayworth.

Her legs were long and sexy—dancer's legs, with just the right amount of muscle tone and the right amount of allure. Her torso, arms, shoulders and neck looked as if they were sculpted by one of the great artisans of the Medici period of the Renaissance. Her face was gorgeous, simply gorgeous, with its perfect bone structure and jawline, petulant full lips and sophisticated yet seductive eyes. But her hair, her incredible hair, a luscious auburn mane, thick and silky, parted on one side, cascading down over her shoulders in waves, had men dreaming about her, and Howard was no exception. She was "The Love Goddess," that's what *Life* magazine called her in 1947, but Howard didn't need *Life* to tell him who Rita Hayworth was. He had known it from the first time he saw her sing and dance "Put the Blame on Mame" in *Gilda*. Like the rest of the male population, he had been wild over Rita from that moment on. But there was a difference between everyone else and Howard Hughes.

Howard had the time, patience and, above all, the money to make his dreams come true.

Rita was already a star when she made *Gilda*. Her studio was Columbia, and she was the biggest star they had. Her agent, Johnny Hyde, had recently negotiated a new contract with Columbia's legendary boss, Harry Cohn, that gave Rita an unheard of 25 percent of the net profits from all her future films. Her motion picture career was only getting bigger and better. But her personal life was quite another matter.

From Howard's usual sources—gossips, informants and Noah Dietrich's reports—he was well aware of Rita Hayworth's personal life. He knew she was born on October 17, 1918 in Brooklyn, New York, the daughter of Volga and Edwardo Cansino of the dancing Cansinos. They named her Margarita Carmen Cansino. When the family moved to California in 1927, Rita went on the road with her father as his dancing partner. She was discovered dancing in Tijuana, Mexico, and signed by Winfield Sheehan, the chief of production at Fox Studios. Her first appearance on screen was a non-speaking part as a dancer in *Dante's Inferno*, starring Spencer Tracy, and her first speaking part was a featured role in 1935 in *Under the Pampas Moon*. Fox eventually dropped her contract, but she was signed to a seven-year deal by Harry Cohn at Columbia, who suggested she change her name from Margarita Cansino. She shortened her name from Margarita to Rita and took the maiden name of her mother, and Rita Hayworth was born. The year was 1937, and she was on her way.

She was also married for the first time that same year to Eddie Judson, a hustler who wanted Rita to do anything and everything it took to further her career. The marriage ended in 1942 with Rita giving him everything he wanted just to get out of the marriage. By that time, she had started seeing Orson Welles, who had gone mad over Rita from a publicity photo he had seen in a magazine. Before he even met her, he bragged to friends that he was going to marry her. He was considered a genius in the wake of his famous *War of the Worlds* radio broadcast about Martians invading earth, as well as his triumphant motion picture *Citizen Kane*. Welles chased Rita and they were married on September 9, 1943. Howard could never forgive him for making Rita cut her hair and bleach it blonde for a movie they starred in together, which Welles also directed, *The Lady from Shanghai*. Their marriage was already on the rocks and the word around town was that Welles was just as interested in proving his power and his hold over Rita. The gossip was that she went along with it just so that Harry Cohn would have a heart attack. Rita finally got fed up and filed for divorce on November 10, 1947. Howard was also aware of her affairs with Victor Mature, Glenn Ford and, most recently in March and April of 1947, with David Niven.

It was in late 1947 that Howard began his pursuit of Rita. She had just returned from Europe. It was one of the few times that there wasn't a steady man in her life, and she was vulnerable. The timing was right. Rita had just begun shooting *The Loves of Carmen*, and flowers began arriving every day on the set, as well as at her home in Brentwood. This was standard operating procedure for Howard. But this time he played it differently: Instead of sending a card with the floral deliveries, he sent nothing. He wanted to keep her guessing. And he kept the flowers coming for over a month. Then he sent a fabulous watch with a diamond band—but still no card. Rita was going crazy trying to figure out who her secret admirer was. Her entourage at the studio, her hairdresser, makeup man, costumer and fitting people were all playing the guessing game along with her. And then, using the subterfuge that only Howard Hughes could employ so well, he planted the rumor among Rita's people that it was he who sent the gifts. No one seemed to know how they knew, but they all knew it was Howard Hughes, and they kept it secret amongst themselves. And then the phone calls started. This was Howard's pattern. He would call her at all hours in her dressing room and, of course, at her house. But he was always solicitous toward her, very much aware that at that moment in her life she was wounded and extremely vulnerable. He knew he fit the bill as another powerful man to fill the void left by Orson Welles. He knew he had the stature and credibility to entice her. The time was right, the time was now.

As Howard had hoped, Rita looked forward to his calls. Even though she was busy shooting *The Loves of Carmen*, there was an emptiness, a void in her life. From early on, she had always had a man in her life, whether it was her father, who forced her into an incestuous relationship and dominated her life, or her first husband Eddie Judson, who would have her do anything for money, or Orson Welles, who had to prove he could control and manipulate her. Even in her affairs, she was subservient to her men. It had been ingrained in her from early in her childhood that the man was dominant, that the man was the leader, that the man should be obeyed. Even though Rita had millions of adoring fans, even though her personal entourage would obey all her commands, even though she was the reigning figure in her own personal world, Rita followed the lead of the men in her life just as she had followed the lead of her dancing partners. Rita didn't mind obeying the men in her life, and if it would make them happy, she didn't mind letting them live out their fantasies with her. No, Rita didn't mind at all. And now Howard Hughes was calling and pursuing her— the fantasy lover he had been dreaming about ever since he had seen her for the first time in *Gilda*. Well, she would become that girl again, for him, and perhaps both of their dreams would come true.

Howard had just hung up the phone with Rita. He couldn't believe it. She had consented to act out the scene from *Gilda* just for him. He had been thinking about it for two years, and now it was about to happen. They had arranged for Howard to come to her home in Brentwood at one o'clock in the morning. She had to keep their meetings secret, since her divorce from Welles wasn't final. Keeping it secret was no problem for Howard; it only made him feel closer to Rita, and he loved the intrigue. From the many phone conversations he'd had with her, they had built a very strange but special relationship. They both seemed to know each other, and more importantly, knew what the other one wanted, and it was their mutual need—more lust on Howard's part—that brought them together.

Howard had acquired a copy of *Gilda* and watched it from beginning to end again, but only once. He wasn't interested in the storyline, or the wonderful direction by Charlie Vidor, or the performance of co-star Glenn Ford. Howard focused only on the scene in which Rita sings and dances "Put the Blame on Mame." He ran that scene over and over, more than 50 times. He knew every move, every step, every nuance that Rita had expressed in that scene. He had memorized all the words to the song and sometimes would sing along with her. He was aware that it was Anita Ellis' voice that had been dubbed for Rita, but it didn't matter, because he was totally enthralled by the sensuous movements of her body, which was just barely contained by the black satin strapless gown designed for her by couturier Jean Louis. Howard was both enchanted and aroused by Rita's natural elegance as she swung her hips and locked her sultry gaze on only him from the screen. The more he watched, the more he had to have her. Thank God the time is now, thought Howard, because the fantasy was so intense that the ache in his loins had become unbearable.

It was one a.m., Howard had just rung the doorbell at Rita's house. He had been sitting in his car across the street for more than an hour. From behind the steering wheel in his car, he had watched as a delivery was made to the house 45 minutes before. Everything was going according to plan. The delivery was from Howard, of course, two bottles of Cristal Champagne, 1939, set deep within a huge sterling silver bucket of ice along with two flutes. There were also two packages along with the champagne. One contained an exact duplicate of the fabulous Jean Louis gown that Rita wore in the film, along with the long black gloves she had worn with them. The other package contained a 78 rpm record of "Put the Blame on Mame" sung by Anita Ellis. With Howard's influence and connections, it had been no problem for him to obtain these items.

He was thrilled when he saw that it was Rita herself who came to accept the delivery. He knew that meant she was alone in the house and he was that much closer to living out his fantasy. Howard could see from his car that she was wearing a housecoat and had her fabulous hair pulled high on her head, but her makeup was already expertly applied and her luscious red lips were luminescent against her teeth even from across the street. She searched for a card, but there was none. Rita looked again at the enormous bucket containing the champagne. Something caught her eye, and she wiped away the condensation that had formed and was dripping down the sides. As her hand wiped the dampness away, she saw the word "Gilda" engraved into the silver, and a knowing smile appeared on her lips. This delivery confirmed that her rendezvous with Howard Hughes was about to take place.

Howard continued to observe as she had the delivery man follow her into the house with the champagne and packages. It was less than a minute later when he saw him leave. He sat in his car, watching and waiting, counting the minutes until one a.m. He sat there fantasizing about Rita, envisioning what was about to happen, growing harder by the moment.

He rang the bell, but there was no answer. He was about to ring again when he saw the handle turn and the door slowly swing open into the house. Howard started to tremble at what he saw. In his wildest dreams, in his most erotic fantasies, he was not prepared for what he saw. Standing in front of him wasn't Rita Hayworth. No, standing there was a fantasy come true: Gilda. She had transformed herself into Gilda. She had stepped off the screen, out of his dreams and into the flesh, and she was standing there, waiting just for him. Howard felt his head spinning and grabbed on to the door to support himself. Rita ran up to him and took his arm as a look of concern crossed her face.

"Howard, what's wrong?" He leaned on the door and against her, catching his breath. Perspiring, he took off his snap-brim Stetson and wiped his brow.

"I just didn't expect it. Seeing you in the dress and the gloves, and with your hair just like in the movie." Rita was smiling warmly as she led Howard into the living room. "I've been fantasizing about you, about Gilda, running that scene over and over. But I never expected it to be so real, I never expected it to really happen. My God, Rita, you're so gorgeous." Howard was babbling on like a nervous teenager with his first girlfriend. Rita laughed, throwing her head back, and her magnificent hair fell all about her face and shoulders, just like in the movie.

"Howard," she said, "Let's not waste this magnificent champagne you sent," and she poured a glass for each of them. Tossing down the first glassful almost at once, she held out her empty flute for him to refill it. Howard had never been much of a drinker, but the feel of the ice-cold bubbly in his hand, combined with the dryness in his throat and Rita's own delightful, sensual exuberance, made him decide that tonight would be an exception. He held his glass out to her and toasted "to Gilda." Rita touched her glass to his and whispered, "No, not Gilda, to us."

She took a deep swallow and said, "But you came for Gilda, so first you're going to get Gilda, then us."

For more than an hour they sat on her couch, with Rita asking him questions about himself. She was especially interested in his plane crash and the other women in his life. Howard was on his third glass of champagne and was feeling quite light-headed as he told her about his narrow escapes from death. And he found himself bragging about some of the other women in his life, which was most unusual for Howard. Rita wanted to know the intimate details of his affairs, especially with the other actresses she knew. But he maintained discretion to a degree. Rita finished the second bottle of Cristal and began telling Howard about her childhood and what her father had made her do. She then took delight in telling him about Orson and how he would always want her to wear sexy lingerie so that he could make love to her. She told Howard that she hadn't minded dressing up for Orson, and that's why she got so excited when Howard told her he wanted her because of *Gilda*. He wanted her to look like Gilda. To *be* Gilda. And she was.

The package that had contained the dress was sitting on the coffee table. Howard looked inside it and found the long black satin gloves. He held them out to Rita and smiled as she put them on. He asked her where the other package was, and she said she had already put the record on the phonograph, and all she had to do was to turn it on. Rita walked about the living room, turning off one lamp and dimming the overhead light. She continued to the record player, turned it on and lowered the arm onto the recording. It was everything that Howard Hughes had ever dared imagine—everything and more. Here he was with Rita Hayworth, the reigning sex goddess of the world, and she had become Gilda, exactly as on the screen and in his fantasy, all just for him.

The music began and before his eyes he saw her change from the shy, inquisitive woman of a few moments ago, who had been laughing and drinking with him, into the sultry seductress who had enticed the entire world. Her movements were exactly as he remembered them from the movie. She threw her head back and her hair fell at exactly the same moments. She swayed her hips and turned her back and moved her hands and arms precisely as she had done in the film. Anita Ellis' voice was coming from the phonograph, but Rita was singing too.

Every time she dipped, Howard would try to get a better view of her breasts, which seemed about to explode from the dress. As she turned, her incredible legs would flash into view through the high-cut slit in the black satin gown. She was magnificent, enchanting, alluring. Howard was anticipating the end of the number, when Gilda provocatively peels off one of her long gloves and tosses it out to her audience. He had watched it on the screen and played it in his mind far too many times. She was turning him on so much, and he had become so hard, that he was afraid he was going to embarrass himself. Howard found he had put his hand inside his pants and begun stroking himself, and he had to force himself to stop.

Singing with abandon, Rita finally tossed her glove at Howard, and it hit him in the face. He was so caught up in watching and fantasizing that, for the moment, he forgot that this was real, not a movie. A minute later, the music stopped, and Rita, staying true to the movie, took a deep bow to Howard's applause and then tossed the other glove to him. This time he caught it. Rita was Rita again, and she was laughing as she walked toward Howard. He shouted for her to stop, and told her that she had to ask the question.

"What question?" she asked with a truly puzzled look.

"Rita, don't you remember? This is the part I'm always dreaming about. It's when you hold your arm up and look at the zipper in the side of your dress and say, 'I'm not very good with zippers, could somebody help me?'"

Rita, smiling coyly said, "You're a naughty boy, Howard Hughes, but you're right. I guess I forgot my lines. Are you ready?" With his heart beating twice as fast as it should have been, he nodded. He had played this out many times in his thoughts, and now it was really going to happen. Rita struck the pose and she slowly lifted her arm and looked invitingly at her zipper. With a smouldering look, she gazed directly into Howard's eyes and breathed, "I'm not very good with zippers, could somebody help me?"

Howard's eyes lit up and he took his cue. "I'm an expert, Gilda," he said as he walked up to her. He put his arms around her and pushed her hair out of the way as he started running his tongue up her long neck, just as he had done a thousand times before in his dreams. As she smiled up at him, Howard gradually unzipped her dress, and the gown fell to the floor. Rita's magnificent breasts burst free and Howard cupped them in his hands as he kissed one nipple and then the other, just like in his dreams.

As Howard moved his tongue down Rita's belly, he felt a tap on his shoulders. He ignored it as he continued down toward his objective. But then he felt another tap, and another. Tap,

tap, tap. What's this? This wasn't in his dreams.

"Mr. Hughes, Mr. Hughes." It wasn't Rita's voice. "Mr. Hughes. That's it. You're doing fine. I've installed a steel pin in your hip, and the operation was a complete success." It was a man's voice. It was the voice of Dr. Robinson, the orthopedic surgeon. And he wasn't in Brentwood about to make love to Rita Hayworth, no, goddamn it, he was flat on his ass in the recovery room of the London Clinic in England.

Howard looked up at the bright overhead lamps, and he could just about make out the face of his doctor. The room began to spin, and the smell of the antiseptic stank in his nostrils. Get out of here, get away from me, leave me alone, just leave me alone.

Inside his head, where only he could hear, Howard screamed, God if this is reality, then *fuck it!*

CHAPTER TWENTY-TWO

THIRD WEEK OF SEPTEMBER 1975

·

*Howard Hughes' Bedroom
Xanadu Princess Hotel, Bahamas*

He felt like Alice, falling down the rabbit's hole, turning and spinning, ever faster, down, down and down. He thought about stopping, he even tried to stop, but he couldn't stop. He looked down and tried to see the end of the hole, searching for the bottom, even a glimpse of the bottom. There was nothing he could see, nothing at all, nothing he could grasp onto, and he knew the worst was yet to come.

It had been a little more than two years since he had awakened in the recovery room of the London Clinic and was informed of the stainless steel pin that had been inserted into his hip to begin the healing process. But instead of leading to recovery, the operation had had just the opposite effect. It was as if it had been an operation to *remove* something from his body, and the something seemed to be Howard Hughes' will to go on, his very will to live. Where was his longing to escape, his hunger for freedom, his need to be in control again?

Ever since he had been brought back to his room at the Inn on the Park, and ever since he had been moved from London to the room that he now occupied in the Xanadu

Princess Hotel in Freeport, Grand Bahamas, Howard had remained in his bed. Lying on his back staring at the ceiling—which looked just like the ceiling of all the other rooms in all the other suites of all the other hotels in all the other cities to which he had exiled himself—Howard reflected on how he had allowed himself to get into this position, and more to the point, on why he didn't care.

Howard remembered that a day or so after leaving the hospital and being brought back to the Inn on the Park, Bob Hunt had come to visit and discuss plans to get him up and flying again. He remembered Bob telling him something about the head mechanic breaking security because he couldn't locate Tony Blackman. And that everything got fucked up from that moment on. He remembered Bob assuring him that once he healed, he'd have him back in the air, and this time there would be no screw-ups. But what Howard didn't tell Bob was that it was already too late. He was back on the medication again. He needed it. His doctors told him so. The aides told him so. He felt better with it. He felt safe with it. And goddamn it, he wanted it. He didn't tell all this to Bob that day, that he didn't give a shit anymore, because he didn't want any more disappointment, and besides, the warmth of the magic of the medication made everything seem all right. But Bob gave Howard his snap-brim Stetson and told him to hang onto it: He'd be needing it when they went up flying again.

One of Howard's team of private doctors, Dr. Lawrence Chaffin, who was in his eighties, would look in every few days and try to get him to start his exercise rehabilitation program, as prescribed by Doctor Robinson. Dr. Chaffin was the only one of Mr. Hughes' private physicians who would demand that Howard follow the rehabilitation program. Chaffin had ministered to Howard in 1946 after his near-fatal plane crash in Beverly Hills. Howard hadn't listened to any of his doctors' advice when he checked out of the hospital, and he wasn't listening now. He procrastinated or just outright refused to try to walk, even though it was in his best interest and his hip was on the mend. Bob Hunt and Stan Dean tried to get him up, but to no avail. Howard's own stubbornness and psychosis, exacerbated by the terrible hip injury and his deepening dependence on his medication, had enabled the triumvirate of Gay, Davis and Henley to take over almost total control.

Howard remembered being awakened from one of his fitful sleeps and being told they were moving from London to the Bahamas. Normally, a move of this magnitude would never have been undertaken without his prior acknowledgment and permission. But they weren't dealing with the Howard Hughes of old. They weren't dealing with the Howard Hughes of even a year ago. The triumvirate was in charge now, they were giving the orders, and Howard didn't even argue. He was told that the IRS was about to crack down on him, and he would have to appear in court if he stayed in England. They had to get to a country where there were no extradition arrangements with the United States. Howard Hughes' legal history had been a series of skillfully avoided court appearances, except on rare occasions when he was a much younger man. So when they told him he had to move again, he didn't argue with the aides. He had issued only one order: to get him his snap-brim Stetson. He wouldn't travel without it.

Very early on the morning of December 20, 1973, Howard and his entourage left London in secrecy, just as they had arrived there. They were off to the Grand Bahamas and took up residence at Freeport's Xanadu Princess Hotel, which was owned by another mysterious billionaire, Daniel K. Ludwig, a man who had made his primary fortune in the shipping business, but unlike Hughes, hadn't let his penchant for secrecy control him.

Even though there were only 10 or 12 people in the group around him, the aides were so accustomed to gracious living that two entire floors were booked to accommodate their needs—the penthouse and the floor below it. As usual, the windows were closed, and the drapes taped shut. He also had his movie projector and screen—along with an endless supply of films both old and new—to help him pass the time. For all intents and purposes, nothing had changed in the very closed and private world of Howard Hughes.

The fact that Howard had more or less made up his mind not even to attempt walking again made his aides' job that much easier. Maintaining control was no longer a problem. The more movies the "boss" wanted, the more he would get. The more ice-cold Poland water he wanted, the more he would get. The more medication he wanted, the more he would get. Deeper and deeper down the rabbit's hole he went. Howard no longer showed any interest in world affairs, or even in his own business affairs. He was slowly withdrawing even from the help that Bob Hunt kept trying to offer him. He would only stay in bed, watch his movies, stare at the ceiling or sit on the toilet for hours at a time, cramped with painful constipation. He was slowly departing, deserting life itself, without even the fight or stubbornness that had been so much his trademark. And instead of helping him to fight, making him fight, insisting that he fight, those around him did their best to ease, and accelerate, his descent. They were just following his orders, right?

None of the aides knew who gave the orders for the move to the Bahamas. But once they got there, they all agreed that it was a good thing. Not only did they enjoy the fabulous food and accommodations, and an easier schedule than ever before, but they got the news that there really was an IRS investigation under way that they had escaped from by leaving London. Mr. Hughes had also been indicted by a Las Vegas federal grand jury, investigating his earlier takeover of Air West. Someone in Hughes' head office in California must have had information of the government's intensified interest in the organization. They must have known of the forthcoming indictments and the need to get Mr. Hughes out of harm's way.

Fully aware of Hughes' true mental state, and of his rapidly deteriorating physical condition, the Gay/Davis/Henley ruling elite maintained the facade and continued to conduct business as usual. No one outside of the private world of Howard Hughes knew what they knew—that the boss was no longer in control. And they didn't want anyone to even have an inkling of just how far out of control he really was. As long as they could keep up the illusion, the deception that Howard Hughes was calling the shots, they would remain in charge. When Chester Davis learned that the Bahamian government was invalidating their extradition treaty with the United States in early December 1973—effectively stopping the U.S. from extraditing the notorious renegade financier Robert Vesco—an immediate decision was made to spirit Mr. Hughes away to the newly safe haven of the Bahamas.

Howard was blissfully unaware of the whirlwind that was swirling around his former empire. He simply stayed in his bed and watched his movies, occasionally being helped to the bathroom and taking ever-increasing dosages of the medication. Meanwhile his former chauffeur, secretary and attorney did battle in his name with the various agencies of the United States government that were pursuing him. Howard was completely oblivious to the fact that there were two separate IRS investigations going on. He didn't know that they were trying to subpoena him as an indicted defendant in the Air West case. He had no idea that a series of events that came to be known as Watergate had taken place, and that government investigators were trying to link both his organization and himself personally to it. He believed that the super-secret ship called the "Hughes Glomar Explorer" was truly a research vessel and was ignorant of its true mission, which was searching for sunken Russian submarines. Even when he was informed that there was a break-in and robbery at his old Romaine Street offices and many very sensitive and secret personal papers and records had been taken, his main concern was not the sensational nature of the documents, but his old motion picture equipment and some old prints of the films themselves. He was only aware of and told about the waiting IRS agents, the waiting subpoenas, and the fact that he would be taken into custody if he stepped on U.S. soil.

Bill Gay and Nadine Henley knew long ago that they would eventually have this power over their employer. Early on in his capacity as the first personal aide to Mr. Hughes, Bill Gay had seen what he recognized as the first signs of psychosis. He saw Hughes' constant washing of hands, his obsessive fear of germs, his inability to make timely decisions. But he knew that the eccentricities about meetings in cars and planes were due to hearing problems and not an early sign of mental illness, and he was wise enough to distinguish between them. He discussed his observations with his benefactor, Miss Henley, and they had decided to bide their time and eventually use this knowledge to their benefit.

Nadine, for her part, made it her business to acquire as much knowledge as any psychiatrist regarding Mr. Hughes' mental condition. She instructed Gay that the aides were to do Mr. Hughes' bidding, no matter how bizarre. She knew he would have the capability of carrying on logical, even analytical discussions and conversations about such topics as aviation or motion pictures, while at the same time he would be incapable of taking care of even his most basic personal needs. So while they carried out all his orders without question, complying with his every eccentric and outlandish request while deliberately ignoring his obvious need for help, they made Howard Hughes more and more dependent, more and more helpless to resist.

While Howard lay confined in yet another bedroom, with the outside world taped tightly closed from him and while his mental and physical condition continued to grow worse with each passing day, Gay, Davis and Henley congratulated themselves on the huge financial contracts they had recently voted for themselves, for the aides and for two of Mr. Hughes' personal physicians on September 10, 1975. Bill Gay was content to run the Hughes empire out of the offices that he had opened secretly in Encino, California. Nadine Henley's time was filled trying to get Mr. Hughes' permission for construction of a building for a TV station, KLAS, in Las Vegas that was owned by Summa. She was also attempting to get his O.K. to have the flying boat known as the Spruce Goose donated to the Smithsonian Institution. It wasn't that she or her partners were becoming philanthropic, but the Spruce Goose was costing Summa about one million dollars a year in maintenance costs and they could get a tax write-off by making it a gift.

Chester Davis, meanwhile, was endeavoring to wrest control of Summa's business investments by submitting various complex plans through the aides for Mr. Hughes' approval. Even though he and Nadine Henley and Bill Gay were in control, they still didn't own any stock in Summa. There was only one stockholder, Howard Hughes. Legally, they needed his permission for any major decisions involving large purchases, transfers or loans of funds. Even in his degenerated mental condition, Howard understood what was going on, and he would only give his consent when he truly understood the need to do so, or when he just couldn't fight any longer—but it was always in his own good time.

The triumvirate realized that an investigation of their awarding huge financial benefits to themselves might lead to conflict of interest charges sometime in the future. So to prevent that ever happening, they wanted the insurance and assurance of the boss' approval. That meant his will. Almost from the moment that the entourage moved from London to the Xanadu Princess, they had made a decision to set into motion a plan that soon became a full-time project and, eventually, became an ongoing crusade to get Mr. Hughes to disclose the whereabouts of his will. One aspect of the crusade was that if the aides determined that there was no will in existence, they were then to persuade Mr. Hughes, by any means available, to write a new will favoring the triumvirate as well as the aides and physicians. Almost daily, one or more of his aides would make a polite inquiry. Sometimes they would outright question him about the location of his will, saying it was for his own good. They were shameless, resorting to any approach from pleading to coercion that might elicit the information they wanted so desperately to obtain.

Even in his declining state, Howard knew what was going on. He knew that the triumvirate would need his stamp of approval on what they had gleaned for themselves at his expense. And he would be damned before he would give in on this last battle. In fact, he quite enjoyed the daily routine of the aides coming into his bedroom with their various ploys to pump him for information about the will. They were all so pitiful in their obvious deceptions. But Howard grew to love the game, this last game in which he got to call the shots. Did these fools really think I would tell them about a will I made years before and update it in their favor, or that I would actually dictate a new one naming them as beneficiaries? I may be heading down the rabbit's hole, but this is one battle they will never win.

Howard was staring at the light on his empty movie screen. *Ice Station Zebra* had just finished playing. He called out for an aide to bring him his medication and also a dose of Surfak, a medicine for people with chronic constipation. Entering the room, Glenn Kaiser was assaulted, as always, by that dank, foul odor. At times, due to his physical deterioration and gradual loss of will, Howard would go to the bathroom right there in his bed. Kaiser gave him the Surfak along with Poland water from a bottle that he had to open in front of him as per his orders. Kaiser asked the boss if he needed to go to the toilet. Howard didn't acknowledge him. Kaiser asked if he was hungry. Again no response. Howard just pointed at the movie projector and motioned for Kaiser to start it up again.

"But Mr. Hughes, you've watched that one three times today."

Howard turned his gaze on Kaiser and stared at him with utter contempt and disdain. "Put the goddamned movie on. I don't need you to tell me how many times I've seen it. I'll watch it a thousand more times if I want to!"

"Yes sir, Mr. Hughes." Kaiser began to rewind the film and after a while gathered his courage to once again bring up the subject of the will. The tack he took today was to say how important it was for his family to be provided for, that Mr. Hughes would be performing a humane and decent act by writing a new will or at least a codicil to provide for the families of his loyal aides. When he saw a smile appear on Mr. Hughes' face, he thought that approach might be working and kept on talking.

Listening to the sorrowful story from Kaiser, Howard

kept smiling as he turned his gaze to the ceiling, taking solace in the power he still held over them, and he allowed himself to begin daydreaming. He remembered back to another time when he was in a room with a movie projector, and the projectionist was running a movie for the fifth time just for him. He was in his private screening room at Goldwyn Studios in Hollywood, the year was 1948, and the movie was *The Return of October*, starring Glenn Ford and a girl who was driving him wild with desire: Terry Moore.

He had taken over control of RKO Studios in May of that year, but Howard continued to maintain offices and a private screening room at Goldwyn in Hollywood, just a few blocks from his Romaine Street headquarters. He was dressed in a white, long-sleeve, pima cotton shirt, the first two buttons unbuttoned at the neck, beige, tropical-weight, pleated, wool trousers and cordovan wingtips which he propped on a large footstool as he reclined on one of the worn but sumptuous leather chairs in his screening room. The volume was turned up louder than normal to accommodate his hearing problem, but the loudness of the soundtrack didn't bother anyone else, because he was the only viewer. Howard had just ordered Carl, the projectionist, to stop the film in the middle. He had just watched it from beginning to end five times in a row.

"Anything the matter, Mr. Hughes?" Howard heard Carl's voice through the intercom on the console next to his chair.

"No, it's OK, Carl, take a break, I'll call you when we're going to start again." Howard had been watching *The Return of October* consecutively with no break since around nine o'clock that morning. He hadn't eaten breakfast and continued watching straight through lunch. It was now four in the afternoon, but he didn't find himself craving food. It was a different—but even more familiar and compelling—hunger that he felt, an appetite for that sweet, naive girl with the big blue eyes and turned-up nose. In the movie, her character believes that her uncle is going to come back to life as a horse, and Howard felt she was too damn convincing to be just acting. Could she really be that sweet and innocent? Howard had to know. He had to find out. He had to have her.

"Get me Harry Cohn over at Columbia," Howard ordered the operator at Goldwyn from his private telephone in the screening room, "and let him know it's Howard Hughes on the line, and that it's urgent." After a three-minute wait, the phone almost popped out of his hand at the bark of Harry Cohn, raising his voice so that Howard could hear him. It only made the feared and powerful head of Columbia Studios sound even more gruff and coarse than usual, if that was possible.

"Howard," Harry Cohn shouted, "what the hell is so god-damned urgent that you pull me out of a meeting with my head of production?"

"Hold on, Harry, I've been over here in my screening room at Goldwyn the whole damn day running your new movie *The Return of October.*"

"Yeah, so? What do you think of it?"

"I like it. As a matter of fact I like it a lot. I've run it five times, and I may watch it some more."

"Yeah, so. So you're a fucking nut. Why waste my time to tell me you're going to set a record for watching a movie the most times in a row, like the one you set for flying around the world?"

"No, Harry, nothing like that. I have a couple of questions for you."

Harry Cohn's curiosity was piqued, especially since Howard had recently bought RKO. "So what have you got on your mind?"

Howard waited a moment before replying. He knew that Cohn was very protective of the female stars he had under contract, and especially someone new like Terry Moore, whom he had just starred opposite Glenn Ford. That meant he was grooming her for major stardom, and Howard knew Cohn was well aware of his reputation as a Hollywood playboy.

"Well, Harry, I'm interested in your female lead, Terry Moore."

Cohn's reply was emphatic: "No."

"What?"

"No!"

"Why?"

"You tell *me* why!"

"Well, I, uh, I," Howard was stumbling, "I was taken by her naiveté. She has me believing that she really thinks her uncle is coming back as a horse. I was hoping you could give me the lowdown on her, because I'm thinking of borrowing her from you for a picture."

"Listen, you son of a bitch," roared Cohn into the phone, "don't bullshit a bullshitter. I don't want your fuckin' hands on her! She's a true innocent, and you're not going to spoil this one. Keep away. Just keep the fuck away."

"Now, Harry, take it easy. You got me all wrong. I'm just interested in the girl for a picture on RKO's schedule."

"What the hell are you talking about, Howard? Don't you even know what you got when you bought RKO?"

"What are you talking about?"

"We loaned Terry to RKO earlier in the year, before you took over, for the lead in *Mighty Joe Young*. You know, the follow-up to *King Kong*."

"Well, I'll be goddamned," said Howard as a large smile appeared across his face, "You mean I own an un-released film of hers already?"

"That's right," answered Cohn. "So since you already got a picture with Miss Moore in it, there's no need to continue this conversation. Good-bye, Howard."

"Wait, Harry, wait!" Howard screamed, making sure Cohn didn't break the connection, "This picture I've got is perfect for her, and I'm sure we can work out a fair price." There was silence on the line for about ten seconds. Howard knew how protective Cohn would be of a new star on the way up, and when the new star happened to be female and looked like Terry Moore, it was anybody's guess what else Cohn had in mind for her. But Howard also knew that Cohn, like all the other Hollywood moguls, first and foremost looked upon his stars as properties, the same as currency. Howard knew what drove them—greed, power and profit. So he hinted to Cohn that he could work out a deal to borrow Terry. Howard knew that if Cohn took the bait, he would have to pay through the nose, but what the hell, that's what money was for.

"Let me tell you, Howard," said Cohn finally, "it's going to cost you a hell of a lot more than when we loaned Terry to RKO earlier in the year. You know she's starred in two pictures now." Howard breathed a sigh of relief. He knew he had won over Harry Cohn. Now came the hard part: to win over Terry.

"OK, Harry, we'll work out the right price. Now tell me about her."

"Howard, all you want to know is right there on the screen, right in front of your eyes. She's young, sweet and very innocent; she's got big blue eyes and even bigger tits. What else do you want to know?"

"You got me all wrong," Howard heard himself repeating, but he knew Harry Cohn had pegged him dead right. You *couldn't* bullshit a bullshitter, and he knew Cohn was already counting the money he was going to make off Terry, so Howard continued the charade. "C'mon Harry, I want to know all about this girl, how she came to your attention, how she got the role. I'm very interested in her—for my movie, I mean."

"You know Howard, you should have been an actor, I mean it, I really mean it. If I didn't know what a skirt chaser you really were, you could have convinced even me. Nevertheless, I'm going to fill you in, because this girl is really legit. I've owned the script *The Return of October* for quite some time. We always felt it was a good property, but our big problem was finding a girl to play the lead."

"You've got plenty of girls to pick from right at Columbia," said Howard, "or you could always borrow a star name from another studio."

"Yeah, I know, but we couldn't find anyone who was naive enough, or had enough of that innocent look to make us believe that she really was that naive—on screen, at least." Cohn took a moment to let that sink in and continued. "Then one day this girl shows up with her mother. She looked too good to be true. She's got that turned-up nose and those big innocent blue eyes and we test her for the role. Well, all my people go crazy for her—she's just as good on the screen as she is in person. You get the feeling you could sell her the Brooklyn Bridge and she'd thank you for it. She's a living doll, really an innocent who has to be protected. Her real name is Helen Koford. No one felt we could use that as her stage name, but she was so right for the part of Terry Ramsey in that movie that we changed her name from Helen to Terry."

"How'd she get the name Moore?"

"Well, since her last name is Koford, we shortened it to Ford, but we knew that wouldn't work; a movie starring two Fords, Glenn Ford and Terry Ford. Her mother told us her maiden name was Bickmore. It just so happened I had a letter on my desk from Colleen Moore, and I took it as a good omen. So I dropped the first part of her mother's maiden name and wound up with More. I added an 'o,' and that's how Terry Moore was born. She's really that sweet, and you should know, Howard, she's a Mormon. The whole family is Mormon. This girl doesn't drink, doesn't smoke, doesn't even curse. So whenever you use her, remember to keep your fuckin' hands to yourself. You hear me, Howard?" A moment or two had gone by and there was still no reply. "Do you hear me, Howard?" roared King Cohn.

"Yes, I hear you, Harry. Thanks," said Howard as he hung up the phone. All he could remember was Harry saying that she really was that sweet and innocent. That meant she was the rarest of the rare in Hollywood: a virgin. Howard knew, no matter what he had to do, he *really* had to have her now.

An agent Howard knew set up the introduction. After bumping into Terry and her date at a celebrity tennis match that November, the agent insisted that they join him for a drink at the Beverly Wilshire Hotel in Beverly Hills. A little while later, when they all met at the hotel, the very same agent just happened to notice a tall, lanky man sitting at a table in the corner all alone, and asked if he could introduce the stranger to Terry. The stranger, of course, was Howard, and he was smitten from the moment he first saw her.

Howard was relentless, like a pitbull in heat in his pursuit of Terry, but the methods that worked with other women only led to a stone wall with her. What he hadn't counted on was that she really was a true innocent. Unlike many other young actresses who came to Hollywood, Terry grew up in California, and came from a strong family background where her mother, whom Terry called "Mama Blue," was her best friend. Furthermore, she still lived at home with her parents. Howard had never been up against a situation like this before. He had to practically romance Terry's mother as much as he did her daughter. He would barrage Mama Blue with almost as many flowers as he would Terry, and it seemed that every time he called, he would speak to Terry's mother first, since she always answered the family phone. It was driving Howard crazy, but he swore he wouldn't give up.

Over time, he saw his opening, and it made him desire Terry even more. In his conversations with her, he discovered that she loved movies and had a desire to learn to fly. Well, nothing could make Howard happier than to teach her to fly, and he knew she would love to watch movies with him in his private screening room at Goldwyn. He loved the fact that she was completely unaware of her sexual magnetism, the irresistible appeal that had drawn him to her. He couldn't wait to show her, to demonstrate to her, to teach her, what deeply fulfilling use that appeal could be put to.

It had been six months since Howard had been introduced to Terry at the Beverly Wilshire, and things had been progressing slowly, but nevertheless progressing as far as Howard was concerned. If patience is a virtue, then Howard Hughes was indeed a virtuous man, for his patience never ran out. He had all the time, patience and money in the world and besides, this was a new game for him, and he was making up the rules. As time went by, Howard was getting more assertive with Terry, and little by little, step by step, he knew, he felt, he hoped, that he would get his way. But something else was happening, something strange, something he hadn't felt since Katie Hepburn years before. Terry Moore began to unlock something in him. She adored the adventurer in Howard, and she admired the hero that he was. She saw and began to love only the noble, only the good in Howard, and she never noticed, she never even glimpsed the dark side. She was too young, too naive, too innocent to know.

If he was going to win her, Howard knew he had to remain noble in her eyes, to nurture what she saw in him, while at the same time figuring out a way to get her into bed. He had followed her on her tour around the country promoting her movie *The Return of October*. When he couldn't be there, he called and, of course, sent flowers. When she returned, he started her flying lessons. And he invited her to watch movies with him. At first her mother or a friend of Terry's would accompany them to the screening room, but these last few times he was alone with her. Howard became more daring, bolder, just short of forceful with Terry. He wanted her so badly that he was shameless in his attempts to get her into bed. He would use any weapon he had to gain his goal. He used his maturity to try to reason her to bed, he used his guile, he explained to Terry the advantage of his experience, and as a last resort, he tried to win her over with his wealth. All to no avail. Terry was not jumping into bed with him. But that didn't stop Howard from trying.

The last few times they were alone, there was some heavy necking, and the very last time, light petting. Howard remembered the contour and the soft yet firm feel of Terry's full young breasts, even though she had only allowed him to put his hand under her sweater. For three days, since the last time they had watched movies together, Howard had fantasized about what was under the sweater and especially what was inside her panties. As the movie that he had playing was coming to its end, he was trying to get Terry's hand on the erection that hadn't left him since their last time together.

Howard's tongue was lightly licking Terry's neck as "The End" flashed across the screen. Peter Lorre had just solved another mystery as Mr. Moto. The lights came on and Carl asked through the intercom whether he should start the next film, *The Thin Man*, with William Powell and Myrna Loy, but

Terry pushed Howard away and told him she was hungry.

"We're going to take a break for dinner Carl. We'll start up again in about two hours." Taking Terry by the hand, he led her into his adjoining office, took her into his private bathroom and proceeded to wash her hands. He had done this twice before and Terry didn't consider it unusual any longer, since he had gone to great lengths to explain how important it was to make sure all the germs were removed from their hands before eating. She actually found it quite fascinating that he would take the time to wash her so lovingly, and she found it rather exciting, too. Howard would take about ten minutes to complete the cleansing process, and all the while he would answer the questions she asked him about his past. She would question him usually about his past flings with famous actresses she had read or heard gossip about. But today she was asking about the "Spruce Goose."

Carefully bathing her left hand, he said, "Helen, I told you never to call it the Spruce Goose." He always called her Helen, her real name, never by her stage name. "It was always known as the Flying Boat, and its actual designation was the HK 1. I hate that stupid name the press gave it, the Spruce Goose."

Like a wide-eyed child about to discover something new, Terry asked, "Well, why did you call it the Flying Boat?"

While he kept on with the hand washing, Howard began to tell the story of the famous giant aircraft. "It was near the beginning of World War II and the Allies as well as the U.S. were losing tons of war supplies and ships—as well as men—to Nazi submarines, the U-boats. It seemed that almost every one of our convoys were attacked, with ships lost and sunk. Henry Kaiser, the great shipbuilder, came up with an idea to build planes as big as the boats that carried our troops and munitions. He wanted to build "flying boats." The trouble was that he and his company knew nothing about airplanes, so he came to me, since I had a reputation as an aircraft innovator. I shouldn't have, but I let him talk me into going partners with him in building the first flying boats."

"What do you mean you shouldn't have, Howard?"

He continued scrubbing her hand. "The project was damned from the beginning. Kaiser said he could get all the aluminum we would need to build the planes, but it turned out he couldn't get any. The contract didn't allow us enough time to complete the initial plans, let alone the aircraft. And no plane that big had ever been built or even dreamed of before."

"So why didn't you just get out of the contract?"

"I should have, but I wanted a government airplane contract for Hughes Aircraft, and I was committed. I was afraid I'd be a laughingstock if I pulled out. Kaiser had sold me a bill of goods, and I fell for it. So I tried to pull off a miracle. Working 18 to 20 hours a day, we built the biggest hanger ever built just to house it, and when it was done, the flying boat was 750 feet long, 250 feet wide and 100 feet high. All made of wood. Since we couldn't get the metal I needed for the plane, we constructed it out of spruce plywood, layer upon layer. I had to fight even to get the engines for the flying boat. But when it finally was finished, it was the largest wooden structure ever made—and the biggest airplane in the world. It weighs over 200 tons, the wingspan is longer than a football field, over 300 feet." Terry could see Howard's eyes light up as he told her the story.

"Well, by the time we finished the prototype," he went on, "the war was over, Kaiser had pulled out of the deal, and I was stuck with the expenses that the government didn't want to pay. And let me tell you, Helen, it cost me millions. And on top of that, Senator Ralph Owen Brewster from

Maine, who was fronting for Juan Trippe, the boss of Pan Am, started a witchhunt and had the Senate conduct an investigation into the Flying Boat. The son of a bitch launched a smear campaign against me and my company, and practically called me a thief and a liar.

"Well, I fought fire with fire. I called up my good friend William Randolph Hearst, who I've known for quite a few years, and asked if I could write a column under my own byline that could be carried in all his newspapers. W.R., being a good friend and knowing that my column would sell a hell of a lot of papers, gave me the go ahead. I counterattacked Brewster and his committee by asking very embarrassing questions in my column. In fact, Helen, I think I could have been one hell of a journalist or even an author."

"I'm sure you could have, Howard," she said looking up at him with adoring eyes, mesmerized by every word.

Cleaning Terry's nails, Howard went on: "I had to go to Washington to testify before the Senate committee, and I checked into a suite at the Carlton Hotel. I had Noah Dietrich with me, and I told him not to discuss our strategy there because I thought the place was bugged."

"What do you mean bugged?"

"You know, I was afraid Brewster's people had put listening devices, microphones in the suite. Well, Noah told me I was crazy, that I was overreacting. But after we were back home, we got word that I was right. The place was bugged. Well, anyway, I did real good in front of the committee. A lot of people were already dissatisfied with Brewster, and we showed that he had lied on many occasions and was indeed a shill for Pan Am. My Hearst newspaper columns had a big effect on the press and they generally treated me well. I told the senators how Louis B. Mayer said he would take my word and handshake on a deal before he would take the signed notarized contract of anyone else. Noah and my lawyer Tom Slack brought up my flying accomplishments and I told the committee that if the test runs I had planned for the Flying Boat were a failure, I'd probably leave this country and never come back." Howard had finished washing Terry's hands and was carefully wiping them dry with a large white terrycloth towel.

"Would you really have left the country?" she asked.

"Let me tell you, it had me damn worried after putting my ass on the line in front of the Senate Committee and the whole country. Well, I wasn't planning to fly the boat during the test, just do some trial taxi runs on the water at Long Beach." Standing behind her, Howard could see that he had Terry's total attention as he began rubbing her neck and shoulders while he went on with the story. "On the first run I held the speed to around 45 miles per hour and taxied for three miles. It felt great, and I invited the press aboard for the next run. The waters were choppy, but the Flying Boat smoothed out the sea and this time I taxied at 90 m.p.h. The plane handled perfectly and the crew and I were very pleased. The reporters asked if I intended to fly it that day and I answered, truthfully, no. I let them off so they could report in to their offices on what they had experienced."

While he was talking, Howard slowly slipped his hand inside her brassiere and was caressing her nipple. To his surprise, Terry made no attempt to stop him. With his other hand, he was unfastening the buttons on her blouse, and he thought that this was to be his lucky day. He was imagining what it would be like to have this knockout's 18-year-old body completely naked and teaching her all that he knew about the finer points of making love.

"Then I decided we would do one more taxi run," he went on, "but a headwind came up just as we started the run, so I increased speed to compensate, and she was gathering power as we roared down Long Beach harbor. Just for the hell of it, I put the flaps down, and the damn plane felt so buoyant that it actually felt light. You never would have believed that it weighed over 400,000 pounds. I felt the power from the engines coursing through the controls, into my hands and up into my arms and body."

He was reaching a crescendo simultaneously in his story and in fondling Terry. Her blouse was completely unbuttoned, and he was staring down at her breasts, straining against her bra as her diaphragm moved rhythmically with her breathing. Emboldened, he took her hand and began to move it behind her toward his penis, which was swollen against the inside of his slacks. But she jerked her hand away and Howard snapped out of his reverie as he heard her say, "C'mon Howard, what happened at Long Beach? Go on with the story."

Howard was astonished. She was standing with her top practically off, but she still wanted to hear how he flew the flying boat. Didn't she realize that he needed relief? Didn't she know she was driving him crazy? Was she really that innocent or was she the cleverest of them all? He had to know. Howard went on with the story as Terry continued to let him caress her breasts.

"We were driving over the water at better than 100 m.p.h., and I know we didn't plan for it, but it felt right, so I pulled back on the stick and there we were, airborne. None of us could believe it. We were all smiling and laughing. I took her up to about 70 feet and held it there for about one mile. And then, very gently, I set her back down in the harbor. Surprisingly, you could barely feel it touch the sea. I've had bigger bumps in my single-engine racers. Well, everyone had stuck around and they were cheering and yelling all over Long

Beach. It was covered by the world press, and it sort of took the pressure off me from that damned Senate investigation. Well, what do you think?"

The whole time he'd been talking, he hadn't stopped fondling Terry. "Oh Howard," she said, turning around and putting her arms around him. Gazing at him rapturously, she kissed him first on the cheek and then on the mouth. Howard at once put his tongue inside her lips and, at the same time, undid her bra expertly with one hand while cupping her now free breast with the other. He stood back just a little and looked at her, admiring her beauty, and asked if he could take off the rest of her clothes. She moved closer and kissed him again. His hands were all over her in a flash. But she looked him in the eyes, holding his head in her hands, and said firmly, "That's as far as you go, Howard. In my family, the way I was brought up, there's only one way we're ever going to go any further." She was silent for a moment while Howard stared down at her. Then she broke the silence with only one word. "Marriage."

They stood there looking at each other, searching for a sign. Howard was mad for her, crazy about her. But he knew from the determination in her eyes that if he wanted Helen to go all the way with him, he was going to have to go all the way with her.

Lying there in bed at the Xanadu Princess, Howard remembered back to that unforgettable moment, back to those days of making movies and making love, when life was still an adventure, when life was still a challenge—a challenge he was up to. How long ago it all seemed. How many years in the past. What had happened to the time, where did it all go, when did it all go? The only relief for him now was the friendly warmth of the medication as it took away all the pain. The pain of remembering as well as

the pain of the present. The only comfort left, the only triumph left, was knowing he still controlled these greedy little parasites by dangling the promise of the will. Spinning
faster, falling faster, down, down, down; he was beginning
to see the bottom of the rabbit's hole.

CHAPTER TWENTY-THREE

APRIL 2ND, 1976

.

Howard Hughes' Bedroom
Acapulco, Mexico

Everything seemed the same, but it wasn't. It was worse, much worse. How much worse could it get? He knew. He could see the bottom. He was spinning, hurtling down, faster than ever before. The end was in sight, but the end wasn't coming closer to him, he was moving closer to the end. It wasn't that he was afraid, it was his lack of strength, his almost total lack of will, that made Howard Hughes almost welcome the inevitable.

The windows were closed and sealed, and the drapes were taped tightly shut over them, just as in all the other rooms that preceded this one. The projector and screen, the same size bed, the night table next to it, the refrigerator stocked with Poland water, even that dank, acrid odor. Yes, the room seemed the same, but it wasn't, it was different; it was worse, much worse. It had another odor to it, one he hadn't smelled before, one he hadn't recognized until now. He was sure his doctors and aides recognized it as well. It was the stench of approaching doom. The smell of impending death. His death.

What Howard felt was rage, rage that he had let it come this far. Anger at himself for being stupid enough to allow himself, to actually *make* himself, a prisoner of his own guards. The very people he had hired, had trusted, had put his faith in to keep him insulated from the outside world, had finally, totally and irrevocably turned the tables on him. He was indeed their prisoner, kept in a prison of his own making, a prison that moved from city to city, continent to continent—and as a final irony, one that he had paid for.

He knew he had no one to blame but himself, and that got him pissed. Why should he put the blame squarely and solely on his own shoulders? Hadn't he hired these people in good faith? Hadn't he given them more than they deserved or were qualified for? Hadn't he allowed them to move into positions of power and authority? Hadn't they known what they were getting into when they signed on? He never hid his idiosyncrasies, his obsessions, his compulsions. All he asked was secrecy and loyalty. Secrecy he had received, and loyalty to a point. But what he hadn't counted on, what he hadn't seen coming, what he hadn't seen until it was too late, was the greed.

He should have known, but Howard was an innocent when it came to understanding just how far other men would go in their quest for money and power. Their driving force was greed. His never was. He only wanted to be the best. The best golfer, the best flyer, the best motion picture producer, the best lover. Even Howard couldn't believe that no matter what he did, he made money. When he bought RKO Studios, it cost him a fortune, and all the years he ran it, it lost money. But when he sold it, he made millions. He couldn't come to a decision on the financing of jets for TWA, and incredibly, when he was facing certain disaster and was forced to sell his stock in the airline, he had made an unbelievable profit of more than half a billion dollars. Hughes Aircraft, which he started so that he could set his fastest speed records, had turned into a giant multi-billion dollar company. Throughout all the years, it wasn't as though Hughes Tool was making drill bits, it was more like it was manufacturing money. In spite of his interfering in his own businesses—in fact, in spite of himself—Howard Hughes made money. He had the Midas touch, the goddamn Midas touch. But instead of bringing him tranquillity and happiness, it had brought him here, to the very brink of disaster. He was right to feel enraged. He was right to be pissed, pissed at himself for not having the strength to have kicked that fuckin' drug habit. But worst of all for not seeing what was coming, for being blind to their greed until it was too late. All he could see now was the bottom of the rabbit's hole, and it was clearer than ever as he moved toward it with ever increasing speed.

Right from the moment they arrived at the Acapulco Princess in Mexico, Howard had a feeling, a sixth sense that this would be his last hotel stay. It was while he was coming in through a service entrance to avoid being seen, and being brought up in a wheelchair on a freight elevator, that Howard felt the first cold pangs of foreboding. When it came to moving him from location to location, all arrangements had always been meticulously planned and carried out with military efficiency. But the Acapulco move was different.

This time the orders came without prior notice or warning. The move was disturbing even for the aides, who had settled in and become quite accustomed to the amenities that the Bahamas afforded. But for Howard it was terrifying. He had become set in his ways, in his despair, during their stay in the Bahamas. All he'd had to deal with was the constant ongoing battle concerning his will, and his deepening dependence on the medication. Then, all of a sudden, his routine had been disrupted when he was told they were going to move to Mexico. He tried to summon the strength to resist, but they told him that the reason for the move was that he couldn't receive his supply of medication in the Bahamas any longer, and he was stunned. A new supply would be waiting for him in Acapulco. He agreed to go willingly, for he could not bear the thought of life without at least the hope of relief through the magic of the drugs.

But when they arrived in Acapulco, there had been no advance man to check if the door to the freight elevator was working properly. Howard was in a wheelchair wrapped in blankets staring at his hands folded in his lap, surrounded by his doctors and aides, waiting for the door to the freight elevator to close. There was no sound in the elevator, and none of the men were talking. To Howard, the silence was becoming louder, almost deafening. It was starting to hurt his ears, and he had flashes of pain behind his eyes. All the while he kept staring at his hands, his once masculine, powerful hands, but instead, he saw only the bony, blue-veined, spotted, grayish-colored hands that he knew couldn't be his.

Suddenly the silence was broken by the loud crashing of the elevator door slamming closed and then opening again. Over and over again. Howard cupped his hands over his ears to shut out the noise that was invading his head. This was just the kind of mishap that the people with him in the elevator were most afraid of, exactly the kind of incident they prayed to avoid, because it could unnerve the boss for weeks. But this time Howard was more than unnerved. He took the stuck elevator door as a sign, as a terrible omen.

The stay in Acapulco had gone downhill from there on. The accommodations were first class, the best the hotel had to offer, but not on a par with what the aides had become accustomed to in the Bahamas. And the fact that none of them spoke Spanish only added to their discomfort. In the Bahamas, as in London, all they had required in the way of special foods and supplies of everything—from yellow legal pads to peanut butter—had been no trouble to obtain. It was quite a different story in Mexico, where even for the Hughes entourage, importing what they needed into the country—even the most basic things—presented a major logistical problem.

They couldn't even find a chef they were happy with, changing one after another. And of course, because it was Mexico, they had to triple-order the bottled Poland water that Mr. Hughes drank to make sure there was enough for all of them. Worse than any of their personal discomforts were the electrical problems that ran rampant in the hotel. The stuck elevator door that first day was only a forerunner of the mechanical problems that lay ahead. And when the electrical system went out, that meant the air conditioner went out too. As the entourage found out only too often, there was nothing worse than that hot, muggy weather without air conditioning.

But the aides found relief from all the breakdowns and frustrations in their luxurious new lifestyle, with the whole of Acapulco, and all it had to offer, at their fingertips. They went everywhere, ate anywhere, and simply charged whatever they wanted or needed. What the hell, they were on expense accounts. And so, for them, Acapulco became just another vacation spot, another stopover on their roving tour of the world's great luxury hotels—all financed by Howard Hughes.

But Howard was beyond such pleasures and pastimes. Way beyond. Before Acapulco, even the most insignificant change in his routine could bring on a tantrum, but that all changed after a few weeks in Mexico. Howard simply couldn't cope with the interminable interruptions in his private world. When he found himself in the mood for a motion picture, it seemed the electricity would go out just as he got interested in it. His precious Poland water was never cold enough. As soon as the temperature in his room became cool and comfortable, the air-conditioning would break down. At first he would go into one of his customary outbursts, but as the faults continued, and the breakdowns recurred, it was as if it took the last of his remaining strength. Instead of fighting, he began to give in to the inevitable. The aides were frightened. They had never seen him react like this before. And one day, he simply stopped eating, just plain stopped. It became a major accomplishment if they could get him to eat even a tiny piece of chicken or a sip of milk.

The only energy Howard had left was spent on two orders of business. The first concerned the constant arguing with the aides about his will. He refused to give in, to give up what little control he had left. Confounding them with it, he would tease them about a holographic will that he claimed existed. The aides would question him about the will that he had made Nadine Henley type and retype for him, but Howard knew for certain that he had never signed it. He would still promise that he was leaving a large amount of money to whichever of the aides or doctors would speak to him about it. Even in his grave condition, it would give him a chuckle to raise the hopes of these greedy little bastards. Let them look under every rock, let them look for a thousand years. Fuck' em!

As for the second order of business, he used up what little energy and strength remained in him simply in reaching for the little metal box that contained his "medication." The box was always at the foot of his bed, or on his bedside table. It had become a major effort for him to reach for the box, open the lid and take out one of the hypodermic syringes that was always inside, then to fill it with the liquid magic that turned his nightmares into sweet dreams of days long past. The codeine that those closest to him always made sure was in constant supply to fill his ever increasing demands. He was so weak that occasionally he didn't even have the strength to press the plunger of the hypo all the way in and would just leave the needle dangling from the veins in his arm.

His refusal to eat was becoming a major concern for the aides. They were near panic at Mr. Hughes' dramatically accelerating decay. The aides knew his condition had turned grave, and they looked to the boss' two personal physicians, Drs. Chaffin and Crane, to somehow reverse or at least arrest the downward plunge. Instead of recommending that Mr. Hughes be moved to an Acapulco hospital, the aides were advised simply to try to get him to eat and drink on a regular basis. And they were calling Los Angeles twice daily, advising Bill Gay and Nadine Henley of his condition and begging for orders on what action to take. They explained that something had to be done or, in their opinion, they were going to lose Mr. Hughes. While the triumvirate argued over what to do, the only orders they received were to wait for new orders.

Howard's condition was worsening hour by hour. His doctors finally took blood and urine samples from him, and the results showed that he was dangerously dehydrated. Time was now beginning to run out. Time had always been Howard's ally. The time that he'd always had in seemingly unlimited supply, the time that he had savored, flaunted, used and finally abused, had now become very precious to him, very precious indeed. Time had become his enemy. Would the orders to move him come in time? Could they get his fluid levels back up in time? Could they try to reverse all the years of abuse and neglect in time?

Howard felt too frail and too fragile to move, too weak to even piss. He heard voices telling him to eat, telling him to drink. Worried voices. Who the hell are they kidding? They're worried what's going to happen to them after I'm gone. And that gang of thieves back in the States. You can bet they're worried too. Where were they all these years when I was worried? Where were they when I needed their protection? Where are they now, when I need their help? Why don't they help me now? What did I do to hurt them? I gave them all what they wanted. Why do they want to hurt me? Why did they let me hurt myself?

Howard felt the warm flush spread through his body as the smoke-colored liquid raced toward his brain. It was through sheer will-power that he had been able to shove the needle into his arm and send the drug on its way. He lay back on his bed, his head propped up by the pillows and his eyes open, staring at the ceiling. He had heard the same stories that everyone else had—that a drowning man sees his life flash before him. And that's how he thought of himself, as a drowning man. But the heat of the liquid finally reached his brain and the pains of the present began to melt away as the white ceiling of his bedroom magically transformed into the white background of a giant movie screen as Howard watched scenes from the past, when life was fun and nobody hurt him.

At first the images were blurred, but slowly they began to come into focus for a moment, flashing by only to be replaced by another one before Howard had time to identify what he had seen. Concentrating very hard, he found he was able to slow them down—not much, but just enough so that he could recognize them as they rushed by. Flash, flash, flash. And in the instant he saw them, he recalled the time, the place, the person, the event, the emotions he had been feeling. It was incredible, he really was reliving everything, only it was happening so fast.

His mother, his father, the Hughes Tool Company in Houston. Chief Beard and Camp Teedyuskung. Buying out his relatives and owning all of Hughes Tool. Ella Rice. Noah Dietrich. Flash, flash, flash. Getting his pilot's license. Starting

Hughes Aircraft. San Simeon, Hearst Castle. Setting air-speed records. New York City, ticker tape parade. TWA. The Flying Boat. The Beverly Hills airplane crash. RKO. Las Vegas. Flash, flash, flash. He was riding a flood of emotion, happy and sad at the same time. Howard had forgotten so much of the past, but now it was all coming back and rushing by. Flash, flash, flash. Concentrating harder than before, he focused on happy memories, on the many women he had lusted for, and chased after, and he tried to remember them, those he got and those who got away. Flash, flash, flash. Billie, Katie, Ginger, Ida, Gene Tierney, Linda Darnell, Ann Miller, Joan Crawford, Bette Davis. Flash, flash, flash. Cyd Charisse, Katherine Grayson, Ava, Lana, Rita, Jane Russell, Jean Harlow, Faith Domergue, Elizabeth Taylor, Terry, Joan Fontaine, Olivia de Havilland. Flash, flash, flash. Susan Hayward, Gina Lollobrigida, Carole Lombard, Jean Peters, Mitzi Gaynor, Yvonne de Carlo, Hedy Lamarr, Shelley Winters, Janet Leigh, Ingrid Bergman. Flash, flash, flash.

He was talking in his sleep, mumbling, but the words were running together. One of the aides opened his bedroom door to look in, and he bent close to Mr. Hughes, trying to make out what he was saying, but to no avail. He stood back and was amazed to see a grin forming on the boss' face. No one had seen him smile in years. He would have given anything to know what was going on inside Mr. Hughes' head. If he had a million guesses, he would never guess what—or who—had put the smile on Howard Hughes' face.

Flash, flash, flash. Howard remembered back. It was late March 1952, he was in Bungalow 19 at the Beverly Hills Hotel. It was in the days when he would still answer his own phone, and the receiver in his bungalow was equipped with a voice amplifier to accommodate his hearing problem. The hotel operator had just rung through to ask if he was accepting calls, because she had a party on the line. He said yes, and the next thing he heard was a breathy, little-girl voice saying, "Hello, Howard." He knew it was Marilyn Monroe, and he started to get excited.

Sitting on the arm of the couch, stretching his long legs out in front of him as he held the receiver tightly to his ear, he was totally erect as he recalled their brief but intense affair of three-and-a-half years before, and the reasons he'd had to end it. It was on the cover of a magazine in either '45 or '46, he couldn't remember which year, that she had first come to his attention. He'd had Noah Dietrich run a report on her, and Howard learned that she was born Norma Jean Baker on June 1, 1926 in Los Angeles. Her mother Gladys had spent time in mental institutions, and Norma Jean passed a good deal of her adolescence in foster homes. From that report, Howard had felt something in common with her because he always thought of himself as an orphan. It was a ploy he had used over and over again, telling the girls how lucky they were to have a family, while he was an orphan. One by one, in their attempts to mother Howard, they seemed to wind up in bed with him.

Reading on, he learned that Norma Jean had won her first contract with Fox. That's when she and the studio changed her name to Marilyn Monroe. When she wasn't renewed after a year, Columbia signed her to a six-month contract in March 1948, but it ended without the studio picking up her option in September of that year. Howard had always been intrigued with her, and he knew of her marriage to, and divorce from, a man named James Dougherty. He was also aware of an affair she'd had with Fred Karger, the vocal coach at Columbia. It was strange that Marilyn had moved in with Karger, since he was living with his mother and young daughter along with his sister and her children. She had become friends with his mother and it was a large enough house, but it was still unusual. Marilyn fell desperately in love with Karger, who was tall and good looking as well as in good financial shape. She wanted to marry him and was relentless in her pursuit. But Karger felt that Marilyn, as an aspiring actress, wouldn't make a good substitute mother for his daughter, and when he broke off their romance, Marilyn was devastated.

While she was under contract to Columbia, she had taken acting lessons from the studio drama coach Natasha Lytess. Born in Russia, Lytess, a most intense woman, dark and wiry, who spoke English with an accent that was both Russian and German, had come to the States just before the outbreak of World War II in Europe. She took an immediate liking to Marilyn and told her she was destined to become a star. When Columbia dropped her contract, Lytess quit the studio to devote herself full-time to Marilyn. This was around the same time that her romance with Fred Karger ended, and Marilyn moved in with Lytess, renting a room from her. Howard figured this was the perfect time to begin his chase of Marilyn.

It was the usual inundation of flowers and constant phone calls, and since she was living with Lytess, Howard made it his business to swamp *her* with flowers as well. He even included Natasha on their first dates—lunches, dinners and dancing—and he took her along when they went flying. He was out to impress Natasha almost as much as Marilyn, for he knew Natasha had complete control of Marilyn's private life as well as her career. He'd heard the rumors that Natasha and Marilyn had become lovers, but he couldn't and wouldn't believe it. In any case, he had taken over RKO earlier that year, in May, and he knew that, as much as he wanted to impress Marilyn and Natasha, they wanted to impress him just as much.

It was on his very first date alone with Marilyn that it happened. Everything he had fantasized came true. Only he didn't expect it to happen the way it did. He had just picked her up at Natasha's house in one of his old Chevrolets. He was driving, and no sooner were they a block away that Marilyn told him to pull over to the curb and turn the motor off. In the next second, she was kissing his ear and running her fingers over his fly. She had her tongue on his lips and then in his mouth, all the while rubbing her hand over him. Being on a public street seemed to add to her excitement, but Howard was getting nervous. He was also uncomfortable, his long frame stuck behind the steering wheel. Was she crazy? Didn't she realize he could take her to the best suites in any hotel in the world? She didn't care, and after moving him to the middle of the front seat, Marilyn opened her blouse, released her breasts from her bra, and as she darted her tongue in and out of his mouth, began giggling. Howard asked her what was so funny and she told him that his mustache tickled. Howard had been wearing the mustache ever since his Beverly Hills plane crash to cover a scar on his lip that he refused to have repaired by plastic surgery.

Unbuckling his belt and unzipping his pants, she let out a squeal when she saw he wasn't wearing any underwear. Taking his cock in her hand, she slowly stroked it up and down, making it even harder then he thought was possible. With his legs extended up onto the dashboard of the Chevy, Howard felt like a contortionist trying to reach for her breasts as she moved her face between his legs. Looking directly up at him, she kept her eyes locked on his as she guided him expertly into her mouth. Howard felt himself start to tremble and then, suddenly, in less than ten seconds, he exploded.

He didn't know what to say. It had never happened to him that fast before. Marilyn just smiled and soothed him, telling him it was just the beginning; there was a lot more where that came from. And she was right. Over the next three months or so, Howard was living out his sexual fantasies almost daily. Marilyn was insatiable, unstoppable. But there was something else, and it frightened him. Marilyn, almost from the start, started talking about marriage. She told him how much she wanted a child. He knew her background, he knew about her mother's as well as her grandmother's mental problems. Howard didn't want a child, especially not with someone with a history like that. He was also fastidious about cleanliness; it was beginning to become an obsession with him. Marilyn would sometimes go without bathing, since she thought her natural body odors were a sexy turn-on. They had the opposite effect on Howard, and combined with her incessant suggestions about marriage, she became a turn-*off* to him. He hated giving up the wild sex, but finally he broke it off. After calling for a month or so, she finally accepted the fact that their affair was over. But Howard had always kept a soft spot in his heart for Marilyn, and continued following her career, hoping to help her if the opportunity arose.

The opportunity did arise almost three years later in the form of a phone call from RKO's assistant head of production, Jerry Wald. "You're not going to believe what I'm going to tell you, Mr. Hughes."

"I don't believe anything you tell me. So what is it?"

"Yeah, ha, ha, well, I got inside information from a friend of mine out of Chicago. They've got themselves a calendar that's selling like hot cakes."

"I'm not in the calendar business, Jerry."

"Well, what's making this sell is the nude girl on the calendar. I got it right in front of me. And guess who it is."

"Marilyn Monroe."

"How the hell did you know?" There was shock in Wald's voice. "She doesn't even look the same. But I recognized her. She's lying down, stretched out on a red sheet, or red velvet. It's a fabulous shot, and they've called the picture *Golden Dreams*."

"Does it show her pubic hair?"

"No, just her knockers, and they look great. I'm telling you, Mr. Hughes, no one could recognize her, she looks so different now with her platinum hair. If this story breaks it could ruin her, and Zanuck and Fox will go crazy."

"Okay, Jerry, I want you to keep this under your hat. Don't breathe a word."

"You got it, Mr. Hughes, but tell me, how did you know?"

It was in May of 1949, about four or five months after Howard had stopped seeing her, that she had posed in the nude. Three months later she called Howard to tell him what she had done, and to seek his help in trying to get the pictures back. She told him it had been a low point in her life and that she needed money desperately for her rent and her car payments.

"You should have called me, Marilyn."

"You had broken it off, and I didn't want you to think I was after your money." She went on with her story. "I had modeled many times for Tom Kelley, who always wanted me to pose nude. Anyway, he was a nice enough guy and his wife Natalie more or less talked me into it. I was at his studio on Seward in Hollywood, she put Artie Shaw on the phonograph and before you knew it, the session was over. I only got 50 bucks, but it was enough to take the dogs off my heels. The reason I'm calling you, Howard, is to see if you could help me out by buying back the shots before they're sold. I'll pay you back, I promise, I'll do anything for you."

"Let me see what I can do. I'll get back to you."

Howard told Noah Dietrich the whole story and asked if

he could buy the photos without letting Kelley know that he was involved. About a day later, Noah reported to Howard that they were too late. The photos had already been sold to a firm in Chicago, Bowker and Company. Kelley had kept his word: Marilyn's name wasn't used. Noah felt the best thing was not to pursue the photos so as not to bring undue attention to them. Howard concurred, and he hadn't given it another thought until Jerry Wald's call three years later.

It was December of 1951 and Jerry Wald was casting a movie for Howard at RKO called *Clash by Night*, starring Barbara Stanwyck, Paul Douglas and Robert Ryan. He hadn't yet cast the part of a young, voluptuous siren. Marilyn had heard about the role from her friend, director Elia Kazan, who told her she would be perfect for it. He let her know it was being made at RKO, and didn't she have a friend there? Marilyn picked up the phone and the switchboard at Romaine Street connected her to Howard in his office at Goldwyn Studios. She begged, pleaded and practically auditioned for the role on the phone. Howard told her not to worry, he thought she was perfect for it. Leave it all up to him.

Howard placed a call to Wald and ordered him to give Marilyn the part on a loan-out from Fox. Wald couldn't believe what he was hearing.

"What if they find out it's her on the calendar. It'll ruin us," Wald argued. Howard told him not to worry, he had a plan. Howard also said he wanted Marilyn to have full billing along with the other stars. It would be her first time ever to receive star billing in a movie. Wald thought Howard was out of his mind, but who was he to argue? He hired Marilyn as he was instructed and wondered just what Mr. Hughes had up his sleeve.

It was more than three months later and *Clash by Night* had wrapped. All in all, the shoot had gone pretty smoothly, even though the other stars were pissed that a newcomer like Monroe got equal billing. Marilyn was in the first weeks of shooting her new movie for Fox called *Don't Bother to Knock.* Amazingly, the calendar had been out for a few months and no one had recognized the figure and face of the buxom blonde as Marilyn Monroe. Howard's luck had held out. That's when he put his plan into action. There were many columnists on the Hollywood beat at the time and most wielded enormous power in their syndicated columns. In addition to Louella Parsons, there were Hedda Hopper, Harrison Carroll, Sidney Skolsky, Walter Winchell, Earl Wilson and many others. But Howard chose Aline Mosby, a syndicated columnist for UPI, who was known to do anything for a scoop; same as the others, but who also had a reputation for her poison pen.

Howard told her he had a scoop for her that no one else even had a hint about, but she could have it only if she handled it his way. She readily agreed and gave him her word. Howard had been planning this publicity coup for some time, and now it was unfolding. He told Mosby about the Marilyn Monroe calendar. Next he told her she could break the story, but only after Marilyn told her the reasons why she did it. Howard promised to arrange a one-on-one interview with Marilyn for her within the next 48 hours. In the meantime she should sit tight.

Satisfied that Mosby would follow his instructions to the letter, Howard called Noah Dietrich over to his office at Goldwyn and told him what he had arranged with Mosby. Noah was incredulous, convinced that Howard had flipped.

"You're ruining yourself," he screamed. "When this breaks it'll be a scandal. *Clash by Night* will be a disaster."

"Are you finished, Noah?" Howard had that look of impatience on his face that he got when he had to explain his schemes to his trusted number-one man. "You don't see the big picture, Noah," Howard was calmly expounding as if he was teaching a lesson. "When Marilyn gives her side of the story to Mosby, even that hardened bitch will have to paint her in a good light. I'm betting everyone will feel sorry for the poor little girl. No one will blame her except, of course, the Bible-belters, and they don't go to see her movies anyway. She'll come out of this smelling like a rose. Her name will be on everybody's lips and the public will be clamoring to see her in her newest movie, which just happens to be *Clash by Night*."

"Howard, you are one shrewd son of a bitch. I have to admit, every time, I underestimate you," Noah said admiringly, "you amaze me."

"I only wish I owned that goddamn calendar. It'll probably sell a million copies," said Howard. "But here's why I asked you over. I want you to call up Zanuck at Fox, where Marilyn's shooting *Don't Bother to Knock*, and I want you to disguise your voice or get somebody else to say that you know about nude photos of Marilyn Monroe." Noah's mouth hung open, but he said nothing and kept listening. "Tell him you'll keep it from the press and you'll turn the photos over to him for $10,000."

"Howard, that's blackmail."

"Of course it's blackmail, but it's only a trick. The calendar is already out, but no one knows about it yet. Sooner or later it's going to be front-page news. I want to control it while I can and, at the same time, get that son of a bitch Zanuck plenty nervous. Later on, I'll tell him what I did with Mosby and he'll owe me one. Remember, he's got a seven-year contract with Marilyn, so he's got the most to gain."

"Or the most to lose," added Noah.

"No way. This one's in the bag."

Noah had one of his people place the call, and of course Zanuck hit the roof. Then Howard got an emergency call from Jerry Wald telling him that one of his friends over at Fox said there's a rumor that Zanuck was being blackmailed over naked pictures of Marilyn for $25,000. Howard laughed to himself, Noah must have gotten carried away, I only told him to ask for $10,000. Wald also reported that Zanuck had called Marilyn into his office and was threatening her with termination of her contract, something about a morals clause.

Howard's next call was from a very distraught Marilyn. She was crying and in her little-girl's voice telling Howard that Zanuck was going to fire her and close her picture down. Howard told her not to worry and to listen to him carefully. She was to call Aline Mosby as soon as they hung up and make an appointment for an exclusive interview with her that evening. She was to tell Mosby everything she told him in exactly the same way. "Don't leave anything out," he told her. "Make sure to tell her you needed the money for rent. Admit you did the nude pictures, but say they're in good taste. Try to get her to feel sorry for you and tell her that you're giving her the story because you know she'll be fair. Whatever you do, don't mention my name. Don't even tell her we spoke."

"Are you sure it will be okay, Howard?"

"I'm positive!"

"What if she asks about the photo session, what should I tell her?"

"Tell her the truth."

"What if she asks what I had on?"

"Tell her the truth."

"Well, the only thing I had on was the radio."

Howard cracked up. "Tell her that, she'll love it."

Marilyn had the interview with Mosby that night, and

the next day, March 13, 1952, the story of Marilyn Monroe's nude calendar broke in every UPI newspaper in the world. Instead of having the negative effect that was predicted, Howard was proven right and Marilyn won the sympathy of the movie audience and, indeed, the world. The calendar took off and wound up selling in excess of eight million copies. Howard felt it was a great victory, his instinct for publicity had proven right again.

A day after the story broke, Marilyn called Howard in his bungalow at the Beverly Hills Hotel. Her voice was a little slurred and he could tell she must have been drinking. But she was outrageously happy and told Howard she had to thank him—and show her appreciation. He told her it wasn't necessary, but she insisted. She told him she had a surprise for him, she had it with her and she would give it only to him and only in person. Howard could feel that old sensation starting deep in his groin. He remembered how wild her lovemaking had been three years before. He wanted to say no, he knew he should say no, he couldn't say no. He told her okay, but just so he could get his surprise. She told him to give her an hour and then she would drive over. But he didn't want her driving, so he sent one of his top aides to pick her up.

The aide had been waiting at her home for more than two hours. He didn't know it, but two hours was a relatively short time to wait for Marilyn Monroe. In accordance with Mr. Hughes' bidding, he had an ice bucket with a bottle of 1939 Dom Perignon chilling in the back seat of the green 1949 Chevrolet four-door sedan. When she finally came out of the apartment, the Mormon boy almost went into cardiac arrest. He had never before in his entire life seen any woman that sexy and that blonde. Getting out and running around the car, he opened the back door and helped her in. She said thank you and then not another word as she poured herself a glass of champagne. During the 15-minute ride to the Beverly Hills Hotel, the aide hardly took his eyes off the rear-view mirror, trying to look down her cleavage. Almost there, he made a right turn off of Sunset Boulevard onto Hartford, the street that runs along the side of the hotel and leads to the bungalows behind it. He pulled over to the side of the road not more than 40 feet from Bungalow 19 and its waiting occupant.

When he opened the car door for her, she stepped out carrying the nearly empty bottle of Dom Perignon, and sort of tip-toed her way along the path that led to the bungalow door. The driver was spellbound, wondering how she kept her balance on those four-inch heels as her backside swayed side to side in a rhythm of its own. Her skirt was hiked up fairly high on her thighs and he could tell she wasn't wearing any stockings. He allowed himself to wonder, just for a moment, if she wasn't wearing any panties either. Driving that impure thought from his mind, he watched as she reached the door of the bungalow, opened it and entered. He returned to the front seat of the Chevy to stand guard and make sure they were not disturbed for the rest of the night. It's not fair, it's just not fair, that he should have everything, every time, his way, just because he has all that money, thought Bill Gay as he kept vigil on the bungalow of Howard Hughes from behind the steering wheel of the Chevrolet sedan.

Howard was standing by the large floral-print couch in the center of the main room of the bungalow. He had an Artie Shaw record playing on the phonograph, same as when she had shot the nude photos. The only light came from the lamp on the end table next to the couch. He was dressed in a white pima cotton dress shirt, open at the neck with the sleeves rolled back almost to his elbows, his pants were the pleated, wool, gray-plaid trousers from the double-breasted suit he had worn at the Senate hearings in 1947.

He didn't have a belt on, since he had gained a little weight and the pants were tight at the waist. With his black wingtips, as usual, he wore no socks and his hair was slicked back, parted more to one side than in the middle and he had applied and re-applied his All-Spice aftershave. He was ready, already hard as a rock.

The door opened, she took three steps inside and his mouth went dry. Overcome, he couldn't even speak. The way the light hit her, a vision in white with her platinum hair and winter-white dress with tiny sequins that glittered in the lamplight, she didn't even look real. The dress had a deep V-neck plunge just barely containing her breasts, held up by the tiniest spaghetti straps at her shoulders. The rest of the dress was so skin-tight he couldn't imagine how she walked. It was climbing up her thighs. She wore open-toed clear-plastic mules that gave the appearance of being barefoot. Taking another few steps toward Howard, Marilyn lifted the bottle of champagne to her lips and took a deep swallow. As breathtakingly beautiful as she was on the screen, she was twice as powerfully erotic in person.

There still had been no words spoken between them and in her breathy voice she broke the silence. "Well, what do you think?" she asked as she did a little pirouette for Howard. He opened his mouth, but nothing came out. She laughed and moved closer to him, dropping the empty bottle of Dom Perignon on the carpet.

"I just wanted to make sure you noticed me," she said. As she moved her shoulder, the strap fell to one side and a breast burst free. Howard laughed nervously as Marilyn stood toe to toe with him, reached up and pulled his mouth to hers. Her tongue was all over his lips, his cheeks, his face, and then back in his mouth. Howard still hadn't spoken a word as she moved down his body until she was on her knees. She looked up at him while slowly unzipping his pants. Marilyn smiled when she felt Howard shudder as she took him in her hand and started to play with him.

"I'm glad to see some things never change," she cooed as she caressed him. "I mean, that you still don't wear any underwear." Looking down at Marilyn's gorgeous face, Howard felt his knees going weak as she put him in her mouth. With her head moving back and forth, he heard little cries and moans coming from her. His lips were moving in the same rhythm as hers, his excitement building to fever pitch. Then his knees did give out. They just buckled and he fell backwards onto the couch. He popped out of her mouth, but she held him with her hand and followed him onto the couch, laughing not at him but with him. He still hadn't spoken. It was as if he didn't want to spoil the magic. She got astride Howard, all the time stroking him, never missing a beat and, facing him, pulled up her dress and said, "Here's my surprise for you." Howard's eyes opened wide. He had never seen anything like it before. She had bleached her pubic hair the same color as the hair on her head: platinum white.

"I dyed my pussy just for you, Howard. That's your surprise," she said as she mounted him and slid him deep inside her. Resting her hands on his shoulders, she leaned forward, putting her full weight on him so she could have the leverage she needed to rock back and forth. She was riding him, sliding up and down on him, her breasts bouncing free, moving from side to side as he pulled her closer to him while he held on and sucked a nipple. Putting his hands behind her, he grabbed onto her backside and guided her to the same rhythm as his own. He looked up at her and saw that her eyes were closed as she threw her head back, and he saw her mouth open and he heard her start to moan and then scream as she began to build to orgasm. She was moving wildly, sliding up and down, in and out, harder and harder. Her arms and hands were digging into his shoulders as she was nearing climax. His arms started to hurt. She was leaning too hard on him, and he tried to push her arm off just to relieve the pressure a little, but she went on and on. She was like a wild tiger now. She was screaming, she was shouting, but he couldn't make out what she was saying. His arm was hurting terribly, the pain was sharp like fire, and again he tried to push her off, but she was too strong. She was still screaming, but it didn't sound like Marilyn anymore. It sounded more like someone else's voice, the deep throaty voice of a man— more than one man. How could that be?

The pain became intolerable, he had to get his arm free. "Marilyn," Howard shouted, "Get off. You have to get off. My arm is killing me."

Finally the pressure began to diminish. He heard the male voices again, only this time he could make out what they were saying.

"He's been in and out."

"What was he saying?"

"Sounded like Marilyn, or Maryland, I couldn't make it out."

Howard began to make out the faces of his aides, and he recognized the doctors.

"I think he's coming around," he heard someone say.

"Just one more moment, Mr. Hughes," said one of the doctors, "and we'll have this needle out of your arm. We've had one hell of a time trying to find a vein to draw some blood, but we've got it now."

Howard felt the pain subside as the needle was finally withdrawn from his arm, but he knew it didn't matter anymore. He knew it was the end.

CHAPTER TWENTY-FOUR

APRIL 5, 1976

·

Penthouse Suite
Acapulco, Mexico

Howard had never experienced anything like this before, and he didn't know what to do. He felt like he was watching himself in a play and he had a front-row seat. His aides and doctors were the other actors, but he was the star. He watched the play unfold and saw that all the action revolved around him. He didn't have any lines of dialogue and he wondered why. Then he realized that he was playing the part of a dying man. Only it wasn't a play.

It had started the day before, Sunday, April 4, sometime during the afternoon, when he realized he couldn't move anymore. He knew he was weak, he knew his strength was gone, but he only wanted to reach for a glass of his damn Poland water. It was so close, right on the night table next to the bed, but he couldn't lift his arm. In fact, he couldn't move his head, he couldn't even move his eyes to look for the water. His eyes just stayed open, staring hopelessly at the sealed window of his room. What the fuck is happening, he screamed inside his head. Then came the most frightening thought of all—that he had suffered a stroke and become a vegetable, like old man Joe Kennedy. No, he couldn't bear the thought of it. But the more he tried to move, the more futile it became. He didn't want to panic, he tried to remain composed and reason it out. As his thought processes began to work, a great calm overtook Howard and he realized that, thank God, it wasn't a stroke. For some reason, he didn't know why, he felt at peace as it dawned on him that the end was close, very close, and he had fallen into a coma.

Howard looked like a terribly old man, much older than his years, his skin like dried parchment pulled tight over his bones, giving him a skeletal effect and it was grayish-blue in color, the color of impending death. He weighed less than 100 pounds, and his tall frame of almost 6'4" had shrunk at least a couple of inches, maybe more. The worst, though, was his eyes. They were sunken into their sockets, almost hidden by his protruding cheekbones and the once strong, dark, even fierce, brown color was gone. They looked pale, yellowish, lifeless, and worse yet, they were staring straight up at the ceiling. He was wide awake, fully aware of everything that was going on around him, but unable to move or speak.

Time seemed to be moving faster than normal. Various aides would come into his room to check on him, and Howard could overhear their worried conversations; worried as much about their own future, of course, as they were about his condition. And he could hear complaints that they had received no instructions from the head honchos in Los Angeles. Panic was beginning to set in amongst the entourage.

In serene silence and complete detachment, Howard watched in as Dr. Lawrence Chaffin, the oldest of his doctors and the one who had been with him the longest, came in to examine him. He saw the look of helplessness and fear on the doctor's face, and listened as he ordered the aides to get Dr. Thain to Acapulco immediately. Dr. Thain, Bill Gay's brother-in-law, had become the unofficial head of the private staff of doctors to whom Mr. Hughes' care had been entrusted. One of the aides said that Thain was spending time in the Bahamas and didn't know if he could be reached, and if he could, how quickly he could get there.

Back in Howard's room again, Dr. Chaffin looked ashen as he placed a phone call to a local Mexican doctor, telling him to come over at once, for he had a patient who was gravely ill. Dr. Victor Montemayor seemed to arrive almost as soon as Chaffin hung up, and with all his blankets and sheets pulled back, Chaffin watched while the new doctor studied Howard from head to toe. It was obvious to Montemayor how nervous the other doctors were while he conducted his tests. He was sickened as he examined the feeble old man with the bedsores and needle tracks that ran all over his body.

Appalled at his preliminary findings, he practically shouted that this patient needed to be in a hospital. He couldn't understand why this hadn't been done weeks or even months ago. They protested that their patient was an impossible man who refused to tolerate hospitals, or doctors, or their advice, but Dr. Montemayor would have none of such feeble excuses and told them that if they wanted their patient to live, they had to get him to a good hospital immediately—one in America, not in Acapulco. From his examination, he told them, it was clear that the patient was suffering from acute dehydration, among other things, and he recommended that intravenous fluids and oxygen be administered at once.

The pace had quickened, the action was accelerating, time was moving even faster. Orders had finally been received from the triumvirate They had finally given in to the pleas, appeals and prayers of the aides and the medical men. Ordered to get Mr. Hughes ready for transport to a hospital in Houston, Texas, they were informed that the plane taking him to Houston would be the same one that was already bringing Dr. Thain to Mexico.

It was around 7:30 in the morning when Dr. Thain arrived. Instead of attending to his patient, the aides were shocked to see that Dr. Thain spent precious time in the office of the suite collecting papers from the filing cabinets. Only when that job was completed did he go to see Howard, who was having breathing problems. Without a word, Dr. Thain filled two hypodermic syringes and gave him two shots. But the labored breathing didn't improve and he watched calmly as Mr. Hughes continued to stare at the ceiling with his chest heaving up and down.

The time was speeding by, and it was close to 11 a.m. when the aides wrapped him in blankets and got him ready for the trip to the airport and then on to Houston. Gingerly they lifted him onto a stretcher and picked up the I.V. and oxygen tanks which he desperately needed but were too late to be of any real help. It took them only two steps and they were almost out of the room. How ridiculous, how asinine it was that with all the money in the world, all the money anyone could ever dream of, Howard Hughes would have lived in a room that it only took two steps to leave. How cruel, how tragic it was that with the virtually boundless resources at his disposal, this man was dying of dehydration and malnutrition when all he needed was a goddamn drink of water and a little food.

The aides had cleared the hallways and elevators, and time was moving faster than ever—racing—as they moved him down the elevator and into the parking lot. They slid him on his stretcher into the back of an ambulance, and an instant later, it seemed, they were at the airport and he was being loaded carefully into the waiting white executive jet.

The jet's interior was small, and his stretcher was taking up a good deal of the available room. Dr. Thain and Dr. Chaffin were with him, along with two aides, and they were complaining about how little space there was.

Howard was having terrible breathing problems and the pressure on his chest was awful. Finally the oxygen mask was put back over his nose and mouth, and for the moment, it was easier for him. Somehow he heard the roar of the revving engines and he knew they were ready to take off. Even in his coma, it felt great to feel the jet take off. He knew exactly which maneuvers the pilot was putting the aircraft through to achieve first take-off speed, and then the proper altitude. He was exactly right, to the exact moment, when he guessed that the landing gear would be retracted back up into the wings and the nose of the twin engined jet. He was right again as he sensed the precise moment when they would come out of their sharp right bank over the Pacific and start climbing to their pre-assigned altitude. He knew just what heading they would be following to the northeast for the thousand-mile journey to Houston. For just a moment, Howard forgot the state he was in, and he felt an overwhelming compulsion to get up and enter the cockpit of the plane and take over the controls, to do what had come so naturally to him all his life—to fly. One last time.

Both his doctors were attending to him. He could feel the stethoscope on his chest as it heaved in and out. He heard one of them say the pulse was very weak and he couldn't get a blood pressure reading. Gasping for breath, Howard began to hear a rumbling sound from somewhere far off in the distance. He tried to turn his head and see where the noise was coming from, but he couldn't move. The sound got louder and louder, like the roar of a thundering locomotive, then louder still, like the deafening roar of a tornado. And then, suddenly, it stopped. And just as suddenly, for Howard, there was no more pain, no more anxiety, no more torment. Just a sublime and spreading peace.

Howard's doctors, standing over him on the stretcher, were taking off the oxygen mask. His body wasn't gasping for air any longer. It seemed as if the interior of the aircraft became silent. Totally silent. It was deathly silent.

Dr. Chaffin bent over his body and whispered, "May God forgive us, he's dead."

Epilogue

.

Poor Howard. Early in life he learned that illness brought him the attention he craved. At the age of eight, for no reason that the doctors could diagnose, he suddenly couldn't walk and had to be put in a wheelchair. With his preoccupied parents' love and devotion focused finally on him, he recovered. But not inside. He decided never to let anyone close enough to hurt him, close enough to depend on them, ever again. For a while, though, he let me in, and even after our marriage ended, we remained close—closer than he's ever been to anyone.

But even I couldn't save him from himself. Driven by fears and forces too dark for him to comprehend, he climbed all the way to the top, but when he finally arrived there, he was still alone, empty, unfulfilled, inconsolable. Retreating deep inside, he turned himself into a cripple once again, a victim of his own paranoia, powerful yet powerless, wealthy yet impoverished, lonely and helpless as that small child, but now he was in a world of strangers.

This poor man, who had never dared to trust anyone, reached out once again in desperation, but this time he put his trust in those who ultimately isolated and betrayed him. Most of them were good men, very good men—no dope, no booze, no gambling, no womanizing, church-going men—but the lure of money, Howard Hughes' money, was too great to resist. Absolute greed, like absolute power, corrupts absolutely. They could have saved him. They controlled all communication to and from Howard Hughes. They watched as his life spun out of control, they watched as he took more and more drugs to kill the pain. They even procured the dope for him, kept him in a stupor, under their control, neither dead nor alive, just stood there and let it happen. They watched and waited until Howard began to die. They watched and waited and did nothing as one of the greatest men of the 20th century, a visionary, an innovator, a king maker, one of the richest and most powerful men on earth, the world's first billionaire, whose charmed life had survived five airplane crashes, finally died of malnutrition, dehydration and—worst of all—of a broken heart. But the tragedy was not just Howard's death; it was the death of all his unfulfilled dreams.

Though they had seen the end coming, the aides sat in stunned disbelief while the news was broadcast to a shocked world. For many years, to the general public, Howard Hughes had been an elusive legend, a mysterious recluse, but to his own inner circle, he had become a non-person. It was as if they had become Hughes. They were making all the decisions, they were running the empire; they were living his life. But when he died, their power, their entire meaning in life, died with him. All of them are forgotten today, totally forgotten. But even in death, the man himself lives on. His name is spoken more today than in the final years of his life. Airports, institutions, avenues are named after him, but they are merely monuments. The man and the mystery live on. He will never die, because people will keep trying to decipher the riddle of who he really was: the most misunderstood man of the century. A man so powerful that the only person who could have sabotaged him was Howard Hughes himself.

I hope this book will help to heal that broken heart of his, because my love for him has outlived all the others, outlived even death. He has always been and will always be my Don Quixote, my knight in shining armor.

He will always be...my Howard.

Index

health of, 15-16, 19-20, 42-
44, 90, 118-121,
154-155, 167-168,
194, 202-203, 206,
208-211, 234, 255-
257, 272, 273-277
hip injury and surgery, 209-
211, 212-215, 225,
226-228, 229
and Hughes Aircraft XF-11
crash, 113-124
inner circle, 40-50
Mason and, 6-12
and mother's fears about
health, 77, 78-79, 80
need for power and control,
11, 24, 36-38, 53, 80,
105-106, 133, 157
physical appearance, 8, 15-
16, 35, 90, 104,
162-163, 163-164,
196, 253, 274
psychological characteristics,
10-11, 13, 24, 27,
38, 41, 91-92, 95,
132, 156, 205, 279
psychological depression, in
1958, 128-129
psychological depression and
downward plunge,
in 1975, 226-227,
229, 255
signature, 101
will of, 34, 233-234, 255
and women, 56, 59, 65, 73,

80 (see also names of
women)
Hughes, Howard, Sr. (father),
21-24, 77
partner of, 204
Hughes Aircraft, Burbank, 181
"Hughes Glomar Explorer"
(ship), 231
Hughes Tool Company, 6, 31,
53, 84, 94, 100, 204
Hughes as sole owner of, 53,
60-61, 62, 65, 73,
179, 181
sale of, 45-46, 47-48, 49-50
Hunt, Bob, 106, 127-135, 155-
165, 207, 227, 228
and aides, 193-194, 199-200,
203-204
at Inn on the Park, 129-135
physical appearance, 129
Huston, Martha (aunt), 120-121
Hyde, Johnny, 216

I

Inn on the Park, London,
events at, 17-20, 33-
34, 40-50, 7481, 82-
88, 89-97, 98-112,
127-136, 154, 193-
201, 202-211, 226,
227-228
Internal Revenue Service
investigations, 230-
231
Irving, Clifford, 96, 101